Martin Mansergh: A Biography

Kevin Rafter was born in Waterford in 1969. He holds a masters degree in economics from Trinity College, Dublin and one in politics from University College Dublin. He has worked as a Political Reporter with the *Irish Times*, Political Correspondent with the *Sunday Times* and Editor of *Magill*. He currently presents the *This Week* programme on RTÉ Radio. His previous books include a biography of the late Neil Blaney and history of Clann na Poblachta.

KEVIN RAFTER

RTIN

SERGH

OGRAPHY

**NEW
ISLAND**

MARTIN MANSERGH: A BIOGRAPHY
First published September 2002
New Island
2 Brookside
Dundrum Road
Dublin 14
Ireland

ISBN 1 904301 05 3

British Library Cataloguing in Publication Data
A catalogue record for this book is available
from the British Library

Cover design and interior typesetting: New Island
Cover image and credited interior photographs courtesy
of Derek Speirs; other interior photographs courtesy
of the Mansergh family
Author photograph courtesy of Fergal Phillips
Printed in Ireland by Colour Books Ltd

Acknowledgments

This is an unauthorised biography. When I first approached Martin Mansergh with my proposal to research and write this book, he replied with characteristic politeness that he was a bit taken aback, flattered but really not sure about the subject. He suggested I utilise my interest in Irish politics and history by examining his late father's contribution to Anglo-Irish understanding. However, once the seriousness of my intent was explained, considerable assistance was offered.

The book profited from access to Mansergh family historical papers as well as speeches and cuttings held by Martin Mansergh. I had the benefit of two sit-down interviews as well as several off-the-record conversations.

Over the last year I became accustomed to the question: 'Are you asking as a journalist or as biographer?' The only time I was unsure of my response was when in the middle of researching the book the political advisor decided to turn general-election candidate.

Inevitably the manner in which the information provided has been blended into the text and the interpretation placed upon it will not always be favoured by the subject but I hope he agrees that what I have written is fair, objective and impartial. I owe a debt of gratitude to Martin's wife, Elizabeth, and the other members of the family who must have wondered about the individual furiously transcribing in their front living room.

This book could not have been written without the co-operation of the many people who agreed to be interviewed about Martin Mansergh. Those who spoke on the record are evident in the text but thanks is also due to those who did not wish to be identified. In particular I was most grateful to Fr Alex Reid and former Taoisigh Charles Haughey, Garret FitzGerald, Albert Reynolds and John Bruton as well as the current head of government, Bertie Ahern.

During the course of writing this book I received a Visiting Research Fellowship from the Institute of British-

Irish Studies at University College Dublin. Thanks to John Coakley, the IBIS Director, for agreeing to make office facilities available and to Claire Mitchell and Kevin Howard for the warm welcome.

Faith O'Grady of the Lisa Richards Agency confirmed the value of advice received from Michael McLoughlin: 'Get an agent'. Faith bought into the idea with great enthusiasm and made the introductions with New Island.

Several people read the manuscript and offered sound advice, most importantly my good friend Colm O'Reardon. Terence Dooley pointed me in the right direction on the Big House tradition while John Bradshaw at Clann na hÉireann in Tipperary Town provided invaluable historical material on the Mansergh family.

Many other friends heard little else from me for many months but 'No news, working away on the Mansergh book.' In that group I include Ursula Halligan, Peter Fitz-Gerald, Miriam Donohoe and Martina FitzGerald as well as my parents, family and my wife Oorla.

Finally, two little boys are probably still puzzled about the strange nocturnal activities of their father; always up late, sitting in front of a laptop computer. Hopefully in the years to come Ben and Brian will understand. This book is for them.

Kevin Rafter
July 2002

Contents

Introduction

It was late. The small hours of a mid-week morning in March. There was little traffic on the main road that stretched from Tipperary Town to the capital city of the Irish Republic. The driver could feel the tiredness descending. Fresh air billowed in the car window to prevent him falling asleep. On the motorway into Dublin he decided to pull into the lay-by. Neither the fresh air nor several cans of Coca-Cola were having the required effect. A few minutes sleep and he would be ready to travel the remainder of the journey to his home in South County Dublin.

Some time passed. A light shone in the window. A Garda was inquiring about the driver's well-being. Had he been drinking? Nothing but Coca-Cola. The empty cans on the passenger seat supported the case. What was his occupation? The driver laughed aloud. 'Fianna Fáil candidate for South Tipperary,' he replied. It seemed like hours since he had addressed a Fianna Fáil meeting in Tipperary, after which he set off from Friarsfield House, a property in the shadow of the Galtee Mountains on the former family estate.

Martin Mansergh, Special Advisor to the Taoiseach, had had a hectic start to 2002. On his desk in Government Buildings lay the draft of the Fianna Fáil general election manifesto. There was also an early version of the speech that Bertie Ahern would deliver at the forthcoming party Árd Fheis, in effect a pre-election address to a gathering of the Fianna Fáil faithful. The 56-year-old advisor was set to play a more active role in the imminent contest than he had done in any of the seven general elections since he came to work for Charles Haughey back in early 1981.

Mansergh was becoming accustomed to the description and all that went with the role of election candidate. It offered a novel distraction to the passengers on the government jet as they travelled in March 2002 from Baldonnell Aerodrome in the Irish Republic to the United States for the annual St Patrick's Day celebrations.

Taoiseach Bertie Ahern was seated alongside his partner Celia Larkin. Senior advisors aboard included Joe Lennon and Martin Mansergh. When the Gulfstream IV jet reached cruise speed of 530 mph, the passengers switched off their safety belts, relaxed and were offered light refreshments by the cabin steward. Mansergh opened his briefcase and produced a contact sheet of photographs. Set against a blue background, the person in the photographs was himself. The selection had been taken for use on his election literature and lamp-post poster. "Which one works best?" the advisor asked of the other passengers.

The curriculum vitae of Martin George Southcote Mansergh records his birth in England in 1946; a public school education at Canterbury; a doctorate in pre-Revolutionary French history from Oxford University and a rising career in the Irish diplomatic service cut short by a 1981 move to work for Fianna Fáil.

He was born into a family which had been part of the unionist community in Ireland until the partition of the island in the early years of the twentieth century. In the newly Independent Irish Free State, however, the family moved from that unionist tradition and identity. Martin Mansergh made an even more fundamental shift. He describes himself as an Irish republican, ideologically committed to achieving Irish unity.

A combination of influences have contributed to his reaching this point. There was his father and his academic research on Ireland and Irish nationalism. There were the holidays spent in Co Tipperary. At school and university his Irish background set him somewhat apart from his English contemporaries. There was the outbreak of conflict in Northern Ireland and the nascent passions inevitably raised by the situation in Belfast and elsewhere.

This is the story of an English-born Protestant son of Irish unionist stock and the contribution he has made to the history of this country. Mansergh has been one of the most influential political figures in contemporary Irish life. Despite this, most of his work has been in the background – as a political advisor when Fianna Fáil was in government and as Head of Research for the party when it was in opposition. Few people outside the political and media bubble in Leinster House knew who he was, and even then, few in that grouping had any real idea about his background, his personality or his motivations.

What were those motivations? There was an emotional and intellectual attachment to Fianna Fáil as both concept and political party. There was the desire to see the island of Ireland politically re-united, using peaceful means and with the consent of all the people who inhabited the island. This in turn required an end to the Provisional IRA's campaign of violence.

Martin Mansergh was central to convincing leading Republicans that their conflict had to end, and that the political route would successfully bring about the objective that they all shared. His job description necessitated concentration on the leadership of the Republican Movement. As a consequence he had less contact with the moderate voices of nationalism in the North, led by John Hume and his colleagues in the SDLP. Unionists were also wary; building relationships with Mansergh was complicated both by his family background and his contacts with republicans.

The Mansergh-Adams dialogue, facilitated by the Redemptorist priest Fr Alex Reid, helped transform relations on the island, not only within republicanism but also between republicans and their unionist counterparts. In the absence of the dialogue between Mansergh and the President of Sinn Féin there may well not have been the IRA ceasefires and the Good Friday Agreement. Indeed, the Mansergh family motto – always ready – was never more appropriately applied to a clan member.

To his admirers in Fianna Fáil and the Republican Movement he has been the unsung hero of Irish political life. To his foes in the unionist community and beyond, he has been a hardened ideologue with an uncompromising attachment to one side of political events. But, as this book recounts, friend and foe alike acknowledge the significance of his contribution to the peace process.

Mansergh joined Charles Haughey as an advisor in 1981 and served the controversial Fianna Fáil leader as his close political confidante for over a decade. Mansergh has remained deeply loyal despite all that has emerged about Haughey's financial affairs. He was the only senior Fianna Fáil figure to continue in a pivotal role in the party when first Albert Reynolds and then Bertie Ahern came to power.

Yet, despite this prominence few know the real Martin Mansergh. The characteristic politeness; the convulsive laugh; the understated self-description; the steely determination; the loyal lieutenant; the absent-minded academic; the naive politician; the staunch ideologue. All these characteristics combine to define Martin Mansergh. This book traces the true extent of his influence and reveals the significant part he has played in Irish politics for the last quarter of century.

One

The Unionist Tradition

William of Orange arrived at Carrickfergus in the second week of June in 1690. The King of the Netherlands was also joint monarch of England, Ireland, Scotland and Wales. Motivated by a desire to spread the Protestant faith and reduce the influence of Catholicism across Europe, William led an army of some 36,000 men against that of the former monarch James, who had been forced to abdicate over his defence of Catholics. He had been exiled to France but his arrival in Ireland was the start of a campaign to regain the crown.

The two armies faced each other in battle on the banks of the River Boyne in Co Louth. They fought for three days from 30 June 1690. William knew that his army outnumbered that of his enemy by some 10,000 troops, that it was better equipped and had superior training. His victory at the Battle of the Boyne cemented Protestant rule on the island of Ireland, so much so that even today over 300 years later the memory of the famous Boyne victory rouses members of the Orange Order in annual ceremonies in Northern Ireland.

The famous victory was remembered in stories, songs and paintings. And so it was on the walls at Grenane House outside Tipperary Town, the home of the Manserghs, where a painting hung showing King William of Orange crossing the River Boyne. A Protestant family that had benefited from the confiscation of land from the native Irish population, the Manserghs – like the majority of their class and creed – gave their loyalty to William, the historic hero for the Orangemen in Northern Ireland.

For over two centuries families like the Manserghs were clear as to where their loyalty rested. Over time, subsequent generations came to describe themselves as Irish, but they expressed this national identity within the context of the British Isles and the constitutional association of England, Scotland, Wales and Ireland.

The ascendant position of this landlord class began to erode with the rise of Irish nationalism in the nineteenth century. Then the early years of the twentieth century shattered old certainties. Many whose forefathers had cheered on William of Orange at the Battle of the Boyne faced great challenges to their established loyalties, allegiances and identities.

As elsewhere, times have changed at the Mansergh home in Co Tipperary. The family's painting of William of Orange is now in storage. At the front entrance wall to Friarsfield, the second house on the original Mansergh estate, a young beech tree is protected as it takes root inside the main gates. The tree was a gift from Gerry Adams, one of the leaders of modern Irish republicanism, to Martin Mansergh, the Fianna Fáil advisor who played so central a role in bringing an end to the military campaign sponsored by Adams and his associates.

The Sinn Féin leader had grown the tree from seed and presented it to Mansergh after a meeting in a Dublin hotel. The sight of a middle-aged man in a business suit and overcoat walking through the hotel foyer holding a tree raised a smile with Adams. For Mansergh the beech tree is a symbol of reconciliation, signalling an end to centuries of differences between the two strands of life on the island – unionist and republican, Protestant and Catholic, British and Irish.

The Mansergh name has been in Ireland for about ten generations. The Irish connection – which started a family tree leading to Martin Mansergh today – began some 350 years ago in the seventeenth century when three brothers left England to start a new life in Ireland.[1] An Englishman, George Mansergh, who was born in 1596, married Rebecca Redman from Halton, Yorks. Her brother Daniel Redman was MP for Co Kilkenny. The couple had three children – Brian, James and Robert – who were born between 1624 and 1629.[2]

Daniel Redman moved to Ireland in or around 1641 and his three Mansergh nephews followed, taking the boat on what was then a four-day journey from the land of their birth to start a new life in Ireland. The reasons why they decided to uproot from the Lune Valley are unclear. Emigration at that time was motivated by factors including a lower cost of living in Ireland and the attraction of making money. The latter activity would have been achieved by providing assistance for the Cromwellian campaign in Ireland.

Oliver Cromwell arrived in Ireland in August 1649 as Commander-in-Chief and Lord Lieutenant. His task was to enforce British rule including the implementation of the Protestant land settlement policy and the transplantation of the Catholic population. By the time Cromwell departed nine months later his armies had undertaken a savage campaign against Catholics, Ulster Presbyterians and members of minority religions – slaughtering women, children and unarmed captives. The wars in Ireland from the early 1640s to 1652 left more than 600,000 people dead.

The military campaign was funded by so-called adventurers; those who lent or 'adventured' money for the Cromwellian action in Ireland. In lieu of the outstanding debts the adventurers were offered two-and-a-half-million acres of land in Ireland. The land was confiscated from the defeated Irish and the Old English who were ordered to move west of the Shannon. In 1641 Roman Catholics owned 60 per cent of the land but by the 1680s only 20 per cent remained in their possession.

The New English had started to arrive in Ireland before the Cromwellian resettlement, but their presence increased significantly from the middle of the seventeenth century. Whatever the specific motivation for their migration to Ireland, the Manserghs were part of the Cromwellian settlement of Ireland. Martin Mansergh noted that Daniel Redman "clearly came prior to Cromwellian times, though that did not make him, for a time anyway, any less of a Cromwellian. As Cromwell's rule was particularly oppressive, intolerant and bloody and involved a policy of uprooting a large part of the native population, few families preferred to think of themselves or be regarded as Cromwellian."[3]

Mansergh confined usage of the term 'Cromwellian' to Redman but it must equally be applied to his own direct ancestors. The exact nature of the Mansergh brothers' participation in – and support for – the military campaign is unclear. However, a parchment in the possession of the National Library of Ireland recorded: "Appointment of Brian Mansergh to be a lieutenant to the troop of Capt. Redman in Lord Generall Cromwell's Regiment."[4] Moreover, the Manserghs were direct beneficiaries from the settlement policy.

The Cromwellian settlement created a new landlord class in Ireland, among their ranks the ancestors of Martin Mansergh. They were part of a Protestant elite that over the following 250 years would monopolise all aspects of power and influence in Ireland. The objective of plantation policy was to create a new English class with Protestant values, thereby ending a dependency upon the Old English and Catholics, who could not be trusted to follow the wishes of England.

This class considered themselves the representatives of the imperial state and would in all likelihood have arrived with a sense of superiority. As one writer observed about the mid-seventeenth-century settlements: "They must have viewed the Tipperary landscapes afresh; they came with notions of exploitation and of gaining wealth; they belonged to a growing commercial nation and they were to leave a deep impression on the landscapes and societies into which they intruded."[5]

These Protestants of Ireland were a gentleman class, dominating land, law and politics. Many were absentee landlords remaining in England and controlling their Irish estates through a local agent. However, many members of this ascendancy class put down firm roots in Ireland and became a constant in Irish life. The Mansergh family was in this latter category.[6]

This new landed class – essentially the English in Ireland – quickly gained positions of authority from the Crown. In 1661 Brian Mansergh was appointed a Commissioner in Kilkenny to collect taxes for the Monarch while, some years later, the authorities at Dublin Castle requested that he disarm the Catholic population in the county.

While ancestors of Martin Mansergh arrived in Ireland in the early years of the seventeenth century, the acquisition of the family estate in Co Tipperary took place some years later. Grenane is located two miles outside Tipperary Town. The main residence was a fortified castle-type property. In subsequent years stones from the castle were used to build a country house, more in keeping with the style of residences in England. Other landlord families undertook similar construction work.

Grenane, the main house on the estate dates from around 1730. Friarsfield, the property that is owned today by Martin Mansergh and his brother Nicholas, was built about a quarter of a mile from Grenane in the middle of the nineteenth century.[7]

Mansergh observed: "I know there are people today who think it romantic to own and convert a castle. But to my mind moving out of damp castles into more elegant houses was one of the best decisions our ancestors made."[8] Not that this has lessened his interest in castles, a hobby that family members know to their cost, having climbed many damp narrow stone steps to battlements in Ireland and in Europe.

While part of the Protestant elite, the Mansergh family were never among the wealthiest of their class. One study of 131 gentry families in Co Tipperary – based on data from 1775 – ranked the Manserghs as middle-tier landlords. The ten wealthiest families had yearly estate incomes in excess of £5,000. The Manserghs were included in the group of some 60 families which received a yearly estate income between £1,000 and £2,000.

Nonetheless this status afforded them a lifestyle far removed from that lived by the vast majority of the Irish population. Power and wealth were in the hands of the Protestant ascendancy, the denomination of the vast majority of the landlord class. Catholics were on the margins of power and wealth. They were denied the vote, access to public office and faced restrictions on land leases. Kurt Bowen noted, "The penal laws represented an Irish form of apartheid in which religion served as the fundamental determination of all privileges ... "[9] In turn, religious difference was coupled with differences in national identity. Protestant was associated with England while Catholic and Irish became almost equivalent.

Records indicated that in 1831 over 400,000 people lived in Co Tipperary. Almost 96 per cent of the population in the county were Catholics while Protestants accounted for the remaining four per cent. However, the landed gentry in Co Tipperary, as elsewhere in the country, were different in their origins, creed and outlook from the tenant farmers and labourers. There were class differences, which were augmented by differences of cultural inheritance.

In the years after the 1800 Act of Union the landlord system appeared secure, but was ultimately unable to withstand the social, political and economic changes that marked nineteenth-century Ireland. Popular protest became an almost constant feature of Irish society. These protests were primarily motivated by a sense of economic grievance felt by tenants towards their landlords. The objections were based on demands for higher rents and the payment of tithes to the Church of Ireland.

Relations between Catholics and Protestant varied, although increasingly, religion became associated with distinct political preferences for the governance of Ireland. By the 1820s political agitation and inter-denominational strife had emerged as permanent features of Irish life. The biggest challenge to the ascendancy class emanated from Daniel O'Connell and the campaign for Catholic Emancipation. The foundations of Protestant privilege were crumbling.

There exists considerable evidence that the tension between the two religious groupings in Co Tipperary frequently spilled over into more violent action during the mid-nineteenth century. McGrath noted that "most landlords travelled heavily protected by armed guards in Tipperary, their houses like virtual fortresses with steel shutters affixed to their windows."[10]

As Protestant landlords living just outside Tipperary Town, the residents at Grenane cannot have been totally cocooned from the increasing social and political unrest. The Mansergh family was firmly in the unionist camp.[11]

In the 1820s several tenants from the Grenane estate were arrested for involvement in faction fighting.[12] Four members of the same Hogan family were charged with manslaughter. One of those accused at the trail in Clonmel was the father of five children while another was a six-year-old boy. The four were sentenced to transportation to Australia. A member of the Mansergh family told the court that the Hogans had been tenants at Grenane for over a century. He also wrote an unsuccessful letter to the Lord Lieutenant to prevent their transportation.

Politics and the land issue became intertwined over the following decades. While the Manserghs appear to have avoided any negative impact from the nascent rise in nationalist sentiment, the family directly experienced the campaign to have land for potatoes at a reasonable rent and without payment in advance. Westminster outlawed the traditional agricultural practice of burning land, unless tenant farmers secured the permission of their landlord. The farmers favoured the practice as the ash from the burnt sod helped to fertilise the soil. The Mansergh family received a warning of danger in the summer of 1841 if they did not permit their tenants "to plough and burn the land for the relief of the poor of the county."[13]

English control over Ireland had the support of the Manserghs in keeping with the views of the vast majority of their class and creed. Nevertheless there was a strong sense of decency in the Mansergh management of their estates and the treatment of their tenants. A great-great grandfather of Martin Mansergh's – RMS Mansergh – did not employ an agent. Twice a year he would sit at a table situated beneath a lime tree at the driveway up to Grenane. There he collected rents from about 70 tenants, listened to their complaints and dispensed justice as he saw fit. One of his sons sat with him, often to soften the decisions of the Grenane landlord.

RMS Mansergh was in possession of Grenane during the Famine years of the 1840s. The failure of the potato crop over successive years coupled with poor administration by the Government in London caused thousands to starve to death while many more left Ireland for the United States. A *laissez-*

faire philosophy dominated the approach of the Government. The idea of giving food or money without a return did not have widespread political support at Westminster. A relief work system was started – in return for working on the construction of public works the starving and the destitute received food.

The poor in Co Tipperary were required to whitewash poor-houses, construct sewers and footpaths while also improving roads. As part of the relief work the road from Carthy's Cross to the gates of the Grenane estate was laid. In 1928, one local wrote to the Mansergh family recalling:

> I remember my father who was born in Grenane about 100 years ago, of humble birth, speaking of your ancestor (Richard M) with great respect. When the potato famine was at its height he supplied them with food.[14]

Martin Mansergh himself has argued that, more than any other event, the Great Famine, and the subsequent population decline, discredited the union between Britain and Ireland:

> The solidarity was not there when it was needed, and Ireland was treated by London more as a wayward colony than as an integral part of the United Kingdom. The Famine created a large Irish-American constituency, utterly opposed to British rule in Ireland, beyond Britain's reach.[15]

RMS Mansergh was a close friend of William Smith O'Brien, another Protestant landlord and a friend of Daniel O'Connell. In protest at the British attitude during the Famine years, Smith O'Brien led an abortive rising at Ballingarry in Co Tipperary in July 1848. The event was of sufficient local magnitude for RMS Mansergh to send his immediate family into Tipperary Town for safety reasons, although he remained at Grenane himself.

O'Brien was arrested the following month and he was brought to Clonmel to be tried for treason. RMS Mansergh was foreman of the Grand Jury. It was his responsibility to announce the guilty sentence, which carried the death penalty. Mansergh was uneasy about the verdict and following representations the sentence was commuted to transportation for life.

According to family tradition, the whole episode greatly upset RMS Mansergh: "The anxieties connected with the trial and the fate of his friend are said to have undermined Richard Martin's health."[16] In a June 1935 diary entry, Nicholas Mansergh wrote: "It was said that it was three years before he smiled again."[17]

Despite a benign attitude shown by the Manserghs towards their tenants, social interaction between the classes was limited. The gentry lived a life of splendour and plenty. They attended lavish parties, enjoyed the thrill of the hunt, relaxed with games of tennis and billiards and were waited upon by servants. It would have been no different at Grenane where RMS Mansergh was quite a character. In his old age he became crotchety, smoked nothing but cigars, yet would allow no one else to smoke, always drove in a carriage by himself to church, where he sat in the square family pew, spread a handkerchief over his face and went to sleep.

The Grenane estate in 1876 consisted of just over 2,000 acres, some of the most productive and best-endowed land in Co Tipperary.[18] Rent from the land and properties generated considerable income but the Manserghs, like many other landlord families, were experiencing financial troubles.

The process of modernising Grenane House started in the late nineteenth century. However, the family overspent on the renovations so the estate was let for the first time from 1882 to 1906. The original furnishings and many family portraits were sold. There was a lively market for the contents of the Big Houses – many landlords sold paintings, libraries of books and other heirlooms. The money raised was used to clear debts, to maintain an established lifestyle and also to provide financial settlements for family members and dowries for daughters.

At the time of the Grenane letting there was an offer of £95,000 to purchase the estate but it was refused. Martin Mansergh observed: "By the early 1880s collecting rent had become a tricky business. The international economic depression of the late 1870s, coupled with land agitation, was putting pressure on landowner's incomes."[19] Family tradition had it that the ownership of racehorses did not benefit the finances too kindly either.

The Protestant domination of the southern 26 counties was in decline throughout the nineteenth century. The pace of that decline increased in the last few decades of the 1800s. The discontentment of the Catholic population over land ownership led the Government at Westminster to introduce a series of laws, which facilitated the transfer of land from landlord to tenant. Between 1870 and 1909 the ownership status of almost 13 million acres in Ireland changed from landlords to their tenants. The Manserghs availed of the land schemes that helped tenants to buy out their holdings. The father of republican Dan Breen was one of the Grenane tenants who purchased his holding in the early 1890s.

The line of succession at Grenane was complicated as several owners of the estate died without heirs and were succeed by brothers. Consequently, Philip St George (PSG) Mansergh, grandfather of Martin Mansergh, inherited the house and lands in 1906.

PSG Mansergh was born 43 years earlier in Co Tipperary but would spend many years abroad, leading a colourful life that impacted on the family's outlook during the turbulent years of the Irish revolution. He failed to gain entry to the Royal Military Academy in Woolwich but "owing to exceptional mathematical abilities and fine physique" the decision was reconsidered and he was accepted.[20] However, much to the annoyance of his parents PSG Mansergh had other plans. The 19-year-old left Ireland for New Zealand with £50 in his pocket. He landed in Auckland in 1883 and initially earned a living carrying railway sleepers, although success at poker also generated money.

He set sail for South Africa in 1892 where he made contact with a cousin who introduced him to Cecil Rhodes, the British businessman and founder of the De Beers' diamond empire. Rhodes was driven by a desire to expand British rule across all of southern Africa. One element in his strategy for colonial expansion was to build a railway from Cape Town to Cairo.

PSG Mansergh offered his services as a railway engineer for six months without pay. The offer was duly accepted. PSG Mansergh went on to work as a surveyor under Rhodes and pegged 1200 miles of the Cape to Cairo railway. He was also involved in the construction of the bridge over the Kafue River, three hundred miles north east of Victoria Falls. This work has been described as a "triumph of engineering art."[21] Rhodes was obviously pleased with his Irish recruit – a set of three initialled goblets presented by Rhodes to Mansergh is still in the possession of the family.

Martin Mansergh believed his grandfather's experiences in southern Africa increased his understanding of the desire of local populations for independence from colonial rule. While there is no written evidence to support this view, PSG Mansergh did adopt a neutral attitude to the heightened nationalism that engulfed Ireland after Easter 1916.

The foreign travels of PSG Mansergh were nearing an end by 1906. News reached him of the ill health of his eldest brother who, though married, had no children. Consequently PSG was in line to inherit the family estate in Co Tipperary. He returned home to Grenane and, twelve months later, married his cousin Ethel Mansergh from the Co Cork branch of the family, whose father had had a distinguished career in the British military.[22]

When they married, PSG Mansergh was 12 years the senior of his 31-year-old wife. Their marriage maintained the Mansergh name at Grenane. The couple – grandparents of Martin Mansergh – had two sons: Charles Ogilvy Martin Southcote Mansergh and Philip Nicholas Mansergh. Charles, the eldest son, was better known as Gregor. He inherited the Grenane estate while his younger brother – Nicholas – inherited an adjacent family property, Friarsfield.

When PSG Mansergh arrived home to Co Tipperary in 1906 his first task was to tackle the poor financial situation at Grenane. The era of the Big House was at an end as Ireland underwent enormous social and political change. The vast

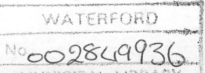

majority of Protestants did not become involved with the nationalist movement. There was little support for the Home Rule bills of 1886, 1893 and 1912.

One writer noted that "their intense suspicions of Catholicism, their segregated social life, and their economic bonds with their more affluent co-religionists were enough to convince even the poorest Protestants that their only salvation lay in retaining the Union."[23] However, by the early years of the twentieth century the capacity of southern Protestants to withstand the nationalist movement was significantly reduced. The era of their monolithic power and influence in Ireland was coming to an end.

The Mansergh family was unionist in outlook, orientation and commitment. Several generations of the Mansergh family either served with the British armed forces or married into families with a tradition of such service in the army and navy. The Mansergh genealogical tree over the last 300 years is littered with references to majors, captains and colonels along with the different regiments units in which they served. Indeed, a relation by marriage of Martin Mansergh's was commander of the forces in Ireland in the 1750s.[24]

Many of those who left Ireland on army and naval commissions overseas were very young, often in their early teens. Martin Mansergh's godfather – General Sir Robert Mansergh or Uncle Bobs as the family refer to him – served in the British army in the Far East during the Second Word War and held the honorary position of Master Gunner. His godson remembered him as a very courteous gentleman, who once said that the Manserghs were too gentlemanly to thrust their way to the top. However, Uncle Bobs rose to become Commander-in-Chief of the Allied Forces in Northern Europe in the three years after 1956.

Many members of the Mansergh family were born outside Ireland because of their fathers' employment in the British forces overseas. Indeed, Martin Mansergh's grandmother was born in 1876 in Dum-Dum in Bengal, the area that gave its name to the lethal bullet. At that time her parents were living in Bengal, the military posting of her father, Major Charles

Stephney Mansergh from Co Cork. Martin Mansergh himself was born outside Ireland on account of his own father's – academic – career.

The family's attachment to the union between Ireland and Britain was evident in a pen-profile of Arthur Henry Wendworth Mansergh. Born in Co Cork in the late nineteenth century, AHW Mansergh was educated at the Royal Military College at Sandhurst. Along with three of his brothers he served with the Crown Forces although he was more fortunate than his siblings who all died on active service.

During his retirement Colonel Mansergh was preoccupied with political events and became actively involved in the unionist cause. A pen-profile in 1914 noted that "his opinions on the subject of Home Rule for Ireland are strong and well-grounded, while he spares no efforts of which he is capable in fighting what he believes would be resultant of irreparable harm to Ireland – the severance of her union with England."[25] These views were hardly consonant with those of his relative, who later worked for Fianna Fáil.

Indeed, the Colonel played an active role in the campaign against Home Rule including taking time to speak at meetings near his home at Warrenpoint. "He sits as a Magistrate for Leicestershire and Co Armagh, and his duties which his devotion to the unionist cause entail upon him include those of Secretary to the Unionist Club and Chairman of the Polling Committee in his district."[26]

He was also a keen golfer at Warrenpoint Golf Club. In 1993, when the club was marking its centenary, Martin Mansergh was an invited guest at the anniversary function. Afterwards he remarked that his unionist relation was: "Secretary of the local Unionist Association, but friendly with the Nationalist MP in the area, as an elderly SDLP supporter told me recently."

Martin Mansergh had a different interpretation of the events in Ireland in the early years of the twentieth century. He noted that as national revolutions go, the Irish one was relatively mild. However, the period from 1916 until the mid-1920s were traumatic for those involved, no matter where their allegiances lay.

There was little immediate impact in Co Tipperary from the Easter Rising in Dublin in 1916. But the situation rapidly changed. During the War of Independence the largest proportion of republican action relative to the total population of the whole country was in Co Tipperary. Moreover, apart from Co Louth, the highest incidence of military action during the Civil War was also in Co Tipperary.

Intimidation and violence were directed at the southern Protestant community. "With their ostentatious loyalism, their ascendancy backgrounds, and their isolated residences in the countryside, they stood out as helpless symbols and as convenient targets for anti-British sentiment," Bowen observed.[27] Throughout the War of Independence and the Civil War this community faced raids, attacks on property, eviction notices and even murder. Peter Hart said: "Protestant experiences of the revolution in southern Ireland ranged from massacres to flight to occasional inconvenience and indifference, from outraged opposition to enthusiastic engagement."[28]

The Mansergh family was in a similar situation to other members of their class when the War of Independence started in 1918. PSG Mansergh ruled that politics was not to be discussed at Grenane. The response was characteristic of many southern Protestants, who adopted a "wait-and-see" stance and generally avoided contact with the army and the police.

The head of the Mansergh household maintained his daily routine of walking into Tipperary Town, but he kept a rifle at Grenane. The first shots in the War of Independence were fired at Soloheadbeg – two miles from the Mansergh estate. The sound of gunfire was heard at Grenane.

The family was fully aware of the dangers. Arrangements were discussed and a plan put in place in the event of an attempt to burn down the property. All those present in the house would be given ten minutes to gather personal and precious possessions before they evacuated. On one occasion, PSG Mansergh confronted several men who were removing the gates at the main entrance to Grenane. Family tradition has it that he approached the men with a toy gun – owed by Martin

Mansergh's father Nicholas – and that they duly responded by putting the gates back up again.

As Terence Dooley has noted, in June 1922, in three districts in Co Tipperary – Templederry, Silvermines and Ballinclough – there was "scarcely a Protestant family ... which had escaped molestation ... Houses have been burned, Protestant families have been forced to leave ... ".[29] Grenane survived the period although the grounds were billeted. Tall trees lined the area around the main house and a deep dike divided the immediate gardens from the farmland. As young boys Gregor and Nicholas Mansergh would hide in the dike watching British troops exercise and train.

Trouble came from both sides in the War of Independence. The Black and Tans shot the family dog on the road outside Grenane. To the amusement of Martin Mansergh, journalist Kevin Myers wrote about this episode in an article in the British current affairs magazine, the *Spectator*. Myers attempted to gauge the turning point in the Mansergh family's political allegiance from unionist to republican. "The year was 1921 and the Black and Tans were bringing their peculiar version of community policing to many part of the Ireland. For reasons which no doubt seemed good to him at the time a certain Black and Tan shot the Mansergh family hound."[30]

It would be more than an exaggeration to ascribe to this particular episode the status of an identity-changing event. However, Martin Mansergh accepted that in a more general sense it was a defining moment in that most Southern Protestants had decided that if the Black and Tans were the price they had to pay for the protection of the Union and their privileged status, the price was much too high. The preference of most southern Protestants was that southern Ireland remained part of the Union, but they recognised the emerging reality.

Furthermore in the particular case of PSG Mansergh, his travels in the southern hemisphere – at the end of the nineteenth and beginning of the twentieth centuries – undoubtedly shaped his outlook and that of his children, including Nicholas, Martin Mansergh's father. PSG experienced first-hand the colonial attitude of Rhodes and his contemporaries in southern

Africa, and before that the question of national identity as it existed in Australia and New Zealand. This may – and Martin Mansergh believes it to be so – have offered him a broader outlook and a wider frame of reference in judging the emergence of an independent Ireland.

His views on Ireland, and Irish identity, left an impression on his son Nicholas and, in turn, his own son Martin. Both father and son shared a common belief in the desirability of a united Ireland. Nicholas would spend his life offering an academic understanding of the beliefs and motivations underpinning Irish nationalism. Martin would become a key participant in a series of events which moved toward closer reconciliation between the different identities on the island.

Two

The Historical Father

In the early years of the twentieth century the vast majority of the Protestant community in Ireland were attached to the union with Britain. Most saw themselves as Irish but in a British context, an identification facilitated by their lifestyle and place in ascendancy society. However, the landed class were about to be forced to confront their identity and allegiance as Ireland became engulfed in political and constitutional chaos with violence emerging as the accepted means of achieving national independence. Change arrived in early 1920 when the Government of Ireland Bill was introduced in the House of Commons. The legislation proposed to establish two parliaments – one for the 26 counties and one for what is now known as Northern Ireland. Northern unionists were happy with this arrangement – subsequently confirmed by the Anglo-Irish Treaty – despite its effective abandonment of their southern counterparts.

The allegiance to Britain of the Irish ascendancy class diminished after 1921, although many landlord families sought to maintain an Anglo-Irish element to their identity. This was achieved by enrolling children in English public schools, by military service and by regular cross-Irish Sea commuting to and from workplaces in England. The writer Elizabeth Bowen observed: "The Anglo-Irish were really only at home in mid-crossing between Holyhead and Dun Laoghaire."[1]

The transition to a new Ireland was more difficult for the older generation of unionists including Martin Mansergh's grandparents at Grenane – PSG and Ethel. Ethel was a unionist and Martin Mansergh suspected she retained that aspect of her identity after independence. He believed his grandfather integrated much easier into the new political order than his grandmother.

The academic Liam Kennedy observed that the consequences of the Anglo-Irish Treaty "dealt a psychological blow of fundamental proportions" to the southern Protestant community, the majority of whom were unionist in political outlook.[2] There was little sympathy for breaking the Union to establish a State that they believed would be Gaelic, Catholic and republican.

Interestingly, the transition to the new independent Ireland may have been easier for smaller landlords – into which category the Manserghs fell. Terence Dooley, who has written about the Big House tradition, observed that these smaller landlords would have been less active in unionist bodies "because they spent more time in their localities and felt susceptible to outrage if they were openly to oppose the will of the majority of the people."[3]

Like Ethel Mansergh, many Protestants lamented the end of the union with Britain but accepted the reality of the situation. This accommodation was achieved in part by social segregation, avoiding controversial subjects when dealing with those from the majority community, and by accepting the nationalist ethos of the newly independent Ireland. Nonetheless, it was a difficult transition amid the violence of the Civil War years, especially given that the landlord class was the target for burnings, lootings and even killings.

Post-independence Irish governments all sought to reassure the Protestant and unionist population that they faced little threat. In the new political order they were numerically small and politically weak. But it was in the interests of the Free State rulers to treat their minority fairly, to demonstrate that northern Protestants would be well treated in a future united Ireland. In general, Kurt Bowen argued: "The minority met with relatively little overt discrimination or open discrimination."[4]

Despite his family background, Martin Mansergh has displayed little sympathy for the position of the landed class during this period. In his judgement, the adjustment to national democracy was difficult because it had been made unwillingly and with much prevarication. "What Mikhail Gorbachev had told Erich Honecker in October 1989 on the fortieth anniversary of the GDR, 'Life punishes those who move too late' is a criticism that may also be aptly applied to the Protestant Ascendancy."[5]

In an essay written in 2000, he touched upon the integration of members of the minority community into all facets of life in the post-1921 independent 26 counties.

> The Free State Government had wooed the ex-unionists, who post-independence and Civil War were still in possession of substantial landed wealth (some of it redistributed by the Land Commission), and who were still a significant force in business, professional and banking life and even in the Civil Service. This phenomenon had not been an unusual experience post-decolonisation in other parts of the world. Post-Civil War, Sinn Féin and subsequently Fianna Fáil recognised the importance of having some links of its own with individuals connected with this milieu, such as Robert Barton who reluctantly signed the Treaty, and his executed cousin's son Erskine Childers who was also recruited. The first President, Dr Douglas Hyde, former President of the Gaelic League, came from the same Anglo-Irish background. The problem with the class, as opposed to some distinguished individuals from it, was a deeply ingrained political, economic and social conservatism, which had held the country back for so long, as well as its lack of empathy with an independent Ireland, particularly one that sought to strike out on its own, and free itself from British tutelage.[6]

The two sons of PSG and Ethel Mansergh were part of the

first southern Protestant/unionist generation to grow up with the newly transformed political and constitutional arrangements. Their forefathers may have joined in the Cromwellian crusade to capture the island of Ireland 300 years earlier, but after 1921 such allegiances were no longer as tenable for the declining ascendancy class which included the young Mansergh boys, Gregor and Nicholas.

Nicholas was born in Tipperary in 1910. He was conscious of the political tumult that coincided with his younger years. Among his earliest memories were the troop trains leaving Tipperary Town for the battlefronts in Europe in 1914-15. He heard the shots that rang out from Soloheadbeg, signalling the start of the War of Independence (which interrupted his primary schooling) and recalled seeing the republican Liam Lynch near Grenane with a gash down one side of his face.

As a young man, Nicholas's father, PSG, had left Ireland for adventures in the southern hemisphere. Nicholas Mansergh also travelled but nearer to home, dividing his time between Ireland and England. These journeys were principally driven by academic endeavours. He studied modern history at Oxford University. Term time was spent in England while university holidays were taken in Co Tipperary.

At Oxford he developed an interest in the Commonwealth. It was an interest which dominated his academic career, allowing Mansergh to produce distinguished research, in particular on Ireland and India. Although at one stage he described himself as "an anti-imperialist," the central tenet of his writings was the relationship between the imperial power and the colonial as the latter sought to attain independence.

> The Commonwealth for my generation had something in common with the Common Market nowadays. I was interested in the Commonwealth to see if it provided a way forward in Ireland itself.[7]

Nicholas Mansergh devoted much time to researching and understanding the settlement reached between Ireland and

Britain in 1921. He argued that the Dominion status given to the new Free State – with, among other things, allegiance to the Crown – was incompatible with republican status. He admired Eamon de Valera's exposition of the concept of external association.[8] It created a situation whereby a post-colonial country could be a Republic, not necessarily within the Commonwealth, but associated with it. The largely undefined Dominion Status suggested that the emerging nation would be secondary and subordinate to the old imperial power. This relationship would obviously offend nationalists and leaders within the nascent Republic. Mansergh believed the British side had seriously erred in imposing Dominion Status on the Irish Free State. It was a lesson that the British learnt well when they drew on Mansergh's analysis of Ireland and the Commonwealth in negotiating independence for India in the 1940s.

Mansergh was also drawn to the related question of partition. In his contribution to a 1997 collection of Nicholas Mansergh's papers, historian Joseph Lee observed that "Mansergh is the pre-eminent authority on partition in the modern world."[9] In that respect Nicholas Mansergh regarded the passage of the Government of Ireland Act of December 1920 as the defining moment in the geographical and political division of Ireland. While many commentators and historians focused on the Anglo-Irish Treaty of December 1921, Mansergh's attention was drawn to the moment with the passing of legislation at Westminster in 1920 when partition received legal basis.

It is an interesting historical quirk that some 70 years after the Government of Ireland Act was passed, Nicolas Mansergh's son, acting as an advisor to the Irish Government, drew on his father's research in the negotiations that led to the Good Friday Agreement. Indeed, Nicholas Mansergh had sought to travel a road similar to his son in terms of building contacts with the various political factions in Northern Ireland. In January 1935 as a young academic, Mansergh met with a Professor Hayes in Dublin and asked for some introductions in Northern Ireland. "I said I should be glad to meet violent politicians of both parties up there but quite firmly he said no: 'There are people up there' he said 'whose politics are no more intelligent than the beating of an orange drum'. And he seemed to think I might be contaminated."[10]

Lee acknowledged that Mansergh, "enjoyed a glittering career by the conventional criteria of English academe."[11] Elaborating on the academic achievements of the Tipperary man, Lee noted that:

> Had he never written a word about Ireland, his standing as a leading authority on Commonwealth history would be secure. But had he never written a word on the Commonwealth, his record as an historian of Ireland would equally ensure him an outstanding scholarly reputation.[12]

The record of scholarship achievement was impressive. Three groundbreaking books on issues on national identity, Anglo-Irish relations and the making of partition were published by the time he celebrated his thirtieth birthday. According to historian Dermot Keogh, Mansergh was "indisputably among the most important Irish historians of the 20th century."[13]

Martin Mansergh offered the following summation of his father's academic career:

> My father sought in his work to raise the level of Anglo-Irish understanding, but in a way that was demanding, rather than of sentimental. He sought to explain to a British audience the depth of the well-springs of Irish Nationalism. He explained to an Irish audience the inner workings of the British official mind towards Ireland as well as the political background to the shifts and manoeuvres that had a disproportionate impact here. He was able to deploy both European and Commonwealth experience to put the problems between the two islands in a larger perspective. While he admired peaceful transition to self-government and independence, it depended a

great deal on the degree of enlightenment that Britain was prepared to show its different possessions. He brought to near-contemporary history and politics a liberal and humane understanding, and was painstaking and judicious in his assessments. He had none of the ingrained pessimism, that sometimes characterise some of the most talented historians of a similar background then and since. He was also little disposed to pass sweeping or dismissive judgements on the ideals and aspirations of his fellow-countrymen.[14]

Although of Protestant ascendancy stock, Nicholas Mansergh believed in the desirability of a united Ireland. Moreover, he found little attractive in the politics of the partitioned six counties. In the summer of 1935 he visited Belfast to observe the traditional Orange Order celebrations. From Donegal Square he watched a 1500-strong Orange procession:

> They were carrying Orange banners with illuminated portraits of Dutch William and other persons of note in the Orange mythology. The music had the merit of a vulgar emotionalism. The parade was obviously determined on trouble and was marching straight for Antrim road. It was not surprising to hear later that there were continuous riots throughout the evening.[15]

Nicholas Mansergh's regular travels between Tipperary and Oxford saw him mixing in senior political and official circles on both sides of the Irish Sea. For example, a diary entry for Saturday 5 May 1934 records meetings in Dublin with the Clerk of the Seanad, the Controller of Prices, an official of the Land Commission and Sean Hayes, a Fianna Fáil TD for Tipperary. Another entry from the summer of 1938 recounts a tour of 10 Downing Street given by a senior advisor to the then British Prime Minister.

The Irish-born academic was as at home in the halls of

Oxford, and the political circles of Dublin and London, as at the local fairs in Co Tipperary. He had inherited the house and lands at Friarsfield in the early 1930s (his elder brother, Gregor, having inherited the Grenane estate). Although there was a farm manager and several other men employed at Friarsfield, the young academic was fully involved in running the farm. His diary entries are full of references to rural life – picking fruit, planting crops and trading at the market. Consequently his fascinating diary entries could refer to tennis at Oxford and a discussion about royalties with his publisher but also to travelling to Ireland to select the cattle to be sold at the fair the following day.

One entry noted that potatoes from Friarsfield were "very easy to sell as they have a high reputation in town".[16] Another entry from January 1935 recorded three hours of haggling at the Cappawhite Fair where the following conversation was overheard:

"An old farmer: 'Who is that?'
Another farmer: 'One of the Mansergh brothers'
1st: 'Are they good buyers?'
2nd: 'They mean business but sell to anyone else if you can for they give bloody low prices.'"[17]

Mansergh was also emerging as an influential scholar: by 1934, he was about to publish his first book which his Oxford supervisor, a Professor Adams, believed would be "quietly successful" on account of its "intrinsic merit".[18] Nonetheless there were some disappointments. When he was unsuccessful in obtaining a fellowship at the university in 1934, he wrote in his diary: "Have an idea that my nationality is telling heavily against me at Oxford."[19] He was an undergraduate at Pembroke College in Oxford from 1929 to 1933 and obtained his doctorate in 1936 at the age of only 26. Most Irish and British officials and politicians, who were involved in the subject of independence for Ireland, were alive and his work benefited from contemporary access. Indeed, his thesis supervisor had been an advisor to Lloyd George and Secretary of the Irish Convention in 1917.

The publication of *The Irish Free State* in 1934 met with

approval and generated a higher profile for its author, leading to increased demand for his services in Ireland. He chaired a meeting of the College Historical Society at Trinity College, Dublin in February 1937, while in April 1938 he participated in a books programme on Radio Éireann. Guests on the programme *I Like This Book* had to speak for 20 minutes on a volume that was a particular influence on them. Mansergh selected a biography of Kaiser Wilhelm II by Emil Ludwig. A subsequent invitation for another programme was withdrawn. Correspondence from Radio Éireann in August 1939 observed that a proposed series had been cancelled because its transmission would have been "difficult in the present state of international tensions" which may have led the material to be "misunderstood by various classes of listeners".[20]

Mansergh remained at Oxford until the start of World War Two working as a tutor in the School of Modern Greats and acting as Secretary of the Oxford University Politics Research Committee. During the war years, he was employed at the Ministry of Information where he was involved with the Anglo-Irish information services and cultural relations. The Tipperary man quickly made an impression, being appointed Head of the Dominions Section in July 1942 while, less than two years later, he was made Director of the Empire Division. This latter position saw him seconded to the Office of the UK High Commissioner in Ottawa from August to September 1944 and, during the same months the following year, he filled a similar role in Pretoria. Mansergh also visited Southern Rhodesia and Kenya. The report of his visit to Canada – marked 'Secret' – observed: "Exiles – particularly Irish exiles – tend to become fundamentalists in politics."[21] It was an interesting comment from a man who was himself in the category of exile.

During the war years two particular exiles were resident in the Ministry of Information in London. One of Winston Churchill's closest confidants quickly followed Mansergh to the Ministry in 1941. Brendan Bracken, a Catholic from Templemore in Co Tipperary, who traded on false claims about his background, education and experience was appointed as political head of the department. He reorganised the wartime

Government's relationship with the media, leaving the print and electronic outlets free to comment on domestic matters while "ensuring that propaganda to neutral and enemy countries was efficiently organised."[22]

Among those working in the British Embassy in Dublin was Rita Dudley, later the wife of Fianna Fáil minister and Irish President, Erskine Childers. Her initial mental picture of Mansergh was formed from phone conversations: "I visualised a small, etiolated figure with a wispy beard and a watch-chain, draped across the front of his waist coat."[23] This impression was overturned when the official at the Embassy in Dublin met the Co Tipperary man from the Ministry of Information. "He was tall, still young, a Tipperary Protestant, and the least dim person I have ever met. He had a Socratic mind which turned work into a perpetual dialogue with one who made all those around him feel like his peers."[24]

One of the objectives of the Ministry of Information was to minimise negative media comment on Ireland's policy of neutrality. Mansergh worked with the poet John Betjeman who would open letters to the Co Tipperary academic with: "Dear old dim doctor."

They arranged for letters from Pamela Hinkson, a Dublin-based journalist, to be published in the London *Times* newspaper. This correspondence was aimed at presenting a better understanding of the policy being pursued by the Fianna Fáil Government in Dublin. The two Ministry men also organised a lecture tour in Ireland for Christopher Hollis, editor of the *Tablet*, who reported back to London on meetings with figures such as de Valera and John Charles McQuaid, the Archbishop of Dublin. The Ministry also encouraged the London press to adopt restraint in its criticism of Ireland.

Mansergh also went on a 14-day, fact-finding mission to Ireland in March 1943. It was his first visit home in 12 months. The role was not to spy – his position would have been known to the civil service, and political figures, whom he met – but rather to gather information to inform British policy on Ireland. His confidential report contained interesting information on Irish political opinion in 1943. The conclusions were formed after meeting an array of individuals such as Eamon de Valera, the editors of the main national newspapers and his bank manager in Co Tipperary. He noted that there was no shortage of wireless batteries and that there was interest in war films which "nobody had seen but everyone had heard about".

The report – which was submitted to the Ministry of Information on the 6 April 1943 and marked 'Confidential' – observed that Lord Haw-Haw's broadcasts were "listened to with no little attention" and that "no one really believes that the Germans have committed atrocities in occupied Europe". Three specific observations stand out in the report – pessimism about the future, concerns about the communist threat and the existence of anti-American sentiment.

"Pessimism about the length of the war is matched by pessimism about the prospects of lasting peace," Mansergh concluded. He asked the Taoiseach for his views on post-war Europe. De Valera "replied immediately that the problems were so overwhelming that one could hardly say how long would be the period of peace. He said there was the outstanding case of frontiers which was almost impossible to settle without goodwill and he did not believe that Russia would display goodwill."

De Valera was not alone in talking about the Soviet Union. Mansergh observed that the country appeared to be "obsessed with the Bolshevik bogey". The prospect of a spread of communism appeared to have created a hostile response to the Beveridge Report that was the inspiration for the creation of the welfare state and the national health services in Britain. Mansergh ascribed this hostility to the costs involved, to a view that it would sap national character and also to the Catholic Church, which was "clearly influencing opinion". Interestingly, in light of Mansergh's own social standing, he acknowledged that he "had no means of gauging working class opinion, but agricultural workers were not enthusiastic".

Mansergh detected widespread anti-American sentiments. He relayed the background to the decision to decline University College Dublin permission to invite Herbert Agar to deliver the Father Finlay lecture. The idea had been suggested by

American diplomats in Dublin, but when UCD sought approval from the Department of External Affairs, two reasons were offered for refusal: the visitor was believed to be separated from his wife and he was also believed to have conducted anti-Irish propaganda in the United States.

As the war neared an end, the possibility of a permanent civil service position with an annual salary of £800 was raised with temporary officials, like Mansergh, who were "selected on the basis of outstanding individual ability". Mansergh's first choice would have been the Dominions Office but he declined – "with not inconsiderable regrets" – a decision influenced by a "rather considerable decrease in salary" and his preference to return to academic life.[25]

The latter wish was met in 1947 when Mansergh assumed the chair of British Commonwealth relations at the Royal Institute of International Affairs at Chatham House. He was also teaching at the University of London. Negotiations on the future status of India were underway in 1947 and Mansergh travelled for the first time to the country on the verge of its independence. He had observer status at the Asian Relations Conference. India was to act as a stimulus for further original work on the nature of relations within the Commonwealth. In subsequent years, on three separate occasions he was Visiting Professor at the Indian School of International Studies in New Delhi.

Upon his return from India, Mansergh delivered a seminal lecture entitled 'The Implications of Eire's Relations with the British Commonwealth of Nations'. The paper was sent to Clement Attlee, who referred it to a cabinet committee that was considering Commonwealth relations. In the course of the lecture Mansergh asserted that newly independent countries such as India could declare themselves to be Republics and still remain within the Commonwealth structure. The paper was also mentioned in a *Sunday Independent* article that prompted media questions to then Taoiseach John A. Costello during an official visit to Canada. Costello was asked about the External Relations Act and whether or not it should be repealed. His response signalled the Irish Government's intention to formally establish the State as a Republic. Mansergh regretted the decision to leave the Commonwealth and was never satisfied with the official explanations given by Costello for the move.

The declaration of a Republic in 1949 signalled a shift in Mansergh's academic interests as his principal area of study – Ireland and the Commonwealth – began to diverge. Over subsequent years the Commonwealth featured less in his work as he focused on India and also Irish nationalism. In 1953 he departed Chatham House for Cambridge University where he was appointed the first Smuts Professor of History of the British Commonwealth. He taught courses in Anglo-Irish history and also supervised graduate research students in the area of Irish history. For many years he acted as an External Examiner for the National University of Ireland.

Mansergh's standing as an academic was such that in 1967 the British Government asked him to become editor-in-chief of India Office Records where all the documents on the transfer of power to India in the 1940s were stored. The influential work *The Commonwealth Experience* was published in 1969. One academic reviewer observed that it was "a magisterial work, the scholarly distillation of four decades of intellectual endeavour in Oxford, London and Cambridge."[26]

In 1969 he became Master of John's College, Cambridge, a position he held over the following decade. The appointment was a break with tradition as Mansergh was neither a college bursar nor tutor, positions held by previous Masters. According to one college report at the time the Tipperary academic was a "strong man and popular company in the senior common room" although it was forecast that he was "unlikely to excite controversy".

Until his death in 1991, Nicholas Mansergh continued to apply his formidable intellect to the study of Ireland and Irish nationalism. His historical work was based on accuracy and on a preference for first-hand sources of information. His interviews with leading political figures made him wise to political life and the limits of political action. Described in the *Irish Times* as "modest, humane and liberal in outlook,"[27] he was an individual who was sufficiently confident in his own national identity as an

Irishman to accept an OBE from Britain, the country in which he resided and worked for almost half a century.

Nicholas Mansergh was fortunate during his years at Cambridge University in having Diana Keaton as his wife. Born in 1919, she was a practical person with an abundance of organisational talents that were applied throughout her life to family, church and scholarship. She was the daughter of the principal of Reading Grammar School; her grandfather was the organist of Peterborough Cathedral.

They met on a tennis court at Oxford University. He was a fellow at Pembroke. She was a student at Lady Margaret Hall and an excellent sportswoman with Oxford blues in tennis, netball and lacrosse. When the couple's engagement was announced one local newspaper carried the headline 'Don to Marry Triple Blue'.

They married in December 1939, and had five children – Philip, Jane, Edward, Martin and Nicholas. As Joe Lee acknowledged, the couple "came to form one of the great partnerships of the university world. St. John's is a big college, a challenge for even her impressive talents as organiser and hostess. But she brought to the task of making all members, undergraduates, graduates and fellows, and not least the Irish among them, feel a sense of belonging, the same imagination and dedication she brought to the refurbishing of Friarsfield."[28] For many years the couple lived between the Mansergh Tipperary home and England where Nicholas pursued his academic career.

Both worked in the civil service in London during the war years, but the new member of the Mansergh family very much took to a life of commuting primarily between Ireland and Britain: "Quintessentially English in the best sense, she eagerly embraced the new Irish dimension of her identity ... " was one summary.[29] She was an active member of the local Church at St Mary's in Tipperary while also serving on the Synod of Ely in Cambridgeshire.

The couple were tolerant and open-minded in their outlook. Later, when Martin Mansergh announced his decision to leave the civil service to work for Charles Haughey no negative words were uttered. "They were liberal in every sense of the term and believed in people pursuing their own career. They never judged things in terms of material risk," Martin Mansergh recalled.[30]

Diana Mansergh was closely involved in her husband's academic career. She undertook the time-consuming and detailed task of compiling the indexes to the books, checking and double-checking sources and acting as proofreader. "She counselled on drafts, seeking to clarify sentence structures that could verge on the excessively complex, as he strove with passionate fair-mindness to fashion a style that would render precisely the infinite nuances of tone, temper and thought inherent in Anglo-Irish relations."[31]

This involvement with the work of her husband continued after his death in 1991 until her own in England in 2001. She oversaw the completion of the manuscript of his last book, the critically acclaimed *The Unresolved Question: The Anglo-Irish Settlement and Its Undoing 1912-1972*. It was a remarkable achievement, given that she was in her seventies and had to work largely from her late husband's handwritten notes. She subsequently collected and edited two volumes of the selected writings of her historian husband.

The posthumous publication of Nicholas Mansergh's Irish papers offers some tantalising insights into the kind of political context Martin Mansergh grew up in, especially given the latter's commitment to Fianna Fáil and to the notion of a 32-county Irish Republic. To begin with, Nicholas Mansergh's assessment of the founder of Fianna Fáil (from hitherto unpublished diaries extracts) was almost consistently positive.

He recorded an election meeting in Tipperary in June 1937 at which de Valera spoke for one and quarter hours – "with warmth but without rancour ... [and] ... his firm refusal to descend to claptrap".[32] By contrast, several days later he attended another election rally, this time addressed by W.T. Cosgrave, who received "a magnificent reception and dealt effectively with interruptions. But the rest of his speech was not so good."[33]

Nicholas Mansergh considered de Valera one of the greatest

politicians to serve in the first half of the twentieth century. In a commentary written in advance of the 1948 general election Mansergh observed of the then Taoiseach: "Austere, but not so aloof as it often supposed in this country, Mr de Valera combines intellectual ability with a shrewd political judgement ... He is a man of inflexible will – ready to compromise when he has got what he wants."[34] This opinion of the first Fianna Fáil leader did not diminish over time. In 1970, Mansergh observed that de Valera was "on any reckoning to be numbered with the great men of our time".[35]

He found de Valera's position in the upper echelons of world affairs as "the more remarkable in one sense in that he became a world figure, not by playing any significant part in world affairs but by becoming by force of character and long survival symbolically representative of a twentieth-century nationalism that had at once discarded the liberal, inter-nationalist trappings of much of nineteenth-century nationalism and sharply repudiated the ideological, left-wing, self-styled internationalism of the twentieth century".[36]

With regard to a commitment to a united Ireland, an entry from 13 February 1938 (Oxford) was highly revealing in terms of the Mansergh family's positioning in the post-independence Ireland:

> Though my own life may prove supremely dull to everyone except myself, I am living at a time when men believe that the foundations of our civilisation are in danger of destruction. Even now when I am 27, I who was born in the last year of King Edward's reign, a citizen of the U.K. of G.B. and Ireland, can remember stories of the Easter Rising of 1916, was fully conscious of the Anglo-Irish war and the Civil War that followed as I was then all the time in Tipperary, where I greeted Republicans and Free Staters alike with equal enthusiasm; I became polit-ically conscious in the last years of the Cosgrave regime, I lived through and suffered financially by the economic war and the world depression... What

else shall I witness? I hope and believe the collapse of the dictators, *the unification of Ireland*, the birth of a new international order – but it may be just a Second World War.[37] [Italics added]

Aside from a nationalist outlook, Nicolas Mansergh was on the left in terms of political belief. When rejecting the idea of writing a pamphlet on Ireland for the Fabian Society, Mansergh pointed out that he was neither English nor "in any party sense, a Socialist".[38] The extent to which Martin Mansergh followed his father's ideological outlook will be discussed in subsequent chapters.

Three

An English Upbringing

Martin Mansergh first came to Ireland at Easter 1950 when he was four years of age. His father was on vacation from his job at the Royal Institute of International Affairs, Chatham House, in central London. The family took the ferry crossing from Liverpool to Dublin before travelling by car to Co Tipperary. This was a fixed routine: school vacations at Easter, summer and Christmas were all spent in Ireland. The Manserghs were living at that time in Surrey in England. Martin Mansergh was born in Woking, 25 miles south west of London, on New Year's Eve in 1946. Indeed, only one of the five children of Nicholas and Diane Mansergh were born in Ireland, the eldest son, Philip, who was born in the Rotunda Maternity Hospital in Dublin in January 1941 – his mother being prescribed Guinness to encourage lactation. The other children – boys, Martin and Nicholas, and girls, Daphne and Jane, – were born in England.

Nicholas Mansergh would commute by train to London every day and his young son would stand on a chair by a window allowing him a good view of the passing trains. When Martin was six-years-old, his father changed jobs, accepting a position on the teaching staff at Cambridge University. The Manserghs set up home in a large country house at Little Shelton about five miles outside the university town.

Clear childhood memories remain with Martin Mansergh from the family's vacation journeys from England to Co Tipperary. The ferry crossing from Liverpool to Dublin; the ensuing delay as it took several hours for cars to be taken off the ferryboat. As they waited the Manserghs would travel into Dublin city centre. "I can still vividly recall the sounds of the horses and carts on the cobbled quays across from the North Wall, and admiring the Guinness train at Kingsbridge Station. There was a genteel shabbiness about Dublin in the 1950s."[1] He also remembered climbing Nelson's Pillar in O'Connell Street in central Dublin.

Car journeys were not always easy on the poor roads in Ireland of the 1950s. Mansergh recalled a heavily laden car with four children squeezed into the back and another in the front. There was the inevitable breakdown or puncture on the bad stretch of road between Kildare and Monasterevin. The family would decamp to the house at Friarsfield, two miles outside Tipperary Town. The property was the home of their father and the residence of his mother. Ethel Mansergh had moved from Grenane when her eldest son married in 1948, although she spent much of the winter in Dublin, enjoying the theatre and visiting art galleries.

Friarsfield House with its view of the Galtee Mountains offered a significant contrast from suburban England. The children revelled in the space and freedom with hens, chickens and pigs in the farmyard and cattle, sheep and oats in the fields. There were trips on the donkey and cart to the local creamery and visits by car to Limerick City to purchase books and records.

The house was a warren of rooms for the children to play hide-and-seek. There were modern conveniences – "the telephone had a handle to it, which had to be turned vigorously to get the local exchange" – but also inconveniences like water rationing when not enough rain collected in the tank above the roof. Drinking-water was drawn from a pump in the farmyard.

Cricket was played on the lawn. His father gave them tennis lessons at the Tipperary Lawn Tennis Club. His uncle Gregor was actively involved with the sport in Ireland for almost half a century. In the winter and early spring months they followed the hunt from Grenane or attended point-to-point meetings. There were visits to the beach in places like Dunmore East during the summer months; trips to watch the planes at Shannon Airport and an outing to Bunratty Castle not long after it opened.

Martin Mansergh recalls: "The Rock of Cashel was great fun,

as we could climb up all the staircases to the open roof, before people worried about insurance claims."[2] Nicholas Mansergh would attempt to convey a sense of place on family expeditions for his children, providing them with the historical associations of everywhere they passed. His son recalled: "the Liberator's house in Derrynane; Parnell's last despairing fling of his arms in College Green as a dying man in 1891; Smith O'Brien's friendship with his great-grandfather, Richard Southcote Mansergh; the ambush at Soloheadbeg; the spot on the Knockmealdowns where Liam Lynch died; Father Matthew's statue near the ruins of Thomastown Castle".[3]

There were servants at Friarsfield. His grandmother had a cook. There was a farm manager and other farm workers as well as several gardeners. The lifestyle was far removed from that experienced by the vast majority of the Irish population. The 1950s were a bleak time in Ireland – the economy was stagnant and jobs were scarce. Only emigration boomed, averaging around 30,000 a year between 1948 and 1958. This stark contrast in lifestyle was acknowledged by Martin Mansergh: "There was great poverty 40 years ago, children going about without shoes, large families living in one or two bedrooms, old women wearing the traditional black shawl."[4]

A local man managed the Co Tipperary farm. Denis McGrath was "an auctioneer, who was active in the old IRA and enormously respected in the locality. He was a fount of wisdom and experience to a young boy like myself".[5] Mansergh also recalled conversations at the creamery and visits to the market to watch how bargains were made and differences split. He said he "picked up quite a lot of the ways of the Irish countryside" from mixing with the people who worked for his father and also his relations in Co Tipperary.

At the start of the 1960s, Mansergh was enrolled at boarding school in Canterbury in the south-east of England. From then on he spent less time at the family home in Cambridge – term was in Canterbury and holidays were spent in Co Tipperary. "Each September, as we left, my grandmother gave us each five pounds, and my uncle marked our height in pencil against the edge of the drawing-room door and wrote in the year."[6]

The 13-year-old Mansergh started at Kings School, Canterbury in 1960. Privately funded, Canterbury is part of the British
public school system. The middle and upper classes in Britain
favoured their children attending public schools like
Canterbury. These schools were a staging post on the steady
progression through to university and then into government or
military service, or the professions. Students were instilled with
a confidence about their place in British society and educated to
exercise authority in the worlds of politics and business. As one
commentator remarked: "The public schools produce most of
the people who run Britain most of the time."[7]

The public schools were – and, indeed, remain – a symbol of
the class-based society in Britain. The BBC broadcaster Jeremy
Paxman, in a book on the British establishment, observed:

> It would be hard to overstate their influence upon the
> institutions of power in Britain. It is not merely that
> they provide a disproportionately large part of the
> elite in so many areas of national life. The very shape
> of organisations, from the financial institutions of the
> City to the Church of England, reflect in some way
> the structures and mores of the public schools. The
> internal hierarchies, the requirements for promotion,
> the assessment of excellence, the masculine clubbi-
> ness, the rewards for loyalty, are all instantly recog-
> nisable ... as products of the public school system.[8]

There were calls in the 1960s for their abolition. Aside from
the elitist ethos, tales of cold baths and bullying were
legendary. In 1964, a newly elected Labour government
established a commission to examine options on the future of
public schools. The Canterbury Headmaster faced up to the
criticism in his annual address in July 1965, when Mansergh
was a final-year student at the school. The Rev. Paul Newell
said the critics preferred abuse to reason: "There are those who
fondly believed that if only one abolished the 11–plus, public
schools, Ascot and the Athenaeum, the millennium would have
arrived ... "

Canterbury traces its origins back to 597 when St Augustine and a group of 40 monks arrived in Kent to convert the local population to Christianity on the instruction of Pope Gregory. With its medieval buildings and sense of history, Canterbury is today one of the most visited tourist locations in Britain. The school is set in the shadow of the cathedral. The young Mansergh was taken by the "magnificent cathedral ... walking in and around the building every day was wonderful".[9]

Kings School is an integral part of the historical cathedral city. Christopher Marlowe – a contemporary of William Shakespeare – and the author Somerset Maugham are among famous past alumni. It takes a mixture of boarding and day students. When Mansergh was a boarder it was still an all-boys school.

Private education in Britain is not cheap and Kings School is among the most expensive of institutions within the public school system. The fees in 2002 were €18,000 per year for boarders and €12,600 for day students. Parents know that in return for these fees their children are offered an environment with wide subject choice, attentive personal tuition and an extensive range of extracurricular activities. The vast majority of students at Canterbury attend university – the school boasts that in 2001 98 per cent of its final-year class went on to university. The ultimate destination of many of these students would be Oxford and Cambridge. And it was no different in the 1960s when Mansergh left Canterbury for Oxford.

An indication of the range of extracurricular activities is evident from the schedule of events for annual end of year King's Week in July 1965. This was Mansergh's final year as a boarder at the school and he wrote previews for many of the events for school newspapers. The school orchestra played Beethoven, Brahms and Hayden; Micheál MacLíammóir performed his one-man show on the life of Oscar Wilde, *The Importance of Being Oscar* while Dudley Moore entertained the pupils with a little jazz. The review of the latter performance is a good illustration of the confident atmosphere that pervaded King's School:

> From the moment he slid on to the stool in front of
> the Steinway at eight sharp until his third curtain call
> and the presentation of a magnum of champagne by
> the school more than two hours later, Dudley Moore
> – surely one of the leading modern jazz pianists in
> the country – had this most unlikely jazz audience in
> the palm of his hand.[10]

Throughout the eighteenth and nineteenth centuries members of the gentry in Ireland sent their children to English
public schools, but in many cases their Irish backgrounds meant
they were not always considered as full members of the elite
class. The British upper classes were not shy of pouring scorn
on their Irish counterparts with their alien accents and
residences in the 'bogs of Ireland'. A member of the Irish landlord class recalling his public-school years, a century before
Mansergh went to Canterbury, observed that the "Irish boys
were ridiculed … especially on St Patrick's Day".[11]

The English-born Mansergh would experience such ridicule,
in various degrees of severity, first at public school and then
later at university. These incidents cannot be discounted when
attempting to trace the development of his nationalist leanings
and loyalty to the Fianna Fáil party. In recent years he
acknowledged:

> as Parnell discovered in Cambridge, and eighteenth-
> century Irish gentlemen before him and Loyalists
> since, no matter what the religious or social back-
> ground, to the English, anyone from Ireland or with
> Irish roots was liable to be regarded, affectionately or
> otherwise, as a person associated with bogs.[12]

The teenage Mansergh was increasingly aware of his split
nationality – English-born but with family roots in Ireland. "I
would have been specifically conscious of it when very
young."[13] He was marked out from his contemporaries at
public school. "I was regarded as different in many ways," he
admitted.[14] This difference emerged from two distinct charac-

teristics – not only was from an Irish background but he was academically very bright.

One of his teachers played on the teenager's Irish background and also his height. Mansergh was given the nickname 'Bog-bean'. He laughs at the label, saying it was worse for his younger brother who also attended Canterbury. Nicholas Mansergh was known as 'Little Bog'.

Micheál MacLíammóir's visit to King's School in 1965 offered evidence of the questioning of identity in the 18-year-old Mansergh. He sat opposite the Irish actor at an evening meal during King's Week and described himself as "Anglo-Irish". MacLiammóir replied: "That's a term we must abolish," before turning to the Canterbury headmaster and saying, as he pointed at Mansergh, "Look, the young William Butler Yeats." Mansergh later said it was "quite the most flattering and inspiring remark ever made to me in my life … "[15]

Many of the ascendancy class lived a dual existence during the early years of the independent Irish State – living and working between Ireland and Britain. But it was an existence that could not be maintained. Most members of the following generation faced a choice. As Mansergh himself described the position, members of that class had to "decide which half of a hyphenated inherited identity we were in practice opting for".[16]

The young Mansergh was one of those descendants of the unionist landlord class in Ireland who had to reconcile a split-nationality after the 1921 Anglo-Irish Treaty. The overwhelming number of landlords, like his grandparents, who remained in Ireland after the 26 counties achieved its independence from Britain, opted for the Irish side of their dual allegiance. For many it was possible to maintain some element of their former identity, but that became more difficult for their children and grandchildren. The newer generations were rooted in an independent Irish State and had little personal memory, if any, of their family association with Britain.

An increasing focus on his Irish roots was matched by a developing personal sense of where Mansergh wanted his identity to be. He had a memory of travelling with his father who was on a lecture tour to the United States in 1956. The trip included a visit to Duke University in North Carolina. The Manserghs were invited to a reception at the Governor's Mansion, a property which had been built before the United States achieved its independence from Britain. The young Mansergh sat in the Governors' chair which bore the inscription 'Representative of George III' – "I remember not liking it one little bit," he said.[17]

As he departed Canterbury for Oxford University in the mid–1960s, Mansergh was increasingly aware of the choice he would have to make: was he English or was he Irish, or was he Anglo-Irish? In fact, he was moving beyond the necessity to merge the land of his birth with the land of the family. Later he would simply describe himself as an Irish citizen. He believed that if he were a Catholic, nobody would ever raise the question of his antecedents. He was prepared to say that his background was Anglo-Irish, but as far as he was concerned the ascendancy was history.

Interestingly, in a highly defensive article written in 1981, Mansergh, who had just started to work for Charles Haughey, challenged "the whole notion that there was such a thing as an Anglo-Irish culture at least in the 20th century, and a *fortiori* that there was a necessary antithesis between this and the 'native' culture".[18]

This wish – almost need – to put the distance of history between himself, his birthplace and the country of his early years, and also his family genealogy, may have fuelled the strong nationalistic leanings which dominated his political thinking in later years.

The strength of such anti-imperialism within the young boy is difficult to determine, but Mansergh was confronted by several factors that influenced his national identity. "If you are second generation you have a choice – a choice of where one wanted to live and a choice of identity. But I suppose it would have been tied up quite significantly with the farm. It may seem odd now to look back at 1950s 'Ireland as an idyllic place but it seemed more interesting and more beautiful (than Britain) and there would also have been holiday memories."[19]

Those holidays in Ireland exposed him to an identity and

national outlook, which would not only have been far removed from the public school curriculum and ethos at Canterbury, but also from that which so dominated his own family history. "I was acquainted with 'the other tradition' in England, as I had a Presbyterian nanny, a Miss Eleanor McCenaghan from Portmagee in the North of Ireland, who was a marvellous friend in every way. But the reaction which her mild anti-popery created inoculated me at an early age from sectarian prejudice. All the same, she told me of the horror of Cromwell's sack of Drogheda, in total contrast to the heroic role attributed to him in the English school history books."[20]

Ireland was not just the home of his grandmother, uncle and cousins. Two formative issues – one at school and another at university – remained in his memory. While at Canterbury there was a transition-type year between state examinations. During this non-exam year his English language teacher gave a class on Irish literature.[21] Discussion of the works of James Joyce and William Butler Yeats fascinated the teenage student. He read Joyce's *Dubliners* and also *Portrait of an Artist* but the poetry of Yeats made the biggest impression.

The attraction to the poet was influenced by the "shared background which inflamed the imagination a little bit".[22] There was some similarity. Yeats, who was born in 1865, lived during the turbulent period of Irish history when nationalism was on the rise; and by the time of his death in 1939 had successfully secured an independent Irish State. The poet also came from a Protestant background and he, too, also aligned himself with the nationalist cause.

"I remember being struck instantly by the 1916 poem," Mansergh recalled.[23] The poem 'Easter 1916' was written by Yeats to reconcile his own feelings about the Rising in Dublin that started a series of events leading to the creation of the Irish Free State in 1921. The British response to the rebellion was to arrest and execute its leaders, a decision that swung an initially sceptical public in Ireland firmly in support of the actions during Easter week in 1916. Yeats took the names of those executed men who led the rebellion and associated them with myth and symbol.

McDonagh and MacBride
And Connolly and Pearse
Now and in time to be,
Wherever green is worn,
Are changed, changed utterly:
A terrible beauty is born.

The 'shared background' diverges, however, when consideration is given to their respective views on the impact of independence upon the Protestant landed class. As noted previously, Mansergh was critical of the Protestant ascendancy for not showing enough empathy with the newly independent state. A reading of Yeats's speech in the Seanad debate on divorce in 1925 has the poet condemning legislation imposed by the convictions of the majority upon members of the Church of Ireland and those of no church. "If you show that this country, Southern Ireland, is going to be governed by Catholic ideas and by Catholic ideas alone, you will never get the North," the poet told the Upper House.[24]

Mansergh's increasing attraction to Ireland and in particular aspects of Irish nationalism may in some sense also be a compensation for his English birth and ascendancy background. He was continuously keen to make family associations with Irish nationalism and also those who fought for an independent Ireland. For example, he stressed that his grandfather stopped on walking trips to Tipperary Town to talk with old IRA men; his father's farm manager "was active in the old IRA" and his anti-Home Rule relation was friendly with local nationalists.

The emphasis on the Irish identity increased further when Mansergh departed Canterbury for Oxford University. It was a seamless transition from elite public school to elite university. Oxford graduates have dominated public life in Britain; half of the Prime Ministers in Britain over the last century, including Tony Blair, studied there. Mansergh was aware of the pre-eminence of Oxford in British life. He said of his own contemporaries: "There was still a small upper crust of aristocrats, but the bulk of students were middle-class."[25]

The three Mansergh brothers – Philip, Martin and Nicholas –

moved from Kings School in Canterbury to study at Oxford University. Their sisters Daphne and Jane respectively studied at Cambridge University and Trinity College, Dublin. Martin Mansergh studied at Christ Church College in Oxford. He may have left the 'magnificent' cathedral at Canterbury, but in Christ Church he arrived at probably the most architecturally impressive campus at Oxford, complete with its own cathedral on site. Founded in 1525 by Cardinal Wolsey as Cardinal College, the name of the college was changed by Henry VIII in 1549 after Wolsey fell out of favour.

Christ Church is estimated to be the wealthiest college within Oxford University. Along with the ownership of some 18,000 acres of land, it is believed to have endowments valued at over £100 million.[26] Graduates of the college include philosopher John Locke, poet WH Auden and broadcaster David Dimbleby. Famous staff included mathematics professor CL Dodgson, better known as Lewis Carroll, author of *Alice in Wonderland*.

Mansergh took a multi-disciplinary undergraduate course studying Politics, Philosophy and Economics. The Oxford University website asks the question – "what careers do PPEists go into?" – and provides the answer – "the financial sector and industry; journalism and the arts; academic research and teaching; public service and politics."[27]

The late 1960s was a period of great international student unrest. Protest movements were in vogue, opposition to the Vietnam War was a unifying cause. In November 1970 Mansergh wrote an article on university agitation for the *Oxford Times* newspaper. The more militant action of the student body was described as sincere but confused. The young intelligentsia were moving to the left, Mansergh observed, because they believed that society was unable to cope with the problems affecting the world. "The self-interest of the powerful corporate bodies, the defence of historic privileges may yet in the absence of a regrouping bring government and democracy to a halt. Not to put too fine a point on it, the present division of society is becoming an anachronism."[28]

The time at Oxford also coincided with the emergence of

popular culture. But the attention of the young Mansergh was captured by many influences. A love of classical music developed at both Canterbury and Oxford. He was a voracious reader but also found time to attend a short horticultural course on growing berries. In later years, several varieties of berry would form part of the gardens at his Tipperary home.

At Oxford Mansergh was confronted by images which re-inforced his privilege ascendancy background, images that made him uncomfortable. "The portraits in the dining hall seemed embarrassingly full of eighteenth-century archbishops of the Church of Ireland, lord lieutenants of Ireland, and prime ministers."

Just as public school had exposed its privileged students to famous and influential personalities, Oxford University offered boundless opportunities to attend debates and meetings at which some of the most senior political figures in contemporary society were guest speakers. Mansergh, for example, attended a public meeting in 1973 that was addressed by the Tory Chancellor of the Exchequer. He recalled "asking a critical question about the inflationary consequences of their expansionary policies, and being disgusted by the put-down of a reply I received, which was 'You did not get much applause for that question'."[29]

He got his first experience of the Rev Ian Paisley when the hard-line unionist politician from Northern Ireland spoke at the Oxford Union. Paisley delivered what Mansergh described as a "crude assault on Catholicism, playing shamelessly to prejudices not too far below the surface of English life".[30]

The appeal of his Irish identity was also conditioned by contemporary changes in Ireland. He read the *Irish Times* at the Oxford Union. "I would go in practically every day. It was Lemass's Ireland and things were on the up. The pragmatic and less ideological Ireland (as opposed to Britain) would have appealed."[31] Once more his Irish background meant there was less than full acceptance by his peers. "Certain members of Christ Church had an embarrassing habit when drunk late at night, of singing 'Land of Hope and Glory' and 'Rule Britannia' at the top of their voices, and accosting unfortunate passers-by like myself and interrogating them on their loyalty."[32]

During the summer of 1969 when violence broke out in Northern Ireland, Mansergh was on holidays from Oxford in Ireland. He had little difficulty in identifying where his sympathies should lie. The Troubles, he said, "forced a final resolution of any problems of destiny and divided identity".[33]

The events of 1969 caught, he believed, the two governments by surprise. The British considered the Irish Question to have been put to bed in 1921 and had difficulty in the 1960s in moving from the majority rule principal. The Dublin administration under Lemass had pursued constructive co-operation with the Stormont regime, a flawed initiative involving southern nationalism and northern unionism that did not cater for northern nationalists. By the time the Troubles started Mansergh was reconciled to moving to Ireland to live and work when his studies were completed. He had settled the issue of identity.

When his undergraduate studies were completed, Mansergh was accepted as a doctoral candidate. His area of research was pre-Revolutionary French eighteenth-century history. For almost four years he delved into the struggle between crown and parliament in France in the late 1700s. A central issue was the viability of an independent absolute monarchy. The research necessitated several study trips to France where papers and records were consulted. His fluency in French was essential. "The high point was probably the month spent in a *chateau d'eau* in the Marne Valley, reading the small but very neat print of a 4,000-page diary kept by a president of the Parlement of Paris during exile to his estate from 1771 to 1774," Mansergh recalled.[34]

The 559-page dissertation was submitted during Trinity Term in 1973. It was entitled: 'The Revolution of 1771 or the Exile of the Parlement of Paris.' In the acknowledgements he thanked "the British taxpayer for giving me the freedom and independence with which to pursue my research for three years." There was also gratitude for his new wife and young daughter.

Mansergh had met Elizabeth (Liz) Young at Oxford in October 1967. They were both attending a reading of a Brecht play at the German Society at Pembroke College. He had "rashly vowed" never to marry someone from Lady Margaret Hall, his mother's old college, a promise that later became a source of much humour. Liz Young was studying modern languages. She was from a Scottish Presbyterian background. "We chatted on the way out and things took off after that," Mansergh recalled, although their initial introduction was not without a humorous incident.[35]

> Plucking up the courage to say a few words to this beautiful, unattached student as we came out of Pembroke College, where my father on modest means had come from Ireland to study 40 years earlier, I invited her to tea in my rooms across the road in Christ Church.[36]

The young Mansergh was living in the Meadows Building, which looked out over the spires of Oxford on one side while from the other it offered a pastoral setting with grazing cattle. After the couple climbed to the fourth floor, Mansergh realised they were locked out – he had left his keys in the room earlier in the day. He made some excuses and left his new friend on the landing before racing to the porter's lodge to get a spare key – "and then, a few minutes later, having run the fastest race of my life, tried to appear unruffled as I reached the top of the stairs again".[37] The embarrassing moment provided Liz with an invaluable insight into practical inefficiencies of her future husband. Martin Mansergh wrote in his diary for that day in October 1967 – "I met the most fabulous girl today."[38]

When marriage was mooted Mansergh received a letter from his prospective father-in-law who wanted to be reassured on two points. How did he propose to support his future spouse and did his own parents approve of the marriage? On the latter point he was fortunate – "They tended to judge people on intelligence rather than on wealth" – while he responded to the first question with "Next year's student grant."[39]

The couple married in September 1969 while still students at Oxford. They purchased a terraced cottage in Charlbury, a village rising above the River Evenlode, about 15 miles from the university town. There followed then a routine of continuous travel between Charlbury and Tipperary. Their eldest child Fiona was born two days after their first wedding anniversary in 1970 while the second member of the family, Lucy, was born in October 1973. They moved full-time to Co Tipperary in 1973 as Mansergh worked on completing his doctorate.

During this time Mansergh wrote letters to the newspapers including the *Irish Times* and the London *Times*. Several letters dealt with the subject of rail travel, an indication of the travel mode most used by the Oxford student in moving between England and Ireland. A letter to the *Oxford Times* in November 1970 on timetabling of the Charlbury-Oxford route was followed twelve months later by a letter to the *Irish Times* objecting to the possible closure of the railway station in Tipperary Town. The lack of co-ordination between the rail and ferry services, and in particular the difficulty in travelling to mainland Europe, provoked further letters to the *Irish Times* in May and October 1973.

Of more interest, however, are a series of letters to newspapers written during the period up to 1974. These reveal a distinctive liberal attitude in response to topics such as contraception, divorce, censorship and equal rights for women.

The sale and importation of contraceptives was illegal in Ireland under legislation passed in the 1930s. A private members' bill to liberalise the law was defeated in the Seanad in the early 1970s, but a debate was underway as an increasing number of people considered the legislation outdated. While conservative groups were prepared to publicly lobby for retention of the status quo, Mansergh was concerned that not enough liberals were coming forward to argue the alternative case. A letter to the *Irish Times*, published in March 1971, clearly placed him in the liberal camp.

> Even assuming the rhythm method worked (to ensure 100% success sexual relations are not to be enjoyed till the 19th day of the women's monthly cycle, and by that time she is beginning to lose her

appetite for them; facts, which, however indelicate, are not conducive to sexual, and thus to some extent marital, harmony), what proportion of the mothers of Ireland know about it, or when they do, are able to work it themselves with the co-operation of their husbands?[40]

He returned to the same subject in November 1973, again in a letter to the *Irish Times*, remarking that "it's notorious that it is easier for the middle-class, the educated and the mobile, whether Catholic or Protestant, married or unmarried, to obtain contraceptives."[41]

A Supreme Court case in 1973 prompted a change in the law on contraceptives. The judgement declared that the 1930s legislation banning the import of contraceptives was unconstitutional. The result was that their importation into the Republic was no longer illegal but their sale was still outlawed. The Fine Gael/Labour Government attempted to change the law to take account of the court's judgement but the Dáil rejected their proposals. The legal impasse was ended in 1979 when, ironically enough, Charles Haughey was Minister for Health. While still someway short of what Mansergh favoured, he later described the Haughey response as "a skilful political compromise. I thought it was a formula of some brilliance".[42]

Liberalisation along the lines supported by Mansergh in 1971 did not happen for another two decades, until a Haughey-led Fianna Fáil–PD coalition – amid some controversy and much conservative opposition – allowed for the free sale and advertisement of condoms.

In December 1972 Mansergh made a case for the introduction of divorce in the Republic in an *Irish Times* letter in which he observed that religious persecution should not be allowed to impact on the decision to remove the constitutional ban which existed. Even among his own creed, Mansergh argued, people should be citizens first and Protestants second.

The pattern of liberal thought went beyond the sexual morality area and included strong views on the value of co-education and the rights of women. He wrote to the London *Times* in June 1972 making a case in support of the admittance of women to men's colleges at Oxford. To those who asked what harm the ban did, Mansergh – somewhat ironically given his own background – observed that "privilege never did so much harm to those who enjoy it. But what about those who don't."[43]

These letters were written during a period when Mansergh was in transition in career and personal terms. His relatively comfortable background afforded him time to complete his doctorate while relocating to Co Tipperary. He had resolved some years earlier that his future was in Ireland. His allegiances were increasingly with the Irish Republic and – over subsequent years – he would give ideological expression to these allegiances through strongly held republican beliefs. The comment of a trade unionist, who sold books and postcards at the Rock of Cashel to the teenager Mansergh, has often been quoted: "Of course, you'll stay." In later years Mansergh would claim he believed the man's words were a "silent expectation that some member or members of my branch of the family would come home for good".[44]

This thinking was not dissimilar to the attitude of the landed gentry a century previously, the belief that they were in a position to rule and do the State some service by joining the military. One writer observed: "Such a choice was seen to be the natural extension of a landlord's perceived duty to lead, something they became aware of at an early age."[45]

In many ways, Mansergh in choosing Ireland as his home – and following a public service career – was mirroring the attitudes of the ancestral class he had politically abandoned. In his own mind his career choice involved some form of repayment: "As a descendant of a minor landowning family which had lived comparatively well off the land, though not free of financial problems in Cork and Tipperary for around 300 years, I felt, growing into adulthood, as I am sure my father felt, that I had a duty to give something back."[46]

In reaching into his family heritage Mansergh chose to turn away from his family's unionist background, which could well have been maintained by remaining in the land of his birth. Instead he accepted his father's Irishness but deepened the attachment by means of an exclusively Irish national identity. "Attachment to the homeland is probably, the most powerful generator of patriotism," he wrote in a letter to the *Irish Times* in March 1974 when making the case for not aligning nationalism with an ability to speak the Irish language.[47] By making Co Tipperary his permanent home Mansergh went some way towards achieving that aspiration.

The inheritance process for the family property at Friarsfield had already started by the early 1970s. For taxation purposes his father had passed over two-thirds of the property to his two youngest sons while retaining the other third. "It was touch-and-go that I would have settled down on the farm," Mansergh recalled.[48] His parents were moderately opposed to the idea. His father told him: 'you have to go to Dublin.' This position was possibly motivated by Nicholas Mansergh's own move from Chatham House in central London in the mid-1950s to university life at Cambridge with the result that he was cut off somewhat from metropolitan life.

But it was Ireland, and not London, that attracted Martin Mansergh. "The Ireland of the 1960s was forging ahead in an exciting manner. I wanted, if possible, to find the opportunity to take part, even though my social background and largely English upbringing might be more of a disadvantage than an advantage."[49]

The Oxford student gave some consideration to an academic career but eventually rejected this employment route.

> People of an academic frame of mind ... if they don't go into academia – who want to do something related to the world they are living in rather than from a university standpoint – well, the next port of call would have been the civil service.[50]

The idea of public service appealed. All thoughts of making money in a private-sector role were discounted. "I was a child of the 1960s. Those were my formative years. I suppose my views would have been moderate-left."[51] This negative attitude toward the profit motive diminished over time. "It is an unreasonable prejudice. I would no longer believe that there is an intrinsic moral superiority in the public service over making money."[52]

The Irish civil service was expanding in the early 1970s. University graduates were being recruited for entry-level official positions. The Department of Foreign Affairs needed additional diplomatic staff to cope with the new demands relating to Irish membership of the European Economic Community (EEC) which Ireland joined in January 1973. The first Irish presidency of the Council of Ministers was due for the first six months of 1975.

Mansergh had been preparing for the recruitment process. One of the conditions for employment in previous recruitment rounds was a working knowledge of the Irish language. As a student of the education system in England, Mansergh had never learnt the language but, along with his wife Liz, he started to attend classes. But the effort was needless, for when the job vacancies in the civil service were eventually advertised, the Irish language requirement was dropped for candidates who were educated outside the State. The new policy was motivated by a desire – prompted by the Foreign Affairs Minister Garret FitzGerald – to attract northern Protestants into the civil service. As Mansergh – English with Irish roots but Protestant – quipped "I happened to get caught in between."

The first civil service interview was dominated by a discussion on the merits of French literature. His interviewer – recently returned from France – was obviously impressed as Mansergh got called for the second round of the recruitment process. The panel at the second interview asked detailed questions about the economy and local history of the home localities of the respective candidates. Mansergh was happy to discuss these subjects in relation to Co Tipperary. On what the Tipperary economy needed, the answer he gave was: "jobs and more jobs." It was a response worthy of a man who would later seek to represent the southern part of the county in Dáil Éireann.

When the interviewer moved to local historical matters, Mansergh was well prepared. His father's interests and also a personal knowledge of the family history in Co Tipperary were invaluable. Questions were asked about historical monuments in Tipperary Town and he was able to talk about the statue of the Fenian activist and writer Charles Kickham. Interestingly, the Kickham monument would, almost 30 years later, serve as a backdrop to a video recording made for the Fianna Fáil Árd Fheis, promoting Mansergh as a general election candidate.

The Oxford graduate finished in first place in the assessment process. In several ways he was an unusual civil servant. First, at 27 years of age, he was older than many of his contemporaries and second, he also had greater financial security. For his first nine months as a civil servant Mansergh was attached to the Political Division of the Department of Foreign Affairs. This was the section where a great deal of preparatory work for the EEC Presidency was co-ordinated.

His first – and as it turned out, only – diplomatic posting was to the Irish embassy in Bonn. He arrived in late 1975 as Third Secretary, a junior official rank. There was some difficulty with the incumbent Ambassador Robin Fogarty, but he admitted it was good training for the years ahead, especially adjusting to working with Charles Haughey.

The Manserghs moved to Bonn with their two eldest daughters, Lucy and Fiona. A son, Daniel, was born in December, 1976. His obviously delighted father left the hospital to celebrate with colleagues in the Embassy. Such was his excitement, however, that he crashed his car into a concrete pillar underneath the Embassy building. But the new father was unscathed. "When I unpopped a champagne cork in the Embassy upstairs, it narrowly missed the late Ambassador Robin Fogarty, who protested he was getting too old for that sort of thing."[53]

There was also great excitement in Co Tipperary at the arrival of the new grandson who would continue the family surname. "When I rang home to Tipperary (it was just before Christmas) my mother ran into my father and informed him: 'Daniel Mansergh has arrived.' He immediately assumed that this was yet another distant relative turning up on the doorstep from California or Australia."[54]

With Liz Mansergh recuperating in hospital, her husband spent a lonely Christmas with his two young daughters eating, by his own admission, "the toughest and most famished turkey from Poland that I have ever had in my life."[55] The Manserghs would have two more children, Harriet and Alice. When Harriet was born in Holles Street in Dublin in 1985, Ned O'Keeffe, a Fianna Fáil backbench TD from Cork, predicted to Mansergh: "Begob, Martin, you will be needing a bigger pocket now."[56]

One of the first tasks of the new Third Secretary in Bonn was to save money for the Irish taxpayer. Mansergh was given responsibility for locating a suitable new property to house an expanding Irish embassy in the West German capital. Having found the property and finalised rent negotiations, agreement between Mansergh and the prospective landlord broke down over payment for car-parking spaces. The rent for the car spaces was greater than what was been paid at the existing Irish Embassy property – DM120 versus DM47. This was double the charge of DM60 that Mansergh had expected.

The young diplomat was unwilling to meet the rent sought and a stand-off developed much to the annoyance of other embassy staff who did not want the deal to flounder with the loss of valuable car parking. The new Third Secretary likened the deal to cattle sales at marts in Co Tipperary. A compromise rent of DM 60 was eventually agreed. "In any negotiations you must be prepared to risk the loss of what you want. I was immensely satisfied and very pleased with my little victory."[57]

In 1977, the Bonn Embassy played host to President Patrick Hillery who was accompanied on the visit by the Minister for Foreign Affairs Garret FitzGerald and his wife Joan. Mansergh recalled the visit because of a "wild goose chase" over a missing coat belonging to Mrs FitzGerald, and also having to find a pair of socks for her husband. The Irish government minister had adhered diligently to a hotel notice advising all departing guests to leave their luggage outside their bedroom before seven o'clock in the morning to ensure the bags were collected. However, FitzGerald had also packed all his socks.

Mansergh recalled the scene: "So when I arrived at his room at the top of the stairs, Dr FitzGerald opened the door and started waggling his bare toes at me, asking could I get him a pair of socks. The innkeeper duly sent me back with two pairs, which earned me the ministerial commendation of a 'most efficient service'."[58] FitzGerald has no recollection of the young Mansergh, although when informed that he benefited from the change in the Irish language rule, the former Taoiseach laughed: "So then he owes his career to me – he never said 'Thank you' – blast him."[59]

A knowledge of German meant senior colleagues would take the Third Secretary to briefings not normally attended by diplomatic staff of this rank. One of the more interesting assignments during his time in Bonn was to represent Ireland at meetings in Finland of the Conference on Security and Co-operation in Europe. It was, he said, a "thoroughly interesting experience" especially given that he met with military personnel from other countries including the Soviet Union.

The posting in the then West Germany left a deep impression. The mid–1970s was the height of the Chancellorship of Helmut Schmidt. Mansergh was impressed: "He was a super-competent head of government. It was a good education in how you can run a modern State in a broad social democratic way."[60]

The Irish diplomat was also very conscious of the example of Germany for the divisions in Ireland. Despite the obvious differences, there were similarities in the constitutions of the two countries. Unity in both Ireland and Germany seemed remote in the 1970s. The crucial difference between the Irish and German cases was the much greater relative prosperity of West Germany and the fact that the people of East Germany had no democratic voice in their destiny. Mansergh was influenced by the policy of developing closer unity between the two Germanys through the creation of greater interdependence.

He saw similarities between the *Ostpolitik* policy of Willy Brandt and the Lemass-O'Neill talks. Egon Bahr – a German political advisor – made a lasting impact with his statement that realities had to be recognised in order to change them. There were obvious parallels with Northern Ireland. Nationalists had to realise that they could not dictate to unionists: the only way forward was through constructive engagement. In later years, when discussing the peace process in Northern Ireland, Mansergh would frequently make reference to the experience in Germany where unity followed the collapse of communism in 1989.

The posting in West Germany allowed time to travel in Europe, and also provided the young diplomat with an opportunity to read, especially on Irish history. He recalled reading aloud to Liz part of the novel *Knocknagow* by Charles Kickham, the Tipperary Fenian activist.

In one of those coincidences of history, the Bonn Embassy staff maintained a watchful eye on an international court case involving the Irish Government and a German arms dealer. The case revolved around a dispute over the net proceeds from the sale of guns bought by a German dealer. It was claimed that the money used in the transaction had been misappropriated from the £100,000 Northern Ireland relief fund sanctioned by the Fianna Fáil Government in 1969. It was a funny twist that saw Mansergh being quoted on the case which was associated with some of the events which led to the sacking of Charles Haughey as Finance Minister in 1970.[61]

After just over two years in Bonn, Mansergh returned to the Department of Foreign Affairs in Dublin. He had been promoted to the rank of First Secretary and was assigned to the Energy Division. Much of his work was associated with energy, science and technology policies within the EEC. The international oil crisis was at its height. But Mansergh was also kept busy with domestic policy. Some of this work was concerned with the proposal to build a nuclear power station in Co Wexford.

Colleagues recalled someone who worked very hard, was fair to junior colleagues but was not the type to go out for a drink after work at the end of the week. "He was a man of few words who always seemed to be churning out stuff, although often it was not directly connected with our section. Ideas always seemed to be coming to him," one former colleague remarked.

The Third Secretary often worked through lunchtime writing papers. When it was finished he might go off for a quick walk. These papers concerned subjects such as the value of a North-South gas interconnector. They attracted the attention of officials in the Department of the Taoiseach who were curious about this diplomat who, as one colleague recalled, was "working outside the box".

Fianna Fáil returned to government after the 1977 general election. Garret FitzGerald departed as Minister for Foreign Affairs. The new Taoiseach Jack Lynch appointed the Tipperary North TD Michael O'Kennedy as the new incumbent in Iveagh House. O'Kennedy served as Foreign Affairs Minister until the change of leadership in Fianna Fáil at the end of 1979. "I was conscious of this bright young man. His attitude was positive and there was only one way he was going and that was up," O'Kennedy recalled.[62]

Indeed, Mansergh did have a bright future ahead of him and, almost certainly, would have been eventually promoted to ambassadorial rank. But by the end of the 1970s he was giving serious consideration to his future in the Department of Foreign Affairs. Another foreign posting would have had serious consequences for his commitment to – and involvement with – the family farm in Tipperary.[63]

In December 1980, the up-and-coming diplomat opted to leave Foreign Affairs. Colleagues were surprised at the announcement. Mansergh decided to accept a position in the Department of the Taoiseach, working for Charles Haughey. O'Kennedy was one of those who expressed amazement at the decision. "It was very unusual, quite unique that someone like that would make such a move, especially as his career pattern in Iveagh House was only going in one direction."[64]

When Mansergh initially moved from Iveagh House to Government Buildings on secondment, there was some resentment among his civil servant colleagues. "The civil service is very territorial. They tend to protect their patch. Mansergh was moving closer to Haughey which would have cut them out," remarked Frank Dunlop, a former Fianna Fáil advisor who was based in the Department of the Taoiseach, where Mansergh arrived as a new staff member in January 1981. Feelings hardened six months later when he left the civil service to join the Fianna Fáil payroll. "Some in Foreign Affairs despised him for going to work for Fianna Fáil," Dunlop added.[65]

Another former Fianna Fáil official recalled: "There were two problems, he not only left Foreign Affairs to work for Fianna Fáil, but he left to work for Haughey. Some of them used to call him 'Dr Mengele' and when Martin heard this I remember him taking great offence."

The role of the advisor will be discussed in chapter ten but at this point it is worth recalling Mansergh's own assessment from 1988 of civil service attitudes to his position as political advisor. "I have no difficulty on this occasion. In this Department they're used to me. I have a role to play and they have a role to play, and I would characterise the relationship as an entirely constructive one."[66] The implication from the comment was that there were strains during his initial period in government working with Haughey. Nevertheless, any antagonism was long gone when Mansergh and several of his former civil service colleagues in the Department of the Taoiseach and the Department of Foreign Affairs combined to make a success of the peace process.

Moreover, in recent times he has defended his former colleagues from criticism levelled by Austin Deasy, a former Fine Gael minister. In late 2000 Deasy said many Irish diplomats "feel they have to mimic the British Foreign Service with their pinstriped suits and Oxford accents".

Mansergh was unimpressed and went public with his criticisms:

> I found extraordinary the timing of an attack on the professionalism of the Irish diplomatic service, scarcely a month after the stunningly successful campaign for a Security Council seat at the UN, after the immensely difficult but hugely important advances in the peace process ... [67]

He added that, as someone who had spent six years studying

at Oxford: "I am not conscious of anyone in the current Irish diplomatic service, which has its own distinctive style and traditions, who has an Oxford accent." He said he believed the only "suspect" was himself, but it was 30 years since he left Oxford and 20 years since he departed the Department of Foreign Affairs. Mansergh quipped that "despite such obvious handicaps of speech and education" he had sought to be of some service to the country. A career move made in January 1981 provided the opportunity to undertake that service.

Four

Joining the Soldiers

Charles Haughey was elected leader of Fianna Fáil in December 1979. The new Taoiseach had had a chequered career. As a dynamic, young minister in the 1960s, he had earned a reputation of being an achiever with ambitions to lead his party. However, his career fell apart in early 1970 with allegations of an illegal arms importation plot involving money from the Irish Government. Haughey, along with other senior party colleagues, was accused of leading an operation that would have supplied guns to nationalists in Northern Ireland. He was dismissed as Finance Minister. Although acquitted by the courts, the whiff of sulphur remained. Moreover, there were rumours, although at that time unproven, about the source of funds for his lavish lifestyle. But Haughey was a doughty politician. After serving his time in the political wilderness, he returned to cabinet in 1977, and two years later was chosen by his party to succeed Jack Lynch as leader.

At that time Martin Mansergh was ready to change jobs. A second overseas diplomatic posting was due during 1981. But he had decided, that if he were to continue being involved in the Tipperary farm, it would be impossible to remain with the Department of Foreign Affairs. There were other considerations at play, moreover. Despite the political neutrality that came with his civil service career, the outlook of the Tipperary man diverged from that of most departmental mandarins who were his contemporaries and superiors in Foreign Affairs. It was unlikely that this divergence of views – not necessarily publicly expressed – would have stunted Mansergh's career path at

Iveagh House. An irrecoverable break was, however, made at the end of 1980.

On Mansergh's 34th birthday on 31 December 1980, Haughey invited him to move to the Department of the Taoiseach on the recommendation of Pádraig O hAnnracháin, a senior civil servant who was close to the Fianna Fáil leader. O hAnnracháin's daughter, Orla, worked with Mansergh in the Department of Foreign Affairs. She had joined as a Third Secretary towards the end of 1979 and was assigned to the Energy Division where Mansergh was the senior diplomat. O hAnnracháin would have heard his daughter talk about her section boss. However, the main interest in the Foreign Affairs official was generated from the material he was producing on issues linked to his brief but considered in a wider policy context. Officials in the Department of the Taoiseach had noticed his work and ideas.

Mansergh joined the Department of the Taoiseach at Principal Officer level and was assigned to the co-ordination and preparation of speeches. However, the time in office was short-lived. Haughey called a general election in June 1981, but the result left him short of a majority in the Dáil. Fine Gael and Labour formed a coalition government. Mansergh left the security of the civil service to join Haughey's backroom team, although with his interest in the family farm he most probably had greater financial security than most of his contemporaries.

He was appointed Head of Research when Fianna Fáil took its place in opposition. The decision to leave the security of the civil service impressed Haughey:

> He took a big risk in following us into opposition. He resigned from the public service and what in those days would be looked upon as a secure pensionable job when there weren't all that many jobs around. But it wasn't just a job to him. He was full of political enthusiasm; committed to the philosophy and ideals of Fianna Fáil. He was a very definite republican and nationalistic in outlook.[1]

71

Mansergh's strong-held republicanism placed him philosophically closer to Fianna Fáil than any other party in the Irish Republic. He was also an admirer of the new Fianna Fáil leader. Moreover, his father had had a healthy respect for the party's founder Eamon de Valera and would have brought home stories from his meetings with the Fianna Fáil leader. Mansergh himself remarked: "In Irish politics the family would have tended to the Fianna Fáil side of the fence."[2]

Mansergh met Haughey for the first time in December 1980 although there was an earlier association with the family. Haughey is believed to have hunted at Grenane with Gregor Mansergh, but the Fianna Fáil politician himself has no recollection of such a meeting. There are several references to Haughey and Fianna Fáil in the correspondence that Gregor Mansergh sent to his younger brother, Nicholas.

Those references confirmed the family disposition towards Fianna Fáil although it was one that was not uncritical, especially in 1982 when Haughey was enveloped in scandal. Nicholas Mansergh was a Liberal supporter in British elections but his admiration for politicians in an Irish context led him to de Valera. However, admiring the Fianna Fáil leader was not always a guarantee of support for the party he led. In the 1937 general election Mansergh made nine impressions on his ballot paper, giving his first preference in the Tipperary constituency to the candidate for the Farmers Party followed by Fianna Fáil, Fine Gael and Labour.

Nicholas Mansergh would undoubtedly have associated personally with the policy platform of the Farmers Party, which contested elections between 1922 and 1932 before regrouping as the Centre Party and then merging into Fine Gael. Its policies were economically conservative and it enjoyed the support of ex-unionists and Home Rule voters.

There were some family misgivings about Mansergh's Departmental change in January 1981 and even more over his career change some six months later. But the young civil servant was attracted to Fianna Fáil's pragmatism and its views on Northern Ireland. Nevertheless, on the face of it the pairing of Martin Mansergh with the party of Charles Haughey was an unusual one. Here was an English-born member of the Church of Ireland from an ascendancy family who had been educated at Oxford University. Fianna Fáil was a conservative-populist party led since December 1979 by a man with a dubious history and motivated, apparently, by an irredentist brand of republicanism.

In 1980 Mansergh had a more liberal outlook than the vast majority of those involved in Fianna Fáil. His views clashed with the party's conservative positioning on issues such as contraception and divorce. However, the new Haughey advisor was able to reconcile those differences as they were secondary to his political outlook. In the more personally important area of nationalism, Mansergh was more comfortable with Fianna Fáil and its attitudes to Northern Ireland than any other party. Indeed, as emerged over time, his own views on the North were probably stronger and more strident than those of the party he went on to serve.

The origins of Fianna Fáil can be traced back to the divisions that emerged in the original Sinn Féin over the Treaty of Independence negotiated with Britain in 1921. Unhappy with the terms negotiated in London, de Valera as leader of Sinn Féin opposed the Treaty terms. He objected to the many British references in the document, including an oath of allegiance to the British monarch to be taken by Irish parliamentarians. There was also criticism that the Treaty would cement the partition of Ireland into two separate political entities.

However, in the subsequent debate in Dáil Éireann a majority accepted the compromise. In the view of Michael Collins, the republican military leader, the Treaty was the means to achieve further independence. In the aftermath of the Dáil vote Sinn Féin split with the pro-Treaty side forming Cumann na nGaedheal – the predecessor of Fine Gael – which governed until the 1932 general election.

De Valera led his supporters into political, and for some time military, opposition. The Civil War that followed the Treaty debate was bitter and divisive. However, the anti-Treaty side ultimately acknowledged the inevitable and ended their conflict with the fledging Irish Free State. But anti-Treaty Sinn

Féin still remained outside parliamentary politics as the party continued with its abstentionist policy towards Dáil Éireann. De Valera was aware of the difficulties posed by a continuation of the policy, underpinned by his party's opposition to the controversial oath of allegiance. A move by the Sinn Féin leadership to abandon the policy was narrowly rejected at a party Árd Fheis, and de Valera soon departed. Disillusioned with political life on the margins, de Valera and his supporters founded Fianna Fáil in May 1926. Six years later the party was in government and remained there until 1948. The main opposition to Fianna Fáil came from the pro-Treaty grouping, which reinvented itself as Fine Gael.

The hostility between the two groupings was exacerbated by the Civil War. However, in reality there were few tangible policy differences between Fianna Fáil and Fine Gael. One writer noted: "Apart from their origins and the personalities of their leaders, it is not easy to trace any sharp distinctions of principle or policy between these two leading Irish parties."[3] That observation was made in 1959.

Over subsequent decades, Fianna Fáil and Fine Gael marked themselves out as parties with broadly based ideologies. Trinity College political scientist, Michael Gallagher observed how both parties offered "pragmatic images ... frequently not backed up by policies at all ... (with Fine Gael appearing) ... like a less-well-packaged version of Fianna Fáil with the same basically pragmatic, problem-solving approach".[4]

The two main parties in the Irish Republic were not, however, exact mirror images of each other. There were differences, although the differences were those of degree and of emphasis. Traditionally, Fianna Fáil was more socially conservative than Fine Gael; it was more nationalistic and it placed greater emphasis on achieving a distinct Irish way of life. One study in 1984 ranked political parties on a scale of zero to ten – with zero being extreme left and ten being extreme right. It placed Fianna Fáil at 6.3 and Fine Gael at 6.8. The Labour Party was ranked at 3.6. By means of comparison, the same left-right scale at that time placed the British Labour Party at 2.3 with their Conservative opponents scoring a 7.8 mark.[5]

Further evidence on the lack of differentiation between the two largest parties in Ireland was available in a study by academic Peter Mair who examined election manifestos from 1948 to 1982. He noted a considerable overlap in the policy themes identified by Fianna Fáil and Fine Gael. Indeed, seven of the ten most frequent themes in Fianna Fáil and Fine Gael election manifestos were common to both. Moreover, five of these themes also turned up in Labour Party manifestos.

In reality, Fianna Fáil prided itself as being neither a party of the left nor a party of the right. It was driven by populism. It was centrist in approach. These features have in recent years meant that Fianna Fáil has had no difficulty entering into coalition governments with parties from divergent ideological perspectives. Mansergh associated with the pragmatism of Fianna Fáil. He provided an illuminating insight into the internal Fianna Fáil perception of its own place on the ideological spectrum in May 2001:

> Fianna Fáil has very broad-based support, averaging 40-50% of the electorate. This, with the single exception of the Swedish Social Democrats, is the most consistent record of any European political party. Fianna Fáil has been deemed as a catch-all party, as one that tries to be all things to all people. Opponents wish that Fianna Fáil would plump for a particular constituency, instead of trying to maintain a broad appeal. While committed to equality of opportunity, rights and treatment, and to outcomes that lift the whole population above the persistent poverty level, we have the advantage of being pragmatic as to means. Certainly, since the 1950s, we can put together a mix of policies, some of which in terms of inspiration come from the Left, and others from the Right. Our critics, needless to say, rarely want to look at the whole picture.[6]

The evidence may indicate the existence of no sharp left-right division in contemporary Irish politics, but Mansergh had no difficulty in identifying just where he believed Fianna Fáil should be placed: "We certainly aim to be the party that occupies the entire ground of Irish politics."[7] And he approvingly noted how a speech delivered by Lemass in Tipperary during the 1965 general election conveyed "a flavour of ... classic Fianna Fáil pragmatism towards public enterprise ... "[8]

This preference for a political party with a broad ideological positioning – or, indeed the lack of one – is one answer to the question of why Mansergh was happy to accept Haughey's job offer in the dying days of 1980. However, it is not a sufficient explanation, especially given the historical passion that motivated Mansergh.

He said two issues – Northern Ireland and social democracy – led him to Haughey and by association, Fianna Fáil. The 1981 career move was certainly driven by a desire to reclaim the republican ideal from the Provisional IRA, and return republicanism to the ownership of constitutional politicians. This goal became part of the Mansergh agenda for the peace process and will be elaborated upon in later chapters.

Moreover, Mansergh also held a deep aversion to the emerging economic agenda of Margaret Thatcher's Conservative Government in the UK which came to power in 1979. Her right-wing economic policies had not fully taken hold by the end of 1980, but the central tenets of Thatcherism were emerging. In 1981 Mansergh may have riled against the anti-union/privatisation agenda of the Thatcher Government, but by the end of that decade, he was advising a Fianna Fáil administration that was pursuing a variation of the British policy to kick-start a depressed Irish economy.

I joined the Fianna Fáil backup team from the Civil Service as Head of Research in July 1981, in an advisory capacity to Charles Haughey, motivated as much by the desire to see Ireland avoid having to take the Thatcherite road, as by the desire to promote a more assertive and thought-out democratic Republicanism. I also felt I had as good an understanding of socialism as many in the Labour Party. Fianna Fáil going back to the 1930s shared many of the same goals and had a much larger slice of the working-class constituency, but was not encumbered by the same ideological baggage.[9]

Mansergh shared many of the values of the Irish Labour Party, including the desirability of economic fairness and the importance of an equality agenda. In comparison with social democratic parties in Western Europe, the Labour Party in Ireland pursues a relatively right-wing agenda. During the 1970s Labour considered itself as socialist in ideological outlook. But Mansergh had a problem with the party's commitment to the nationalisation of industry. Labour was also at that time opposing the European integration process, a movement that Mansergh considered central to the future economic and political development of the Irish Republic.

These differences ruled out membership of the Labour Party. Having said this, it could be argued that the social democratic attitude espoused by Mansergh in 1980 was not far from the philosophical outlook adopted in the 1990s by the Labour Party. Fergus Finlay, a long time adviser to the Labour Party who worked with Mansergh in the 1992-94 Fianna Fáil/Labour coalition, remarked upon these social democratic leanings: "Martin has much more in common with European mainstream social democratic values than some members of the Labour Party – and certainly than a lot of members of the party he worked for so diligently."[10] Indeed, of the four coalition governments that Fianna Fáil has been involved in, the arrangement with the Labour Party was probably the one most favoured by Mansergh.

Nevertheless, at the start of the 1980s, membership of the Labour Party was not an option due to the specific nature of its left-leaning agenda. Any prospect of Mansergh joining Fine Gael was ruled out because of that party's policy on Northern Ireland. He was obviously comfortable with the legacy of history in his attitude to Fine Gael. This was evident in late 1994 when John Bruton became Taoiseach. The Fine Gael leader approached Mansergh with an offer to remain in his position as special advisor on Northern Ireland. Mansergh did not consider the offer a viable proposition. He was unwilling to cut off contact with his friends in Fianna Fáil and also felt that "somebody who sort of crosses the floor politically just to keep a job would arouse suspicion and their credibility wouldn't be the same."[11]

Even without the job offer from Haughey in December 1980, there were pointers as to the political leanings of the young diplomat from the Department of Foreign Affairs. Fianna Fáil was his party of choice because more than any other issue, policy on Northern Ireland was the issue that underpinned Mansergh's political outlook. He observed in 1997 that "the North or the national outlook is still more than anything else the glue that binds most members of Fianna Fáil together, who would otherwise span the right-left spectrum on economic issues and issues of socio-moral legislation."[12]

In Mansergh's own world view, his political outlook was republican in both a political, social and philosophical sense, augmented by a commitment to egalitarianism involving equality of opportunity, and also by a formal separation between Church and State. Over the last 20 years as an advisor to Fianna Fáil, those values and beliefs have been tested time and time again. Sometimes they have been given secondary importance, as in the moral referendums in the 1980s, but on other occasions they have guided national policy, as in the peace process.

From January 1981 onwards, Mansergh became the ever-present member of Fianna Fáil's backroom team. He worked for three different party leaders – Haughey, Reynolds and Ahern – in eight different governments. In office he was Special Advisor to the Taoiseach and when the party lost power he acted as Head of Research for Fianna Fáil. He was a key advisor on Northern Ireland and played a vital role in the peace process. Moreover, he was involved in the negotiations of coalition governments with the Progressive Democrats in 1989 and 1997 and, probably more significantly, with the Labour Party in 1992. Indeed, over the last 20 years Mansergh has been a participant in most of the key dramatic events in contemporary Fianna Fáil history including the controversial resignations of Haughey in 1992, and of Reynolds in 1994. There is no doubt but that Mansergh has been one of the most unusual individuals to serve Fianna Fáil. He stood out when compared with the other individuals who served in advisory capacities under Haughey, Reynolds and Ahern. In the first instance he was the only senior person to serve each of the three most recent leaders of Fianna Fáil. Moreover, Mansergh was driven by an almost intellectual attachment to the concept of Fianna Fáil which translates from Irish as Soldiers of Destiny. This view was expressed by several senior party figures including Séamus Brennan: "For him it's about more than a job. He is really committed to the idea and ideals of Fianna Fáil."[13] One journalist accurately captured the conundrum in 1994: "Fianna Fáil has never been over-burdened with academics and intellectuals, and Mansergh's knowledge and scholarly skills have made him almost indispensable to the party." [14]

An outsider to Fianna Fáil until he went to work for Reynolds in 1992, Seán Duignan observed at close quarters the interaction between party and advisor. The RTÉ journalist remarked:

> Fianna Fáil positively delighted in their own Protestant republican complete with distinguished Anglo-Irish pedigree and Oxford honours. They might joke about him being a cross between Dr Strangelove and Dr Mengele – 'Mansergh pronounced as in panzer' – but they would brook no criticism of him by outsiders.[15]

Fianna Fáil had long been perceived as the anti-intellectual party. Academics and thinkers were associated with Fine Gael and the Labour Party. Protestants such as Erskine Childers, a former minister, and Michael Yeats, a Dublin TD, had served Fianna Fáil, but they were in a minority. Moreover, the last place one expected to find an Oxford-educated member of the Church of Ireland was in the employment of the most conservative party in the Irish Republic.

These interpretations of the dominant attitudes in the different parties – whether real or not – in part explain the status awarded to Mansergh within Fianna Fáil. "For a long time, probably until the early 1990s, Martin was the only bit of serious brainpower on the policy side in Fianna Fáil," a former party officer said. A Government colleague from the 1997-2002 Bertie Ahern-led Government remarked: "For a certain generation of Fianna Fáiler, Martin would be the intellectual epicentre of the party. He would not have consciously sought this position. However, you'd hear it when they'd say, 'We better check that with Mansergh, first'."

The position that Mansergh attained within Fianna Fáil was illustrated by a story involving former Fianna Fáil minister Pádraig Flynn. Newly appointed as European Commissioner in Brussels in 1992, Flynn was on his first visit back to Dublin and scheduled to meet Albert Reynolds in Government Buildings. Several other people were also due to see the Taoiseach and were waiting in the private secretary's office adjoining his office. Flynn was in the queue, as was Mansergh.

The new Commissioner regaled his audience with tales and impressions from his early experiences in Brussels. He was in full flow, animated, with arms in flight, as he described working with Commission President, Jacque Delors. "So like Haughey, all Machiavellian," he said, "and as for his cabinet, full of brain boxes, stuffed with brain boxes." As Flynn referred to "the brain boxes" he pointed his finger at Mansergh, adding "just like you, Martin". The only reply the Commissioner got from the Taoiseach's Special Advisor was a characteristic polite nod of his head.

Fianna Fáil might have turned protective of their Oxford-educated recruit but the initial welcome into the party was mixed. Many Fianna Fáil figures admitted there was some uncertainty within party circles in 1981 at their new advisor. Former Fianna Fáil strategist, Frank Dunlop recalled: "The general reaction was 'Who is Martin Mansergh?' But it wasn't until I met him and heard the accent … I nearly collapsed when I first met him. I thought 'This is going to go down a fucking treat with the lads'."[16]

Michael O'Kennedy, a minister in Haughey's Government at the time, said:

> There were some reservations at first. Most of our lads would never have met someone like Martin. There would have been an inhibition within our tribe but to be honest, and to his credit, I don't think such psychological inhibitions would have occurred to Martin. Within a very short period of time all these things were overcome. They admired his diligence, his availability and his analysis.[17]

Another to admit surprise at the recruitment of Mansergh was Séamus Brennan:

> He started out on the back foot in a way with the politicians of Fianna Fáil. I have no doubt Haughey admired him but the rank and file politicians would have been initially suspicious. The reaction would have been: 'Could we not have a national school teacher with a fáinne and a pioneer pin and a GAA membership card who'd be sound on the national question.' But that was bloody bigotry on our part. All you had to do was meet him and you knew you were dealing with someone very different, with an intellectual understanding of the Northern Ireland issue.[18]

When he joined Haughey's team of advisors and officials in January 1981, Mansergh was initially removed from the party apparatus, the grassroots and even backbench TDs. He tended to move within government and senior Fianna Fáil circles after he transferred initially to the Department of the Taoiseach and later became Head of Research at Fianna Fáil. "He wouldn't have mixed it too much. He wouldn't have been in the bar shouting 'Up the Republic,'" Frank Dunlop said.[19] It is a situation that has changed little over the last two decades – a more recent party official observed: "He is a bit of an independent republic."

There were suspicions about his background, some of which still linger, even if now made known in jest. One former minister when contacted about this biography replied with a laugh: "He was educated at Oxford University, right? Well, then you'd have to ask, who does he work for?" Intellectualism still frightens some sections of Fianna Fáil. One long-standing Fianna Fáil TD observed: "He has a tendency to go off on tangents when you're talking to him. I think he is difficult to talk, to especially with that laugh." Another party official remarked: "There is an other-worldliness about him. He will walk past you on the street, away in another world. And then there's the eccentric dress, the wrongly buttoned shirt and the crooked tie."

When Fianna Fáil returned to the opposition benches in Leinster House after the November 1982 general election Mansergh became a sounding board for politicians about to go on television or radio. Sean Haughey recalled being instructed by the Fianna Fáil Press Office to "Go and see Martin" before an appearance on the RTÉ *Questions & Answers* television programme.[20]

It was a familiar instruction that benefited many party politicians. Mansergh would provide facts and figures to counter policy positions adopted by their critics. Past comments and speeches delivered by Fine Gael and Labour politicians would be produced to illustrate possible changes in policy. "He is respected by the politicians. It's not the usual reaction to advisors who are generally approached by politicians with caution, but with Martin it is different, and I would say that's vindication of his intellectual and personal integrity," one retired Fianna Fáil minister commented.

Mansergh arrived in the Department of the Taoiseach in the early days of 1981 and the environs of Leinster House and Government Buildings quickly became his second home. The advisor experienced office for a few brief months in 1981 and again during the short-lived Fianna Fáil Government in 1982. But with the exception of these two interludes Mansergh spent most of his first seven years with Fianna Fáil when the party was in opposition. The experience served him well and allowed breathing space to learn his trade as the advisor. He certainly had the time and space to become acquainted with – and to judge the mindset of – his political masters, in particular Haughey.

Since 1987 – with the exception of two-and-a-half years from December 1994 to June 1997 – Mansergh played at the table of high office. He may not have had the rank or status of a cabinet minister but, in reality, his influence was greater than most politicians who held senior ministerial position. One Fianna Fáil colleague observed: "Mansergh did not start out as very important – he was young, unknown, spoke funny and had odd manners. His importance is very much based on the personal regard in which he is held by those people he has worked for."

In opposition, the Head of Research was located in Fianna Fáil offices on the fifth floor of Leinster House. During terms in government, Mansergh worked from the central or west wing of Government Buildings on Merrion Street in Dublin. The refurbishment of Government Buildings was completed in December 1990. Haughey performed the formal opening in January 1991. Twelve months later he resigned and since then Albert Reynolds, John Bruton and Bertie Ahern have worked in the Taoiseach's office, which faces out onto the cobbled courtyard with its spouting fountain and directly faces the cabinet room in the parallel North Wing.

The door from Mansergh's office opened onto this first-floor corridor, lined with elegant pillars and crowned by a small domeless rotunda at the central entrance to the Taoiseach's office. All the furniture in the building is Irish. Paintings from the art collection held by the Office of Public Works hang on the walls of most offices. Few officials – and fewer politicians still – were as familiar with these offices and corridors as Mansergh.

Over the last quarter of century he collected volumes of archival material that moved with him between government and opposition.[21] During the 1997-2002 Fianna Fáil/PD Government, Mansergh took over an office farthest away from the Taoiseach's office. The 'geography of influence' theory would suggest that proximity to the fount of influence was critical for advisors. However, it was Mansergh's preference to move to this large office which he needed to accommodate his archival material. Many Fianna Fáil politicians tell of Mansergh's disorganised desk. Former minister, Michael O'Kennedy remembered: "the desk with bundles and bundles of papers. But if you asked him for information on some matter, he had this ability to reach into the bundles and know exactly where to find the relevant papers."[22] When Charles Haughey passed the opened door to his advisor's office, he would frequently shudder at the mess:

> He is the original untidy academic. There were papers everywhere in his office, not just on his desk. Yet he was always able to put his hand on whatever paper or document he needed, no matter how long ago it had been said or published. It was an extraordinary situation when out of such apparent chaos would coherence and accuracy emerge.[23]

Included among Mansergh's papers are notes of meetings with leading republicans made during his clandestine contacts with them in the years and months preceding the first IRA ceasefire in August 1994. Documents tend to make their way to his office for storage. For example, after the death of Jack Lynch in October 1999, his wife Maureen Lynch returned some government papers to the Department of the Taoiseach. Included in the documents were personal statements prepared by Lynch in 1980 dealing with the Arms Trial of 1970. They had significant historical import – "they relate to Jack Lynch's defence of his reputation," Mansergh said.[24] But the documents were not contemporaneous accounts of events and were prepared by Lynch after his retirement as Taoiseach. Therefore, they were not official documents but rather private papers. The civil servant dealing with the documents gave them to Mansergh.

He has been a loyal servant of Fianna Fáil for over two decades, and that in part explains the esteem he is held in by most past and contemporary politicians and officials in Leinster House and Government Buildings. While some colleagues made reference to, what one called, "a mild ego", the one criticism, which united those who have worked with Mansergh in Fianna Fáil, was his almost academic approach to deadlines. "Everything is written out in long-hand and while he is quick at producing material and never lets the side down, he does work at his own pace," one former colleague said. Another party official remarked: "Martin is a three-minutes-to-midnight man when it comes to deadlines. You'd be saying 'Jesus, where's that speech?' He doesn't become fraught but everyone around him becomes fraught."

Over the last two decades Mansergh was the principal speech-writer for all-important Fianna Fáil speeches. He was also the main person responsible for drafting the party's election manifestos. "At meetings he is a good contributor; he gets to the point and is not long-winded," one Fianna Fáil colleague observed. However, other colleagues noted that he could be territorial when subjects he was involved with were being discussed. One official remarked: "He can be stubborn, not in a temperamental way but, for example, he would be quite insistent about his positions on matters at meetings."

The biggest event in the Fianna Fáil calendar is the party's Árd Fheis. It is a weekend-long affair generally held in the Royal Dublin Society in Ballsbridge, Dublin. Several thousand party members from all parts of Ireland gather to socialise and engage in low-key political activity. The proceedings are dominated by the hour-long leader's address, broadcast live on RTÉ television between eight and nine o'clock on the Saturday evening.

Mansergh said of this speech:

> The Árd Fheis speech is different from all others. It has to be a success, and really who makes contributions is a very secondary issue. You have to suppress your ego. Its nice to see what you've written left in, but in the end it's the results that are right, not what you contribute.[25]

Mansergh recalled that before the availability of word processors secretarial staff were "driven to distraction" with changes to speeches. "It was a far more intensive exercise. It's child's play today."[26] This role invariably aided the development of closer contacts between advisor and political master. Haughey was more actively involved than either of his successors in the preparation of the speeches. There was an extensive drafting process, which could often become fraught. However, the two men developed a close working relationship and Haughey was aware of the value of his principal advisor.

The working relationship was clear: Haughey would give an indication of what he required and Mansergh would then prepare a draft that Haughey would duly amend. He would take unfinished speeches back to his home in North County Dublin, making handwritten amendments that the following day would be incorporated into the text by secretarial staff. The Fianna Fáil leader would call upon his advisor at every stage, going through any changes in considerable detail. It was a time-consuming activity, although it was clear who was in charge as Haughey observed:

> To a great extent I was my own speech-writer. I often look back and wonder did I waste too much time on speeches. I see politicians today in the Dáil and elsewhere just reading out what someone else has written. But I don't think you can deliver a speech with confidence and feeling if you have not been involved in preparing it. Normally I would ask Martin for a draft and then put my own stamp on it; revamp it, as it were.[27]

There was a process at work. Drafting was an important part of the Haughey approach to speech-writing and preparation:

> I regarded every speech as important and would have been involved down to the last syllable. It was laborious and time-consuming when we had to rely on typewriters. Later, with the arrival of word

processors, of course it was possible to move the text around on screen and make all sorts of changes, maybe do twenty or more drafts. Before that at most you could only do three or four drafts.[28]

Frank Dunlop recalled that Haughey reacted badly to many early drafts of speeches. "He'd take a draft speech and say 'This is rubbish. How do you expect me to read this crap.' Some people were obviously offended but there was a process at work. But it did get to a stage that what Mansergh wrote was hardly changed. He got into Charlie's mind. He saw the Machiavellian mind at work."[29]

Mansergh recalled researching material for the 1982 Bodenstown address given by Haughey, the first of the annual speeches on republicanism given by Fianna Fáil leaders to be written by the party advisor. Haughey was examining the draft prepared by Mansergh when he looked up inquiringly and remarked of Tone: "He was a bit of a lad, wasn't he?"[30]

Among the many tasks assigned to the Fianna Fáil advisor, greatest satisfaction was derived from writing and editing important speeches. "With a Taoiseach a lot of the time you are pushing out the boat and staking out new ground. That's the stimulating aspect. It is not a static exercise."[31]

However, sometimes the thinking of the advisor on an issue would be ahead of his political master. One former colleague said: "Mansergh would try to slip in a line which he sincerely believed should be advanced. But he would be taking you where the leader or the party may not yet be able to go." Haughey acknowledged this tension: "Sometimes I would have had to rein him in a bit or tone his language down somewhat, but you could always reply upon him to produce the essence of what was needed."[32]

Mansergh was closer to Haughey than either of his two successors as leader of Fianna Fáil. It was a different kind of relationship. Haughey's personality was more dominant and his sense of his own position more obvious. In effect, Mansergh served his apprenticeship as an advisor under Haughey, a politician he viewed as a kind of father-figure. But despite this relationship, the special advisor role was greatly expanded under Reynolds and Ahern. In some respects the latter two leaders relied more on Mansergh than Haughey ever did, a position that developed in tandem with evolution of the peace process after Reynolds replaced Haughey in early 1992.

When Reynolds – some months after becoming Taoiseach – decided to remove Mansergh's responsibility as full-time speech-writer, the advisor admitted to being annoyed with the decision. But he later accepted that it was the correct move in light of his increasing role in the peace process.

There were early tensions as Mansergh adjusted to the new personnel employed by Reynolds. He did not favour the approach adopted by the public relations experts who advised Reynolds, in particular Tom Savage and Terry Prone. They offered "feely-feely over substance", Mansergh said, adding "I am not an admirer of the Terry Prone style."[33]

In March 1992 Reynolds received applause from the Fianna Fáil faithful at his first Árd Fheis as party leader. Mansergh had had less influence on the speech that evening than any Árd Fheis address over the previous decade. He was not impressed, but accepted that with the change in leadership a new approach was required. "I had to say to myself: the days of the classical Árd Fheis speech are gone." Nonetheless, looking back on the Reynolds term in office, Mansergh insisted that there were some "ghastly speeches."[34]

A new approach was also adopted when Bertie Ahern replaced Reynolds as Fianna Fáil leader at the end of 1994. Ahern assigned one person with responsibility for speech-writing but he drew on many sources in shaping important speeches. Mansergh was centrally involved in all keynote speeches, but by then his time was dominated by policy on Northern Ireland. Moreover, the political agenda was altered by an expansion in the number of media outlets in the Republic and the increasingly tabloid-driven nature of daily news. In the latter half of the 1990s, the necessity for a 'news sound-bite' to meet immediate media deadlines lessened the importance of big set-piece addresses. One Fianna Fáil colleague observed: "I think he has had difficulty in adjusting to the speed of the media where news happens much faster than in the past. I think Martin views that development with a certain disdain." Despite his familiarity with the workings of Fianna Fáil, it was clear from party colleagues that few politicians or officials were personally close to Mansergh. "Martin would not be one of life's mixers. He is intensely private, and not very good at chit-chat when it comes to passing time," was the comment of one Fianna Fáil official who worked with Mansergh in various roles over the last decade.

He is well-liked and commands strong respect from party members and Fianna Fáil public representatives. However, there have been occasions when his emergence into the public arena annoyed some in Fianna Fáil. Former Taoiseach Garret FitzGerald recalled a 1982 conference on the subject of Northern Ireland at which Fianna Fáil was represented by Dáil deputy Liam Lawlor. Mansergh was also present. FitzGerald remembered that Mansergh spoke on Fianna Fáil policy "to the utter fury of Liam Lawlor" who complained to Haughey afterwards. The former Fine Gael leader said of Mansergh's conference intervention: "His speech was in no way helpful. He was back at the Treaty. I formed an adverse opinion of him at that time, which of course I did not sustain."[35]

The responsibilities of the Special Advisor varied. In the summer of 2000 the Fianna Fáil/Progressive Democrat coalition experienced a series of crises including the controversy over the proposed appointment to a senior European job of a former judge who had resigned in contentious circumstances. When Hugh O'Flaherty, the former judge, withdrew his name and the dust settled on the affair, Ahern asked Mansergh to meet with disaffected backbench Fianna Fáil TDs. These individual meetings were to appease deputies who believed the Government had lost touch. Mansergh prepared a "political audit" of each constituency that identified local issues that the Government needed to tackle in advance of a general election.

Most party backbenchers were suspicious of the exercise, many considering it a means to generate internal propaganda that consultation was taking place and that the leadership was listening to their concerns. However, many doubters were surprised at the level of detail sought by Mansergh and the follow-up responses on the local and national issues that they had raised with Ahern's top advisor. For example, Seán Haughey received a telephone call from Mansergh who had a scheduled appointment with Haughey Snr at Kinsealy.

"He rang me up to know could he meet me at Abbeyville. My father – who must have been wondering what was going on – showed him into the study where we discussed local and national issues for a good 20 minutes," Seán Haughey recalled.[36] The following week at a Fianna Fáil function the Taoiseach approached Haughey with several observations on the issues he had raised with Mansergh. A short time later, a cabinet minister rang with an update on another matter, which the Dublin North Central TD had also mentioned to Mansergh.

The advisory role developed enormously from 1981 to a situation whereby Mansergh was one of the most influential figures in Fianna Fáil politics with experience that straddled three party leaders. Bertie Ahern explained his value to Fianna Fáil in terms of: "his absolutely clinical, honest advice. If you look at the three guys – Haughey, Reynolds and Ahern – other than the fact that they are three Fianna Fáil people they are actually three very different people. There's an enormous difference – Fianna Fáil is that great coalition of interests – so it would be Mansergh's ability to give honest, straightforward advice. You may not always want to accept it but he'd always give it. He would fight the line. If he thought something was wrong he would not shirk. He's no 'Yes-man'. Mansergh gives the advice fairly strong."[37]

However, over the last 20 years Mansergh emerged as more than just a political advisor to Fianna Fáil. He captured the title of unofficial party historian, in a sense, an in-house 'keeper of the flame'. His writings sought to position Fianna Fáil in a favourable light in historical terms. Indeed, the man who criticised historical revisionism in relation to nationalism and Northern Ireland was an active advocate of a revisionist approach to the events central to Fianna Fáil history. He wrote and spoke widely on the history of Fianna Fáil and, in particular, the legacy of the party's leaders.

The foundation of the Fianna Fáil was, according to Mansergh, "a harnessing of idealism with practicality."[38] The party ethos was one of radicalism and idealism. This historical narrative, on occasion, veered towards hyperbole:

> Fianna Fáil was a successor to the mass movement of popular nationalism in the 19th century, O'Connell's Repeal Movement, especially the Parnellite party at its height in the 1880s and of course Sinn Féin from 1917 to 1921 [...] As its name suggests, in terms of political ideology, Fianna Fáil draws on the Fenian tradition, the Republicanism of 1916 stretching back to Tone and Mitchel, the core beliefs of the independence movement, the intellectual foundations of which lay both in the Gaelic League and Sinn Féin, and the teachings of Thomas Davis. More successfully than Cumann na nGaedheal, which coalesced with other traditions, Redmondite, ex-unionist and a certain undemocratic continental strain of politics ... Fianna Fáil in its early decades remained true to the political, economic and cultural influences of the founding generation.[39]

But there were doubters who did not subscribe to the Fianna Fáil political outlook. In Mansergh's opinion, the party had to contend with much social snobbery: "Fianna Fáil was regarded by the Free State establishment as a collection of ignorant peasants and as potentially dangerous radicals. There were blatant attempts to deploy clerical influence against Fianna Fáil."[40] There is some truth in this thinking, although credit is also due to W.T. Cosgrave, leader of Cumann na nGaedheal, who in the aftermath of the murder of cabinet minister, Kevin Higgins in 1927, moved to get de Valera off the hook on his abstentionist policy and into the mainstream of democratic politics in the new Free State.

This retelling of that particular episode indicated that Mansergh has not been shy of skipping over facts so as to present his party in the best possible light. His explanation for the formation of Fianna Fáil in 1926 for example, neatly downplays de Valera's U-turn on the oath of allegiance:

> De Valera's goal in forming Fianna Fáil was to move towards an agreed constitutional basis for the State that would be independent of Britain, then having consolidated it, address the problems of partition. The subsequent success of Fianna Fáil showed that the people of Ireland much preferred republican politics to republican violence. The republican viewpoint on the Treaty may have been justified, but allowing the differences on either side to spill over into civil war had been a tragedy that should have been avoided at all costs.[41]

Indeed, in his writings on the history of Fianna Fáil, Mansergh was not above party political point scoring. For example, Cumann na nGaedheal, the pro-Treaty party which established the institutions of the new State during a bitter Civil War, and ensured a smooth transition of power to Fianna Fáil in 1932, was dismissed as having "a very limited view of government responsibilities and a defeatist view of the Irish economy".[42]

Moving forward to the 1950s, the opposition parties faced criticism for arguing the advantages of emigration as a cure to the bleak economic environment in that decade while "Fianna Fáil in contrast rarely adopted a resigned and defeatist attitude to emigration and unemployment".[43]

History is rarely so clear-cut and an academic historian would not consider events and legacies in such a partisan manner. Despite his academic training, Mansergh – as Fianna Fáil historian – was not a disinterested scholar. He had been an active participant in most of the significant events in the party's recent history. This involvement undoubtedly coloured his perspective on events and personalities. For example, he repeatedly displayed a tendency to side-step periods and events that were problematic for Fianna Fáil.

There was also a protectiveness of his party that sometimes

blurred objectivity. The 1977 Fianna Fáil general election manifesto exemplified this. The much-maligned document contributed to the expansion of government borrowing in the Irish Republic at a time when the economy was unable to benefit from government fiscal stimulus. However, Mansergh argued: "The years 1977-81, which it is now customary to denigrate, were a period of unique and phenomenal economic and social progress."[44] While the judgement may be ill-founded, consistency has dominated the Mansergh interpretation: several years later he continued to argue that there was "an over-concentration on superficial and populist aspects of the 1977 manifesto".[45]

A clear sense of party political point scoring rather than historical rationale pervaded Mansergh's interpretation of the deficit-funded government activity from the 1970s onwards. When asked what was to blame for the domestic crisis of the late 1970s and 1980s, many commentators and most economists pointed to the expansionary 1977 budget, whilst acknowledging that some slippage in good economic practice had preceded it. But the 1979-81 Haughey Government made the situation worse in spite of tough talk from the new Taoiseach. Despite a deterioration in the public finances, large public sector pay awards were approved as were double-digit increases in current government spending.

The Irish economy hit turbulent times as the international environment was marked by recession. Domestic policy contributed to the economic malaise. Nevertheless, Mansergh continued to defend the post-1977 policies. In 1986 he declared that: "the 1977–81 Fianna Fáil Government has been most unfairly vilified. In comparison with the present Coalition, it was a positively brilliant Government. Employment between 1977 and 1981 rose by about 65,000."[46]

There is little support for his viewpoint. The economy was at rock bottom. The 1977–81 period was just part of a decade-long malaise in Irish economic affairs. Control was lost of borrowing and life was scarred by unemployment and emigration. Garret FitzGerald, a member of the 1973–77 coalition rejected Mansergh's hypothesis: "While things were not perfect we left the

economy in a reasonably good shape. Anything said by Martin
Mansergh about our record is self-serving and propaganda. He
cannot be taken seriously on the matter."[47]

But Mansergh has not been content to simply spread the
blame for the economic woes of the late 1970s. The widely
discredited manifesto was explained away as if Fianna Fáil was
not the party that authored the document:

> The essence of it was a very ambitious attempt to
> achieve sustained full employment, in the face of a
> huge demographic challenge. EC entry had made all
> governments of that period over-confident. Things
> went wrong. Arguably, there were flaws in an
> approach that depended on the public sector
> providing the engine for growth. It was very
> unfortunate that in managing the difficulties, that
> were greatly exacerbated by the second oil crisis-
> induced recession, confidence could not be
> maintained, and that effective remedial action was
> too long delayed.[48]

There have been other issues on which Mansergh sought to
put distance between his party and some uncomfortable truths.
Aside from economic policy, there was the Fianna Fáil reaction
to the emerging liberal agenda in the 1980s and 1990s. Despite
the liberalism evident in newspaper letters in the 1970-74
period, Mansergh remained uncritical of Fianna Fáil's slow
response to the changing social values of Irish society:

> Fianna Fáil has preferred to deal with social change
> as much as possible by consensus, rather than by
> liberal/conservative confrontation. There will always
> be a battle between those who want to move forward
> to an imagined ideal of where we could be versus
> those who want to go back to an imagined ideal of
> where we were.[49]

As discussed in the next chapter, Haughey and FitzGerald

battled for a decade over the issues of contraception, abortion and divorce. Mansergh sided with his political boss regardless of his own personal attitudes. The practice of shedding his own beliefs in part allowed Mansergh to reconcile the obvious differences. But as emerged in later years the one area that was central to Mansergh's philosophical outlook – Northern Ireland – towered over every other policy. In that regard, he was most comfortable with Fianna Fáil.

Alongside rearranging policy issues, the Fianna Fáil advisor sought to place each of the six party leaders in central states-manlike positions, in particular de Valera and Haughey. The Fianna Fáil Forum was told in May 2001 that: "De Valera belongs with other founding figures of the 20th century, like Nehru, de Gaulle and Nelson Mandela, who first liberated a nation and then for a long time after remained the principal embodiment of it."[50]

In his analysis of the contribution of Fianna Fáil to Irish history, Mansergh identified three particular periods since 1926 when he believed the party had been "the driving force in national life" – the 1930s and 1940s; the sixteen years of uninterrupted power from 1957 to 1973; and the years since 1987, which – he said – was "the best period of our history".[51]

The period covering the 1930s and 1940s he described as one when the party "established and defended sovereignty but also stimulated economic activity and built up a very basic network of social services". He also noted of the period that Fianna Fáil policies ensured that:

> Ireland did not succumb to the temptations of either Fascism or Communism, and succeeded in holding its own vis-à-vis intense pressures from Britain and America, so that it was not reduced to pliant dependency status.[52]

The principal driving force behind this position was, according to Mansergh, Eamon de Valera. In the 1990s, a major reassessment was undertaken of the contribution of Michael Collins, the republican military leader, during the

95

period in which the Irish State gained independence from Britain. Several biographies – and a Hollywood movie starring Liam Nelson and Julia Roberts – lent an air of charisma to the revolutionary leader who was shot dead before the Civil War ended. As the reputation of Collins increased, so that of de Valera diminished.

Mansergh publicly became the defender of the de Valera legacy: "The political contribution of Eamon de Valera in articulating the Irish case was at least as important to the achievement of Irish freedom as the military contribution of Michael Collins."[53] It was not that Mansergh discredited the role of Collins. Indeed, a bust of Collins rests on the mantelpiece in Mansergh's Co Dublin home. He remarked: "Less eloquent and cerebral than de Valera, he had the practical qualities of Lemass and shared with him a good financial head and brilliant administrative ability. For the record, in August 1921, as Minister for Finance, he brought in a Book of Estimates totalling £145,000."[54]

The Fianna Fáil advisor became a vocal critic of those academics and commentators who – he argued – "continually stereotyped" his party's foundering leader. Indeed, Collins was cited to mute criticism of de Valera's conservatism. Mansergh established a similarity in their outlook by providing a link between de Valera's 1943 St Patrick's Day vision of "the Ireland that we dreamed of with its simple, frugal comforts" and Collins aspiration for an Ireland where "the beauty will be the outwards sign of a prosperous and happy Gaelic life".[55]

De Valera led the opposition to the Anglo-Irish Treaty in 1922. This action provoked a bitter and bloody Civil War. In many ways the causes and consequences of de Valera's stance in the Treaty debates became the core of Nicholas Mansergh's academic life. However, his son – as party advisor and historian – credited de Valera with the achievement between 1918 and 1921 of uniting the military and constitutional leadership of those seeking independence from Britain.

Even Martin Mansergh found it awkward to explain the position adopted by de Valera over the Treaty: "In judging de Valera's actions … it must be remembered that he was the leader, and like all political leaders, striving to maintain the unity of the movement. He was by no means an absolutist doctrinaire republican, but he knew that with or without him, the Treaty, as it stood, meant a split and that it would not bring peace."[56]

In Mansergh's account, therefore, the role of de Valera was downplayed while stress was placed upon British responsibility. The short-sighted British refusal to accede to the Republic desired by nearly everyone on the island apart from unionists was credited by Mansergh as the principal cause of the Civil War. "The trouble in 1922 was the clash between British constitutionality, accepted to a degree as a matter of expediency by the pro-Treaty side, and the new Irish constitutionality developed between 1916 and 1921."[57]

Mansergh was also to the fore in challenging 'revisionist' thinking in relation to Northern Ireland that essentially threatened the traditional Fianna Fáil narrative on Irish nationalism. Much criticism was directed at revisionist writers who – in Mansergh's view – had undermined national self-confidence by seeking to debunk great figures and inspiring ideals of Irish history. He observed: "The problem with much revisionism is that, while the conclusion may be novel or surprising, the case made for it is not as conclusive or convincing, as the author would like us to believe." In a throwaway comment, he remarked: "You can usually tell revisionist history by the number of book prizes it receives."[58]

This anti-revisionist attitude required many staunch defences of the founding leader of Fianna Fáil, including a newspaper review of the book *De Valera and the Ulster Question 1917-1973*, written by the broadcaster and historian, John Bowman.

According to Mansergh, the book did not recognise "the Fianna Fáil position [as] enunciated by Eamon de Valera which sought a united Ireland in the form of a unitary state". Mansergh was critical of Bowman for presenting de Valera as a 'federalist'. The two men engaged in a series of newspaper exchanges as each defended their respective position on what de Valera's stance actually was.

Mansergh was scathing in his criticism of the Bowman

thesis: "Indeed, Bowman contrives to present de Valera half seriously as the founding father of revisionism, while simultaneously censuring him as a blinkered irredentist. It would be about as sensible for party followers to take de Valera's Northern policy from Bowman, as it would be for Christians to take their religion from Voltaire."[59]

The second successful period in Fianna Fáil history, as identified by Mansergh, began in the late 1950s with the White Paper on Economic Development and ended with membership of the European Economic Community in 1973. There was a real sense of affection and admiration for Sean Lemass who was closely associated with these two events. As a student at Oxford in the 1960s, Mansergh followed the ramifications of the economic liberalisation pursued by governments led and influenced by Lemass. He observed that Lemass had in a quite different way almost as remarkable a career as de Valera:

> Although he had the image of being a great pragmatist, unlike his more ideological predecessor, his approach was in fact informed by a strongly felt political philosophy rooted in a rounded republican ethos which saw social improvement as the most important national mission. His instincts were interventionist, not *laissez-faire*. He both complemented and contrasted with de Valera, who was cast in the legendary role of a nation-builder and constitution-maker. Yet to modern Ireland it is arguably the economic and social national-building identified with Lemass that has much the greater contemporary appeal.[60]

The Lemass mission was to build a viable economy and improve what were – even in the 1960s – atrocious social conditions. This objective was achieved by providing work and housing for the urban unemployed and low-paid. There was some tetchiness about the attribution of the "a rising tide lifts all boats" quotation to the second leader of Fianna Fáil. "The glib *laissez-faire* spirit of the adage 'a rising tide lifts all boats' is neither an apposite characterisation nor a fair summation of his economic philosophy as Taoiseach. Lemass was all too aware of the limitations of the *laissez-faire* approach."[61]

The achievements of the peace process were rooted, according to Mansergh, in the policies adopted by Lemass. He was very clear in acknowledging the changes heralded by the leadership succession in Fianna Fáil in 1959. "Lemass in his style of government had already brought to an end in any meaningful sense civil war politics ... It could be argued that the first real progress on Northern Ireland occurred under Lemass, and that he instituted the first steps of a policy of détente ... "[62]

Mansergh invested much weight in the speech delivered by Lemass at the Oxford Union in October 1959: "One can also see laid out much of the programme of the following 40 years." This speech included references to a British declaration that the problem created by partition could be ended by agreement amongst the Irish. It was a signal for future policy:

> The revised constitutional formulation of Articles Two and Three put to the people in the Referendum of 22 May 1998 drew a great deal on Lemass' ideas with a greater emphasis on people rather than territory, on unity by agreement, and also giving authority for the establishment of institutions with executive powers between the two jurisdictions to exercise functions in respect of all or any part of the island.[63]

The third period of Fianna Fáil history that Mansergh identified commenced in 1987. The advisor credited his party with the achievement of the economic and social advances of recent years, a fact he viewed with considerable pride:

> In 80 years, what has been a backward and underdeveloped province of the UK, with often abject social conditions, and which might have been destin-ed to remain primarily an agricultural exporting

country plus a tourist destination, has been transformed into a highly dynamic, modern and diversified industrialised economy, that no longer has to be content with very limited ambitions. [64]

Mansergh wrote widely on the achievements of de Valera and Lemass while there was also detailed praise for Haughey, Reynolds and Ahern. Jack Lynch featured little. Indeed, there was no acclaim for Lynch's leadership in an address given by Mansergh in 1986 on the occasion of the sixtieth anniversary of the formation of Fianna Fáil. While there was acknowledgement for EEC membership – and there was a defence of the party's 1977 manifesto – only one direct mention of Lynch featured in the text, a passing reference to the co-operative relationship that governments under Lemass, Lynch and Haughey had with the trade union movement.

Given the deep distrust between Haughey and his predecessor, a certain political sensitivity may have influenced the 1986 narrative. Lynch had dismissed Haughey as a cabinet minister during the 1970 Arms Crisis, and although Haughey was later restored to high office, Lynch opposed his leadership bid in December 1979. In subsequent years, Lynch was a confidante of Des O'Malley, Haughey's principal internal rival in Fianna Fáil.

There was a more forthcoming assessment of Lynch eleven years later, again in an address to a Fianna Fáil audience. "The Lynch era was a gentler, less assertive continuation of the Lemass era. Jack Lynch ... enjoyed a phenomenal electoral success, winning two overall majorities in three General Elections. His style was to be understated. His eyes were nearly always liquid. His decency and obvious strength had universal popular appeal."[65]

When Lynch died towards the end of 1999, there was some comment about his treatment by Fianna Fáil after he stepped down as leader. However, as Bruce Arnold, political journalist and Lynch biographer, wrote: "The party he had led did not know what to do about him. Charles Haughey's immediate reaction had been to expunge Jack Lynch and all he stood for from the record. There were no tributes, no references, no sense of any continuum from one leader to the next ... Jack Lynch was deliberately painted out of the picture."[66]

But Mansergh offered a different interpretation. He took exception to, what he considered, "exaggerated statements".[67] Referring to speeches he probably would have written himself, Mansergh listed the occasions at Árd Fheiseanna when Lynch's three successors paid tribute to the Cork politician.

In a newspaper letter, Mansergh wrote: "The memory of Jack Lynch and his leadership of Fianna Fáil will for many reasons continue to inspire the respect and affection of party members and find a noble and fitting place in its annals."[68] Moreover, Mansergh himself observed that the 1966 succession resulted in a new Taoiseach who shared some of Lemass's ideal attributes – "A national consensus-builder and conciliator, a person of simple lifestyle and integrity."[69]

The Lynch controversy indicated just how defensive Mansergh could be about criticism of his party's image. He also condemned some of the treatment of Fianna Fáil leaders by political opponents and the media. For example, there was some controversy when Albert Reynolds as Taoiseach used the word 'crap' in an interview with journalists. Mansergh was annoyed about the fuss. "The Taoiseach repeated a particular four-letter word in an interview, that on other occasions has caused neither John Major nor Bill Clinton the slightest difficulty, but it brought down the wrath of the *Irish Times* in one of its periodic fits of morality."[70]

So with his writings and public-speaking engagements Mansergh developed, alongside his pivotal role as Special Advisor, the position of Fianna Fáil's in-house historian. As is discussed in the next chapter, one area in particular proved to be a blind spot – the Fianna Fáil advisor has only ever gently referenced the excesses of Charles Haughey. "There is within this party an immense storehouse of political achievement and experience and acts of imagination. There is also a pride in country. On the debit side, there have been political failures and personal lapses. While these can and do inspire high moral indignation, our record as a democracy over the past 80 years is one of the best."[71]

There can be no doubt but that Mansergh displayed a defensive characteristic when Fianna Fáil came under the microscope. He showed a strong personal desire to protect its leaders, embellish their achievements and mitigate their failings. On occasion he was less than partial in his objectivity, but at all times he exhibited undivided loyalty, a trait that worked to his advantage in uniquely serving three party leaders over the last two decades.

Five

The Haughey Era

Charles Haughey was in his office in Leinster House. Around the country ballot boxes were being opened and the votes counted. Throughout the morning Martin Mansergh was in and out of the room but Haughey remained seated at his desk. The radio was tuned to RTÉ as coverage of the counting of votes in the 1987 general election got underway. From around 11 o'clock Fianna Fáil tallymen in key constituencies began reporting firm indications of the way the vote would go. The party had spent the previous four-and-a-half years in opposition. The pundits on the radio were predicting eleven possible seat gains for Fianna Fáil with two potential losses.

At ten minutes past one, Mansergh took a call from Ray MacSharry, a senior Fianna Fáil politician with an excellent grasp of election-day manoeuvrings. MacSharry had news from the count in his Sligo-Leitrim constituency. The word from the tallymen was good. They were predicting a seat gain. Fianna Fáil would take three out of the four seats on offer in Sligo-Leitrim. Mansergh put the phone down. Beaming across the desk at Haughey, he said: "I think we're going to win."

In fact, the Mansergh lunchtime prediction – based on the accurate forecast of success in Sligo-Leitrim – was premature. When all the votes in the 1987 general election were counted Fianna Fáil had 81 seats in Dáil Éireann. The outcome was a gain of six seats, but the party was still short of the elusive overall majority in parliament. It was the pattern of the Haughey years – in each of the five general elections contested under his leadership the party narrowly fell short of winning a

Dáil majority; although in each of those elections Fianna Fáil achieved a first preference vote that was well in excess of that won under more recent leaders.

Over the four-and-a-half years since the general election in November 1982 Haughey and his advisors had been preparing for a return to government. The economic situation was disastrous – unemployment was running at 18 per cent of the labour force, annual net migration was around 25,000 while the Republic's economy actually contracted in size in both 1985 and 1986. It was ideal territory for an opposition party. Fianna Fáil hoped to benefit at the polls as voters heaped blame on the outgoing Fine Gael/Labour coalition.

Mansergh heard this viewpoint expressed when he travelled at weekends to the family farm in Co Tipperary. His Uncle Gregor was critical of Haughey over the political scandals in 1982 and also the conservative stance adopted by Fianna Fáil during the 1983 abortion referendum. However, by mid-1985 – at the height of the economic recession – Gregor Mansergh was one of many seeking an alternative to the FitzGerald-led government. "Fianna Fáil can't get in soon enough or everyone will be broke – £1.24 for a glass of Guinness!" Gregor wrote in a letter to Martin Mansergh's father in July 1985.[1]

Set against such a backdrop, the 1987 general election results were a major disappointment for Fianna Fáil. There was an additional blow as the Progressive Democrats – formed in December 1985 out of internal Fianna Fáil divisions – won 14 seats. Fine Gael and Labour were both well-beaten at the polls. But for the fourth time under Haughey's leadership Fianna Fáil had failed to win an overall majority. The party was still adhering to an anti-coalition policy so the most attractive option available to Haughey was leadership of a minority government.

Mansergh embarked on his third period working for Haughey in government. He could only hope for a longer spell than the two previous occasions, six months in 1981, when he joined Haughey's staff as a civil servant speechwriter, and eight months in 1982 when he was Special Advisor to the Fianna Fáil Taoiseach.

At that time the senior member of the Haughey team was

Pádraig O hAnnracháin, a long-time civil servant. He came from a Fianna Fáil background and had had a distinguished career working closely with the first three party leaders. Steeped in politics, O hAnnracháin possessed a razor sharp wit. In the 1950s he had been private secretary to de Valera. From 1957 until 1973 he served as head of the Government Information Service working with both Lemass and Lynch. From Co Clare, O hAnnracháin was close to Haughey who appointed him Deputy Secretary in the Department of the Taoiseach after the 1979 leadership contest.

O hAnnracháin was instrumental in the employment of Mansergh, and in 1983 followed his lead and resigned from the civil service to join the Fianna Fáil backroom team. Throughout the 1980s – along with Mansergh and another Haughey loyalist PJ Mara – the retired civil servant was the principal full-time advisor to the Fianna Fáil leader. During 1987 O hAnnracháin's health deteriorated. With Haughey back in Government Buildings he started to work part-time until his death in January 1988, after which the man he had attracted from Foreign Affairs assumed the leading advisor role.

The initial brief given to the new Haughey recruit in January 1981 focused on speech-writing. However, Mansergh was also involved in research on projects related to North-South relations. His job description was set out in a Department of Taoiseach memo prepared at the time of his arrival in his new position. The memo listed his areas of responsibility as: "Preparation of speeches for the Taoiseach; Government statements. Identification of areas and topics where speeches and statements are desirable."[2]

There was some initial tension mainly because the young official from Iveagh House had usurped many senior officials in the Department of the Taoiseach. At one stage the Department of Foreign Affairs refused to give Mansergh direct access to files. A compromise was eventually reached with the advisor first requesting Haughey's permission for information being sought that was then provided by departmental officials.[3]

Haughey was not the easiest employer. While he could be good company, and was very courteous, the Fianna Fáil leader was notoriously short-tempered. Occasions of rudeness with officials were legendary. Mansergh said there was "one stand-off" shortly after he arrived from Foreign Affairs. During the drafting of a document Haughey was rude to his new employee. Mansergh left the Taoiseach's office, went immediately to O hAnnracháin and said: "I don't have to put up with this. I can go back to the Department of Foreign Affairs."[4]

Relations did improve and, in time, Mansergh became Haughey's most trusted advisor. "I worked very well with Haughey … It was a little bumpy at the beginning when I was a civil servant. I'd say we had a creative working relationship."[5]

Haughey held a general election in June 1981, seeking his own mandate from the voters. The election took place against the backdrop of the hunger strikes in the Maze Prison. Several prisoner candidates polled well, with two winning seats in Louth and Cavan-Monaghan. The Fianna Fáil leader described the election result as a draw. However, the outcome left him as leader of the opposition with only 78 of the 166 seats in Dáil Éireann. Garret FitzGerald became Taoiseach leading a minority Fine Gael/Labour coalition government.

At that stage Mansergh was still a civil servant on secondment from the Department of Foreign Affairs to the Department of the Taoiseach. Given that he worked for Haughey, Mansergh could not have been sure about his prospects with the new administration. His civil service job was safe although there was no certainty about the position he might be allocated. A move back to Iveagh House would have been possible, although that would undoubtedly have been internally problematic.

However, Mansergh had already decided he did not want to return to diplomatic life, especially given his interest in the farm in Co Tipperary. In any event he had other options. The position as Head of Research for Fianna Fáil was offered. He readily accepted and, in late July 1981, duly resigned from the civil service.

It was a turbulent era in Irish politics. There were three general elections in 18 months and considerable political con-troversy, scandal and intrigue. The Fine Gael/Labour government collapsed in early 1982 when its budgetary proposals were defeated in a Dáil division. In the subsequent general election Fianna Fáil was returned to government:

> I was rather pleased with that because that's what you would call knock-out opposition. I mean Garret FitzGerald had come in on the 30th of June 1981; for all anyone had known, he would have been there for four years anyway, despite the tight situation. He (Haughey) was actually out of office for only seven months. I think it was very effective period in opposition. As a matter of fact, I was less surprised than Haughey the night the government fell.[6]

As Fianna Fáil moved in and out of government over 1981-82, Mansergh assumed a more important role in the internal Haughey hierarchy. He was admired for his ability to assimilate ideas, conceptualise material, and then reproduce it in a manner suitable for public consumption. This role developed further after the November 1982 general election defeat, when Fianna Fáil began what would turn out to be over four years on the opposition benches. "He became the guru on everything, producing all the research single-handedly. He was like a machine," another party official, Frank Dunlop recalled.[7] Haughey was in agreement with this analysis:

> Martin very quickly became indispensable. He had a tremendous ability to lay his hands on material. If you were looking for part of a speech or a quotation he would produce it. He had an encyclopaedic command of facts and dates, and also what people said and when they said it. If someone in the opposition made a speech on some issue, Martin would be very quick to point out that, on some other occasion, they had said something different – and he would produce the relevant document.[8]

Mansergh's closeness to the Fianna Fáil leader was becoming

more obvious. Bertie Ahern was Chief Whip during the 1982 Fianna Fáil government. The position gave the future Taoiseach his first insight into the power structures at the centre of the governmental process. He attended cabinet meetings and was based in Government Buildings, where he also had his first contact with Haughey's key advisor.

> He had a big influence on Charlie. There was no doubt about that. Charlie would have seen his capacity to work … the two of them got on very well because they were able to talk about a whole lot of things dear to both their hearts. Both of them were culture vultures; into museums, the arts, heritage, so they had plenty of things in common. But with Martin it would always be a working relationship. Martin would create his own entertainment – he'd go off to the theatre or to the national library to do his own thing. So his relationship with Haughey would have been very much working as an advisor but he would have had a hell of a lot of influence … [9]

During the 1980s, one of Mansergh's objectives was to get Haughey to recreate the momentum of the original New Departure policy when, a century earlier, Charles Stewart Parnell had succeeded in harnessing the support of those who believed that physical force interventions were justified in principle. Moreover, Parnell also successfully won Irish-American support for the national movement. Interestingly, the Mansergh assessment of Parnell's career offered ample evidence for the presentation of similarities with Haughey.

As Mansergh saw it, Parnell's prestige as a leader derived from an ability to know how to act in a crisis. Moreover, Parnell saw himself not merely as a party leader but as the leader of a national movement. There was an attempt to cultivate an aloofness and an air of mystery about him; he led a disciplined organisation that led to accusations of dictatorship; and he had stormy relations with the press. It was not overly difficult to replace Parnell with Haughey to arrive at the traits Mansergh undoubtedly believed were also associated with his own employer.

The Fianna Fáil advisor also acknowledged another historical lesson to be learnt from Parnell: "Any political party that allows outside pressure to dictate who shall be its leader suffers such demoralisation as to put at risk its future."[10] A message was being conveyed to the dissidents in Fianna Fáil.

Not long after his appointment with Fianna Fáil in the summer of 1981, Mansergh was himself making headlines. On 23 August 1981 he wrote to the *Sunday Times* in his new capacity as the party's Head of Research. The letter emphatically rejected the idea of an independent Northern Ireland as a means of achieving peace. "From Gladstone to Lloyd George the island of Ireland was accepted as the proper unit of self-determination."[11] The national daily papers in the Republic picked up on the letter with the following days' editions all carrying stories about the views of Haughey's new advisor.

This proximity to – and by association, apparent influence on – Haughey, generated considerable interest in the new party advisor on the part of the media and indeed Fianna Fáil. Over the first six months of 1981 Mansergh was a civil servant and would have attracted little public attention. However, that position changed with his decision to enter the employment of Fianna Fáil. The *Belfast Telegraph* described him as 'Haughey's man of mystery'. The newspaper's profile described "the tall, gangling donnish figure" as "something of a shadowy figure around the corridors of power".[12]

He gave his first media interview to Sean O'Rourke in the *Sunday Press* in December 1981. The interview was marked by a finely honed political appreciation of the import of his answers. The material was very critical – in an obviously party political manner – of Garret FitzGerald and the priorities of his Fine Gael/Labour government.

The new Taoiseach had announced his decision to seek to change the Republic's 1937 Constitution to eliminate – what he perceived as – the sectarian aspects to the document. On RTÉ Radio, FitzGerald said he wanted "to lead a crusade, a republican crusade to make this a genuine republic". This so-called 'constitutional crusade' involved removing the ban on divorce legislation. There was also a wish to change Articles Two and Three of the Constitution that claimed the area of Northern Ireland as part of the Irish State. These features of life in the Republic were, FitzGerald believed, obstacles to better relations with unionists in the North. However, Haughey and Fianna Fáil rejected the idea arguing that the Taoiseach had presented the enemies of Irish unity with a "a gold mine of propaganda".

Two months later, when Mansergh was interviewed in the *Sunday Press*, he gave full vent to Fianna Fáil positioning on the 'constitutional crusade'. However, there was an additional edge to the Mansergh criticism that could not have been made by Haughey or other Fianna Fáil figures. In fact, only the party's Protestant advisor could so openly dismiss the FitzGerald hypothesis about a sectarian Catholic ethos in the laws of the Irish Republic.

> As a Protestant, I feel the matter is being approached in a somewhat woolly-minded and naive manner. Most Protestants in the South I've talked to disagreed with the Taoiseach and some of them resented him calling this a sectarian state because it implied that Protestants are treated as second-class citizens which they are not.[13]

This was a theme Mansergh would return to and develop in subsequent years. Indeed, it is worth emphasising that Fianna Fáil were able to use their new recruit's religion to good effect. Whatever about Haughey's rejection of the constitutional crusade, Fianna Fáil was able to present Mansergh as evidence that Protestants had a comfortable place in nationalist Ireland. Moreover, as a member of the Church of Ireland, he was better able to make the case than even his own employer. "Speaking as a Protestant myself I feel that it is quite wrong to present the Protestant people of Ireland, as if somehow they were the injured party."[14]

Mansergh was wholly unconvinced about FitzGerald's arguments that the so-called 'confessional element' in the ethos, laws and Constitution of the Republic acted as a barrier to reconciliation between North and South. His reply pulled no punches:

> We can't centre national development around whether or not it pleases the unionists. Nor do I see that one has to go to extreme lengths to accommodate the imputed desires or wishes of those who totally refuse to participate. Anyway I don't think many unionists would approve of the abolition of hanging or the effect on the small Protestant schools of raising the entry age.[15]

By any standards the *Sunday Press* comments were a remarkable intervention from a political advisor. Even today such obviously party political interjections by advisors remain a rarity despite the development of a more structured advisor system in the Republic. Moreover, the extent of Mansergh's willingness to adopt a hardline approach in public was clear evidence that he had taken on board the pragmatic but conservative political agenda followed by his employer. Mansergh would later fill a similar role when Fianna Fáil accepted the arguments of anti-abortion lobby groups for a constitutional amendment to ban abortion in the Republic.

Abortion was already illegal based on legislation. However, concerns were raised by conservative groups following a limited liberalisation of the contraceptive laws in 1979 – a move prompted by a Supreme Court judgement some years earlier. Moreover, these groups were watching the situation in the United States with unease as a liberal judiciary relaxed federal law on abortion. The main Irish anti-abortion group argued that 1861 legislation outlawing abortion could be similarly interpreted in the Republic by a court judgement. To prevent such an outcome, conservative groups sought a constitutional guarantee on the right to life of the unborn.

Pressure on both Haughey and FitzGerald intensified

throughout the 1981-82 period with neither party leader being overly exercised at the idea of a constitutional referendum. However, it was a time of great political instability which created the ideal atmosphere for lobby groups to extract concessions from politicians.

In a study of the abortion debate, Tom Hesketh observed of the 1982 period: "There is firm evidence that Haughey was under considerable pressure from pro-life sources to produce an amendment before the widely anticipated general election."[16] The difficulty was in finding an amendment wording that was legally and constitutionally sound while also being acceptable to the anti-abortion groups.

Mansergh acted as a go-between with church leaders. He held separate meeting with individuals from the Church of Ireland and Roman Catholic Church. At a meeting with the Irish Council of Churches in Belfast on 13 October 1982 – which he requested – Mansergh indicated that a satisfactory form of words for an amendment had "almost been agreed to" and would be ready "by the end of the year".[17] However, with a general election approaching Fianna Fáil quickly moved to dispel any doubts about its commitment on the issue. On 2 November 1982 the party published a draft wording, which Mansergh argued, served only "to preserve the present legal status quo."[18] It was an assessment that subsequent events proved to be wholly incorrect.

The Fianna Fáil wording read:

> The State acknowledges the right to life of the unborn and, with due regard to the equal right to life of the mother, guarantees in its laws to respect and, as far as practicable, by its laws to defend and vindicate that right.

The text was rejected by Dick Spring, newly elected leader of the Labour Party, although his Fine Gael counterpart welcomed it. However, some weeks later following his election as Taoiseach, FitzGerald received legal advice that raised doubts about the Fianna Fáil wording. The advice observed that giving 'equal' rights to the mother and the child raised the possibility that a future Supreme Court which outlaw aspects of existing medical practice. Moreover, the advice from Attorney General Peter Sutherland also warned that the wording could be interpreted as permitting abortion in certain limited circum-stances. Attempts to formulate an alternative wording floundered, and with the support of some Fine Gael and Labour TDs, the Dáil accepted the Fianna Fáil amendment.

Mansergh set out the arguments in favour of the Fianna Fáil approach and the party's wording in a substantial article published in the *Clonmel Nationalist* newspaper in April 1983. The article was noteworthy for its measured and rational tone. In many respects this distanced Mansergh from the more emotional interventions of many others who participated in the debate from all perspectives. The referendum debate was bitter and divisive. The atmosphere in the campaign was not helped by the fact the Fine Gael/Labour government was divided on the issue.

Mansergh was unconvinced about fears for 'hardship cases' especially given the difficulty in limiting such cases to rape, incest or severe deformity. He observed:

> Rape should not be a problem. If promptly reported, it is possible to give medical treatment that will prevent conception. In reality most of the abortion legislation in the Western world is meant to cover only special cases, such as adverse effects on the physical and mental health of the mother. In practice, a demand for an abortion can always be justified in such terms, as pregnancy is apt to be physically and mentally stressful.[19]

The fact that he was prepared to accept the necessity of emergency contraception – which would have included the morning-after pill – placed the advisor at loggerheads with his political masters in Fianna Fáil. However, this divergence of view was not reported upon during the referendum campaign.

The official view of the Church of Ireland was that a

referendum was unwise and unnecessary. Mansergh wrote to the *Irish Times* posing the question: "Are Catholics and Protestants really still so far apart in the ecumenical age that any law or constitutional clause that is of Catholic origin or inspiration is automatically sectarian, divisive and to be rejected by Protestants?"[20]

The 1983 wording was incorporated into the Constitution as Article 40.3.3 having been passed by the people in a referendum. Mansergh was unimpressed by FitzGerald's handling of the 1983 referendum: "Our aim was to create a consensus and I have no doubt that had we stayed in office, there would have been much less division and confrontation on the issue."[21]

This was a moot point especially given subsequent developments. The decision in the abortion referendum in 1983 spawned two decades of debate on the issue in the Republic. The ambiguities in the Fianna Fáil wording, identified in the legal advice given to the FitzGerald-led government, eventually emerged in 1992 when a 14-year-old rape victim was legally prevented from leaving the jurisdiction to have an abortion.

There was less-than-enthusiastic support for the 1983 referendum at Grenane in Co Tipperary where his Uncle Gregor was predicting a large "No" vote. In a letter to Nicholas Mansergh in May 1983, his older brother observed: "Politicians should run the country not interfere in private lives."[22] In another guise Gregor Mansergh's nephew might have shared such a sentiment. The evidence from the early 1970s certainly pointed in that direction.

Indeed, it is difficult to reconcile the liberal Mansergh with the negative stance of Haughey's Fianna Fáil on a succession of issues in the 1980s, including divorce and contraception. It would seem that the advisor was prepared to modify his personal views on individual liberty and personal freedom. Nonetheless, in a speech to a Fianna Fáil conference in 1986, Mansergh defended the party's record on socio-moral issues:

> An attempt has been made in recent years to depict Fianna Fáil as a right-wing party, on the basis of

certain very selected social issues. 'The pluralist society' has been used as an ideological weapon to bash Fianna Fáil, ignoring the fact that any democracy is by definition pluralist. For the record, Fianna Fáil introduced the first inter-dominational schools, the first family planning legislation. It did not oppose the introduction of divorce, but left the decision to the people.[23]

The defence offered by Mansergh in 1986 was probably best described as a defence too far. The first inter-dominational schools were only approved after a long campaign by parents, while legislation introduced by Fianna Fáil in 1935 made the sale or importation of contraceptives a criminal offence. Forty-four years later, following a Supreme Court judgement striking down part of the 1935 legislation, Fianna Fáil updated the law to allow chemists sell contraceptives to those with a doctor's prescription. As the late John Whyte observed: "It was a narrowly restrictive measure."[24]

The examples chosen to argue for Fianna Fáil's liberal credentials were hardly auspicious. In addition, under Haughey's leadership in 1984 Fianna Fáil opposed legislation to allow contraceptives to be openly sold by pharmacies and health boards. That legislation introduced by the Fine Gael/Labour government was itself a long way short of the liberal approach advocated by Mansergh a decade earlier. Moreover, the decision to oppose the proposals precipitated the departure of Des O'Malley from Fianna Fáil – he abstained in the Dáil vote – and the establishment of the Progressive Democrats. The latter was a move that in electoral terms alone cost Haughey and Fianna Fáil dearly.

Fianna Fáil also adopted a neutral position during the 1986 referendum to remove the constitutional ban on the introduction of divorce legislation. However, a majority of party members opposed the proposal of the Fine Gael/Labour government. The reality was that, at that time, Mansergh was more liberal in outlook and disposition than the party he served.

When asked about how Mansergh fitted into Fianna Fáil given its traditional stance on liberal-conservative issues, Haughey only reiterated the claim he made on RTÉ in December 1982: "Fianna Fáil is neither a hostage to the left nor slave to the right, but operates a pragmatism of the centre."[25] Mansergh took a broader view, arguing that members of political parties could never be totally happy with every aspect of their party's policy platform. In later years Fianna Fáil totally changed its stance on issues such as contraception, divorce, homosexuality and, to a degree, abortion. Such policy positions were not altered without considerable internal unease, although the changes were a pragmatic response to changing public attitudes and values. The end result of this process was to create greater unity on social issues in the view of Mansergh and Fianna Fáil.

The December 1981 *Sunday Press* interview also provided evidence of the hard-line stance Mansergh adopted in his approach to Northern Ireland and the unionist community. He told the newspaper that it had been accepted as fact that unionists had opted out of a united Ireland, a scenario that was very different from saying they had a right to opt out. "It is quite wrong to legitimatise the unionist position, which is what the Taoiseach [FitzGerald] is doing in proposing to modify Articles Two and Three."[26]

The interview offered some insight into the type of advice Mansergh was providing to Haughey particularly in relation to Northern Ireland. The Fianna Fáil advisor was highly dismissive of FitzGerald's approach to the unionist community, believing it to be a futile exercise: "Reconciliation and rapprochement will require us all to move. I think the components for the new Ireland for the most part already exist, and do not have to be invented. We are like a jigsaw where the pieces do not appear to fit."[27]

When he was elected leader of Fianna Fáil, Haughey considered finding a solution to the problems in Northern Ireland as his chance to make a mark on history. He was perceived as a Fianna Fáil traditionalist in relation to the North, but he had shown little real interest in policy on Northern

Ireland prior to the 1970 Arms Crisis. Indeed, news of his involvement in an alleged plot to import arms for use in the North surprised most political observers. The events of 1970 – while still not fully explained – marked Haughey out as being rooted in the 'green' wing of Fianna Fáil.

In his first speech as Fianna Fáil leader to a party Árd Fheis in February 1980, Haughey claimed that "Northern Ireland as a political entity has failed".[28] The new Taoiseach added that he looked forward to forging new arrangements for the island as a whole without a British presence but with active British goodwill.

A united Ireland remained the central objective of Fianna Fáil policy. However, there was a key divergence on Northern Ireland policy between Fianna Fáil and Fine Gael during this period. While Haughey and Fianna Fáil took the line that the best basis for a deal lay in an agreement between the two governments, Fine Gael insisted that the communities in the North were central to any agreement. Given his track record, Haughey would have had little prospect of building trust with unionist leaders. If a deal was going to be done, his most productive route was going to be through direct bilateral talks with Downing Street.

So Haughey, conscious of his place in history, was not prepared to singularly play the irredentist card. A successful Anglo-Irish summit was held in Dublin in December 1980 at which the Taoiseach and his British counterpart, Margaret Thatcher, agreed to examine the 'totality of the relationships' between the two islands. A number of joint studies were proposed. The month after the Haughey-Thatcher summit, Mansergh arrived in the Department of the Taoiseach. He was to explore the 'totality of the relationships' in areas such as security, citizenship and economic co-ordination.

The introduction of Mansergh to Haughey's advisory team coincided with a period when relations between the two leaders became increasingly strained. Any initial trust that had been developing dissipated when the Irish side pushed too far what had been achieved at the 1980 Dublin Summit. Thatcher was annoyed at talk of solving partition and achieving Irish unity within a decade. The British Prime Minister was clear about what she envisaged as Dublin's role in policy on Northern Ireland – "The future of the constitutional future of Northern Ireland is a matter for the people of Northern Ireland, this government and this Parliament and no-one else."[29] The 1981 hunger strikes also placed pressure on the relationship.

This occurred at a time when Mansergh was quickly gaining influence in the backroom team as Fianna Fáil adjusted to life outside government. In November 1981 Haughey called a press conference in the Burlington Hotel to react to an Anglo-Irish summit in London at which Garret FitzGerald and the British Prime Minister sought to repair relations strained by the hunger strikes. The two leaders agreed to establish an intergovernmental council. Haughey was unimpressed. But more significant, perhaps, was the presence of Mansergh at the press conference table sitting alongside the Fianna Fáil leader. He later recalled "metaphorically fastening the seat belt" at a number of these press conferences.[30]

Fianna Fáil policy on the North hardened after the failure of the bilateral approach. The inevitability of a united Ireland became a constant refrain from Haughey. The recruitment of Mansergh with his democratic republican principles was also a factor. In any event, whatever prospect Haughey had of developing a fruitful relationship with his British counterpart ended in May 1982, when the Fianna Fáil government expressed reservations about the value of European Economic Community (EEC) sanctions on Argentina. For Mansergh, the Irish position was merely what other EEC member states were saying in private.

During the Haughey years a number of policies and issues were considered as 'core values' in Fianna Fáil. In particular, the party was anti-coalition; strongly nationalistic on Northern Ireland; conservative on social issues and favoured a policy of military neutrality. Haughey recalled:

> Irish neutrality was a major issue in those days. In Europe there was great pressure for a common foreign and security policy. That was something we

had to watch carefully. There was some debate as to whether we were just military neutral or were we totally neutral? Martin was helpful in delineating these issues. We didn't want to hold up integration – I was always and still am for that – but we did have to watch the implications for our policy of neutrality.[31]

Mansergh was strongly in favour of maintaining Irish neutrality defined in terms of membership of international military alliances. Credit for developing the policy was attributed to de Valera and his decision to keep Ireland out of World War Two.

In an address to a Fianna Fáil audience in 1986, Mansergh remarked:

> ... one of the principal benefits of Irish independence is our ability to maintain our neutrality, however, imperfect, and to keep our soil free of military bases, nuclear missiles and not to have to constantly increase defence spending and be prisoners inside an alliance subject to the dictates of the leaders of that alliance. Most countries in Europe are not so fortunate.[32]

The position evolved in subsequent years. By early 2002, Mansergh was posing the question: "Where is the validity in the argument that we should be frightened of militarism, when anyone with eyes to see can observe that Europe is substantially demilitarised compared to the cold war years?"[33] He downplayed Ireland's role in the EU's Rapid Reaction Force, especially given the need for approval by a significant number of member states before it could move into action. A concern was raised about the possibility that Irish involvement in EU peacekeeping and humanitarian tasks might not be possible, should the State adhere to a rigid interpretation of its policy of neutrality.

However, no matter what way the neutrality issue was presented, both the definition and attachment to the neutrality concept fundamentally altered over the last two decades. This fact was evident when the Fianna Fáil/PD coalition in 1999 signed up for membership of the NATO-led Partnership for Peace (PfP) group, a move that would have been unthinkable during the Haughey years.

Mansergh did not favour Europe developing into a military superpower, but he had no difficulty in arguing that PfP would have a liberating effect on the Irish Defence Forces through greater co-operation and training with their counterparts elsewhere. "PfP is not a military alliance, and I personally would be very against giving up our independent foreign policy tradition to join one," the Fianna Fáil advisor argued in an address to the representative body of the Defence Forces, PDFORA.[34]

The move was a good illustration of the pragmatism underpinning Fianna Fáil's political outlook that Mansergh found attractive about the party he joined in 1981. Indeed, during the 1990s, there was a considerable shift in the Fianna Fáil positioning on many issues previously considered as 'core values'. Party policy in 2002 in areas such as Northern Ireland, neutrality, the liberal-agenda and even the economy had moved a considerable distance from that articulated in 1981. It would seem that Mansergh moved seamlessly with those changes. The party advisor was at the heart of Fianna Fáil policy-making for two decades. Moreover, he had also been a close observer – and sometime participant – in the personality clashes that dominated the leadership of the party throughout the 1980s and 1990s.

During the initial years of Haughey's leadership there were considerable divisions within the party. Haughey had narrowly defeated long-time rival George Colley in the leadership contest in December 1979. Many Fianna Fáil TDs and Senators privately shared the view of Garret FitzGerald that the successor to Jack Lynch as fourth party leader had a "flawed pedigree". There were many unanswered questions about his involvement in the 1970 Arms Trial and also how his views would manifest themselves on Northern Ireland policy. Moreover, some commentators raised the issue of his wealth,

although there was no evidence to confirm the extent to which
– as emerged in later years – Haughey was a kept man.

Immediately after taking office the new Taoiseach pledged to
address the deteriorating economic situation but the evidence
from his initial period in power failed to match action with
rhetoric. Senior Fianna Fáil figures were unhappy with
Haughey's failure to get to grips with the public finances, and
also his government's excessive spending while talking of the
need for fiscal restraint.

The cabal of internal opponents included senior party
figures such as Colley, Martin O'Donoghue, a former economic
planning minister, and Desmond O'Malley, the Limerick man
who had been promoted to cabinet during the 1970 Arms
Crisis. All three men were loyal supporters of Jack Lynch. They
were the visible leaders of the anti-Haughey wing within
Fianna Fáil.

A move against Haughey was first mooted after the
February 1982 general election when Fianna Fáil – for the
second successive election under Haughey – failed to secure an
overall majority in the Dáil. His opponents saw their
opportunity when it was evident that, as the party had only
won 81 seats, the support of independents and small parties
would be required to secure a Dáil majority. The anti-Haughey
faction backed O'Malley as their challenger for the party
leadership.

The issue was scheduled to be resolved at a meeting on 25
February 1982, when a motion to re-elect Haughey as leader
was to be debated. The media speculated that between 30 and
40 members of the Fianna Fáil parliamentary party would vote
against Haughey. But on the day itself the dissidents stopped
short of challenging the incumbent. O'Malley's prospects were
damaged at the meeting itself when one of his most visible
supporters, Martin O'Donoghue, spoke of the need for unity
behind Haughey as leader.

There were rumours of intimidation but Haughey was free
to form a minority government dependent upon the support of
Neil Blaney, a former Fianna Fáil TD who had also been sacked
from government in 1970 over the arms crisis allegations; Tony

Gregory, an independent TD from Dublin and Sinn Féin: The Workers' Party, a Marxist party that had its roots in the Republican Movement in Northern Ireland.

The new Fianna Fáil government took office on 9 March 1982. It lost a motion of no confidence on 4 November and, as such, the year ended as it had begun, with a general election. The eight months of the minority government's life were full of scandal and the controversy that only added to the view that Haughey was unfit to hold public office. Indeed, the life of the second Haughey administration had started in controversy over a deal done with Gregory, a newly elected Independent TD. In exchange for support in Dáil votes – and most importantly on the division on the election of Taoiseach – Gregory extracted a written programme of public investment for central Dublin.

Mansergh distanced himself from the 1982 period, observing: "I was the Northern Ireland political advisor during that period, so I suppose I was mainly involved on that side of things."[35] That assertion is open to question, however, since there is evidence that Mansergh was more centrally involved. Specifically, Mansergh was involved in setting up the Gregory deal in return for the latter's Dáil vote:

> Haughey would have told me who to talk to about this and about that, and before he went to see Gregory the first time, you know, I would have given him a paper of Gregory's position on different issues. I think he was quite well prepared going into meetings both with Gregory and with the Workers' Party.[36]

The Gregory Deal was – as soon transpired – a relatively minor controversy when set against other events that occurred during 1982. Dick Burke, a Fine Gael TD, was approached with an offer to become Ireland's European Commissioner. His acceptance of the position was intended to increase Haughey's voting strength in the Dáil but the victory of another Fine Gael candidate in the by-election caused by Burke's resignation as a

TD only served to damage the reputation of the Fianna Fáil leader. The move smacked of 'cute-hoorism' although it was probably not as damaging, or as personally embarrassing for Haughey, as when his election agent, Pat O'Connor, was charged with vote fraud.

However, by the far the most serious difficulties encountered by the 1982 Fianna Fáil government centred on claims that the administration of justice in the Republic was being abused by certain political figures. For example, the police in Northern Ireland detained a witness who had been due to give evidence in a court case involving the brother-in-law of Sean Doherty, the Minister for Justice. There was also a row about the transfer of a Garda from Co Roscommon, the home county of the Justice Minister.

Then during the summer of 1982 a murder suspect was arrested in a flat owned by the Attorney General who subsequently resigned. There were also rumours of illegal phone tapping. Conor Cruise O'Brien, a former Labour Party minister, coined the sobriquet 'GUBU' to sum up the various controversies – grotesque, unbelievable, bizarre and unprecedented. The words had been uttered by Haughey to describe the unusual series of events engulfing his minority government.

The sequence of controversies encouraged further talk about the leadership issue in Fianna Fáil. Several months after their first abortive coup, O'Malley and his supporters were forced to move directly against Haughey's leadership of Fianna Fáil. Discontent was growing within the party. This was confirmed in October 1982 when one of the TDs who had assisted Haughey's accession in December 1979 tabled a motion of no confidence in the party leader. To the surprise of the O'Malley-Colley faction, Charlie McCreevy, a backbench Dáil deputy from Kildare, precipitated the heave. O'Malley was in Spain on holidays when news of McCreevy's no confidence motion reached him. The Fianna Fáil parliamentary party was to meet on 6 October to vote on the motion.

Mansergh owed his professional employment as a political advisor to Haughey and had developed a strong sense of loyalty to the Fianna Fáil leader. He was by Haughey's side throughout these leadership battles. "I would have to admit that the adrenaline flowed. I am not someone who went out looking for political battles."[37]

Despite his position in relation to the Fianna Fáil leader, the anti-Haughey group never identified Mansergh as a target for the type of criticism levelled at other officials and advisors during leadership heaves. Séamus Brennan, one of the ringleaders of the anti-Haughey faction, said Mansergh was not considered as partisan in the various internal party struggles:

> He was seen as a Haughey stalwart, an advisor and a protector but I don't think the anti-Haughey people held that against him much. They saw him not as a politician but as the tactical political strategist. He wasn't seen as a political advisor who leaned over Charlie's shoulder and said: 'You'd want to get rid of that fellow.' So he didn't draw the ire of the Lynch-Colley-O'Malley side of the house.[38]

The October 1982 leadership contest was high political drama. The Fianna Fáil grassroots rallied to Haughey. Once more there were stories of intense pressure being brought to bear on TDs and Senators considering voting against Haughey.

The meeting in the Fianna Fáil offices on the fifth floor in Leinster House went on all day and into the early hours of Thursday 7 October. The corridors of the parliament buildings were crammed with Fianna Fáil supporters from all over Ireland. There was hardly room to move in the Dáil bar. When word of the result seeped out there were wild scenes. In an open roll call vote the no confidence motion had been defeated by 58 to 22. When they emerged from Leinster House members of the anti-Haughey group were verbally abused; one was struck and their cars were kicked and thumped.

Haughey survived as his critics withdrew to assess the situation. Another general election defeat – and further revelations including a phone tapping scandal – followed. There are several references to the political events of 1982 in the correspondence that Gregor Mansergh sent to his brother, Nicholas. In early June 1982 Gregor wrote: "Haughey's antics with Burke and Eileen Lemass ... has (sic) gone down pretty badly."[39]

Towards the end of the same month Mansergh's uncle observed: "I don't care for Charlie Haughey's manoeuvrings at all and I feel it can end only one way, a disaster of some kind – any remarks I've heard at race meetings or in the market for instance view him with great distaste. I've told Martin to watch out."[40] The opinion hardened further and by October 1982 Gregor Mansergh was writing of his nephew's employer: "In common with lots of others I can't stand CJH any longer and hope we're rid of him as soon as possible."[41]

Haughey had emerged democratically as Fianna Fáil leader in December 1979 but there was a considerable section of the party which had never accepted the legitimacy of his leadership. The dissidents' numbers were strengthened as Haughey failed to deliver at the polls and also emerged discredited from the scandals associated with his government. On 7 February 1983, another no confidence motion was debated by the Fianna Fáil parliamentary party. The motion followed a general election defeat in November 1982 and subsequent revelations that the phones of two journalists had been tapped during the life of the short-lived 1982 Fianna Fáil administration.

The third leadership heave was, according to Mansergh, "the most desperate leadership crisis". He observed: "Early February represented a dangerous period for Irish democracy when the Dublin media with all the force it could muster were trying to force Fianna Fáil to change its leader ... "[42] He also suspected the involvement of British intelligence in an attempt to discredit the Fianna Fáil leader.

As the confidence vote neared there was increasing speculation that Haughey was going to be beaten. Mansergh recalled:

> I would be more conscious in hindsight, perhaps, how close to the precipice I was stepping than I would have been at the time. It was a very intense period

but, mind you, I suppose lots of people had a belief in Haughey's capacity to fight and survive.[43]

The leadership contest looked lost when Haughey and his supporters did a tally of the parliamentary party members. Haughey considered stepping down as Taoiseach and Fianna Fáil leader. He drafted a few lines for a resignation speech and asked Mansergh to develop the script.

> I did some further work but my heart wasn't in it. I certainly remember his response when I said he should try and gain some time. He said: well if I thought that (he could play for time), he'd fight. Charlie did a lot of soundings so I'm not suggesting that anything I said to him had any particular influence. I mean I would have been one voice among others, that's all. I would have helped him throughout the period. I would be sort of proud of having helped him fight his political battles.[44]

The vote was taken by secret ballot. After another marathon meeting, Senator Donnie Cassidy emerged with the news: "Charlie by 40 votes to 33." Once more Haughey emerged the victor. The crowds that had gathered at the gates to Leinster House on Kildare Street started to chant: "We want Charlie. We want Charlie."

The 1983 leadership battle was the last fought by Des O'Malley. While the former minister continued to oppose, a point was eventually reached and Haughey was forced to move against his political foe. The Limerick politician broke ranks with Fianna Fáil in May 1984 over responses to the report of the New Ireland Forum. The party whip was withdrawn. Nine months later O'Malley was expelled from Fianna Fáil after he abstained on legislation to liberalise contraception law.

Haughey opposed the attempt to liberalise the law, although Mansergh recalled that the party leader had mixed views on the stance Fianna Fáil was proposing, especially as the measure was a limited liberalisation of his own 1979 legislation. But leading members of the party front bench favoured opposition based upon conservative and political motivations: "Haughey went into outright opposition over that partly against his better judgement," his advisor recalled.[45]

Mansergh was at Haughey's side as he emerged out of Leinster House on the night in February 1985 when O'Malley was expelled from Fianna Fáil. "Most TDs after they fall out with the party go through a period of quarantine and then edge back, but with O'Malley it was clear the rift would go on widening," Mansergh remarked.[46]

The Limerick East politician went on to form the Progressive Democrats. There was a remarkable reaction to the new political party with regional meetings attracting huge crowds while established political figures like Mary Harney and Bobby Molloy from Fianna Fáil opted to switch sides. There was much speculation about the intentions of other senior party figures such as David Andrews and Séamus Brennan. Mansergh recalled the time: "We were not overly concerned. There was no panic. The view was that it will pass and let's keep the defections to a minimum."[47]

The emergence of the PDs was only one of the challenges faced by Fianna Fáil in opposition in the mid-1980s. Mansergh said one of his principal achievements as an advisor was simply helping to sustain Fianna Fáil in opposition from November 1982 until early in 1987. The Irish economic position was bleak. Over a quarter of a million people were out of work, the blight of emigration had returned while government borrowing was out of control.

It was a terrible time to be in government but worse to be in opposition. While internal dissent within Fianna Fáil continued, Haughey adopted a singular strategy in relation to the Garret FitzGerald-led coalition – oppose. "Haughey's style in Opposition was robust. People nowadays are critical that the Opposition is not robust enough. People were certainly interested in politics at that time and people were sort of passionately pro- or anti-Haughey," Mansergh said.[48]

Little that the Fine Gael/Labour coalition achieved found favour with Fianna Fáil. On almost every policy from the economy to Northern Ireland, Haughey and his colleagues found justification for criticism and opposition. The Taoiseach Garret FitzGerald considered the strategy unscrupulous. "Oppositions also opposed but I have to admit they were more negative than was reasonable on everything except when to do with national security."[49]

Nevertheless, both Mansergh and Haughey shared the same positive assessment of the Fianna Fáil tactics between the end of 1982 and the general election in 1987. Haughey remarked: "If I may say so we were a very active opposition in that period. By 1987 we were ready for government. We had policies and we knew what we wanted to achieve. Martin Mansergh and, when we were in government, Pádraig O hUiginn would have had a major input into our economic policies and policies generally."[50]

But the policy of outright opposition caused several problems for Fianna Fáil – some in relation to Northern Ireland, others with more lasting damage to the party's dominant position on the Irish political landscape. The most immediate downside was the exit of O'Malley and the creation of the PDs. A former advisor colleague of Mansergh's argued this point: "Yes, we knocked the stuffing out of the government of the day but we also created the PDs. We ended the broad family that was Fianna Fáil and that has been a loss to the party ever since."

Fianna Fáil has been short of a Dáil majority in all general elections since 1977. However, since the 1989 contest the party has not even been in a position to form a single-party minority administration. In 1989, 1997 and 2002 deals had to be done with former party colleagues to attain power while in 1992 Fianna Fáil formed a coalition with the Labour Party. If Haughey had moved to accommodate O'Malley and his supporters in the mid-1980s, it is possible that the dominant electoral position of Fianna Fáil could have been sustained somewhat longer.

During that period Haughey took advice from many quarters but Mansergh was his full-time policy co-ordinator. Mansergh was in effect providing Fianna Fáil with a shadow civil service while the party was in opposition. "Between 1983 and 1987 nobody did anything without referring it to Martin Mansergh," a Fianna Fáil TD said.

The extent to which Mansergh emerged as an all-round confidante was evident when Haughey was interviewed on RTÉ radio by Pat Kenny during the June 1989 general election. The phone-in programme lasted for 90 minutes with Haughey fielding questions on a variety of topics. Over 200 callers got through to the programme phone number although there was only time to actually put 25 questions directly to Haughey on air. For the duration of the programme Mara was in the control room while Mansergh actually sat in the radio studio alongside Haughey as he faced his interviewer.

During the 1980s the three principal Fianna Fáil advisors in Leinster House were Mansergh, O hAnnracháin and Mara. By that time O hAnnracháin had retired from the civil service after a long and distinguished career. He had a wicked sense of humour that was frequently directed at his colleague from Co Tipperary. Haughey enjoyed the office banter:

> Martin had a certain charming naivety about some things and O hAnnracháin, who had a great affection for him, loved to rib him by saying such things as: 'Mansergh, that's just your Trinity prejudices,' knowing the deliberate mistake would get the immediate response: 'I wasn't at Trinity, it was Oxford.'[51]

Mara had joined the Fianna Fáil staff as press officer in Leinster House in 1984. He was a long-time Haughey supporter, having backed him during the 1970 Arms Crisis. They travelled together to Fianna Fáil functions during Haughey's period in the political wilderness in the 1970s. Born in Dublin, Mara was outgoing, gregarious and a treasure chest of funny and often scandalous stories. The new press officer was a long way from Mansergh in terms of either background or personality. However, the two men worked well together, combining to achieve their shared objective of getting Haughey and Fianna Fáil back into government.

Haughey was particularly sensitive to everything written about him and would frequently lose his temper over adverse media commentary. On one occasion, O hAnnracháin observed of the mood in Haughey's office: "He's eating children in the raw state."[52] There was a memorable row on the morning that *Hot Press* magazine published verbatim an interview with Haughey with expletives included. Mansergh was in Leinster House when Haughey arrived but before Mara had appeared. The atmosphere was explosive. Along the corridor all party officials heard was a loud verbal exchange between the Press Officer and the Fianna Fáil leader: "Mara – you've finally blown it. I'm ruined. Get out of my sight."[53]

Mansergh was equally sensitive about media coverage but without the tempestuous nature of the Fianna Fáil leader. Every morning the advisor would pore over the political reports in the newspapers. He would despair about what he deemed poor quality criticism of Haughey and Fianna Fáil. Mara would regularly receive long and detailed memos from Mansergh that set out the factual errors in particular reports as well as reasons why analysis or comment articles were ill-founded.

One of the most severe critics of the Haughey leadership was Bruce Arnold of the *Irish Independent*. Mansergh believed Arnold's articles were well-written but flawed in their assessments and conclusions. He took some revenge when the *Sunday Tribune* asked that he review Arnold's book *What Kind of Country?* It was a vitriolic review: "The bulk of this book is a fairly pedestrian narrative of some of the events of the last 15 years." When Arnold later wrote a biography of Haughey, Mansergh observed that it was "a polemical but not exactly profound biography."[54]

Mansergh acknowledged his sensitivity to the media: "To be continually attacked by a columnist should often be regarded as a compliment, a badge of honour, a source of amusement even, not a cause of annoyance or embarrassment. But it is not always easy to persuade political leaders or even oneself of that in all such situations."[55] However, over the years Mansergh adjusted somewhat to adverse media coverage, as he explained in 1996 at the Listowel Writers' Week:

Political leaders, most of them, have a tendency to be paranoid about their critics. Perhaps they should occasionally look at the situation through the eyes of those critics, because they might see a somewhat more reassuring picture. Imagine the frustrations, when an intelligent but politically driven critic has to endure for years and years the political success of someone whose public reputation and prestige they have repeatedly, week in, week out, in vain sought to attack and demolish. I am told it was carpet-eating time, in some of the upper echelons of the *Irish Times*, when they discovered to their horror in December 1992 that Albert Reynolds, litigant extraordinaire against the newspaper of record, was going to be helped to a second period of office courtesy of Dick Spring.[56]

Mara was at the receiving end of Mansergh's memos on the quality of the fourth estate's view of Haughey. But he did extract some humorous revenge. Haughey's press officer was blamed for some of the more colourful aspects of life in the Mansergh household that appeared in newspaper articles in the mid-1980s. One such piece was written by journalist Sam Smyth in March 1987: "An unlikely Fianna Fáiler, he still carries the clipped tones of Oxford, wears duffle coats, makes his own jams and pickles, and carries a deep-seated suspicion of British intent in Northern Ireland."[57] Nevertheless, there was some truth in the description. As a student at Oxford University, Mansergh had taken a course in berry growing – today he grows several varieties of berry at his farm in Co Tipperary – while his wife Liz makes sloe gin.

Whatever about their obsessions with the media, both Mansergh and Mara worked exceptionally well together without any real friction. However, one incident lodged in Mansergh's mind. Fianna Fáil had returned to power after the 1987 general election. Mansergh and Mara were in their respective offices in Government Buildings. Mansergh wanted clarification on a newspaper report and rang Mara. "To my surprise, he started hectoring and shouting down the phone at me, and treating my questions as very stupid, in a colourful way that I sometimes heard him use to put down obtuse young reporters with a tiresome line of enquiry. When he put down the phone, he called out to his clerical assistant: 'Sinéad, who was that?' When he found out, he came running into my office, next door along the corridor, apologising and laughing profusely."[58]

The novelist Colm Tóibín experienced the advisor's fervour during a train journey from Belfast to Dublin in June 1989. Tóibín was at that time writing for the *Sunday Independent*. He was returning from an SDLP conference – "slightly hung-over" – with a colleague. By his own account Tóibín was preparing to settle in for the train journey with a bundle of Sunday newspapers. Mansergh, who had been at the conference, was also returning to Dublin on the same train. Tóibín recalled:

> And then this guy arrives, full of quotes from Gladstone, de Valera and Charlie Haughey. His mission was to explain Fianna Fáil policy to us, and he did this for most of the journey without cease. He looked at us through his glasses, he spoke to us in his British accent, and it never seemed to occur to him that both of us were steeped, perhaps to our detriment, in Irish political culture, and one of us at least, in the ambiguous, complex and rich culture of Fianna Fáil. This didn't deter him … I almost bailed out at Dundalk.[59]

Haughey respected and admired Mansergh for taking a risk in following Fianna Fáil into opposition after the June 1981 general election. In the months that followed – and especially after the general election defeat in November 1982 – there was certainly a deepening in the relationship between politician and advisor. Sean Haughey, a son of the Fianna Fáil leader who was also elected to Dáil Éireann in 1989, recalled that Mansergh became a frequent visitor to Abbeyville. "He was not at social functions. It was clearly a working relationship, a very close one."[60]

Mansergh compiled and edited a collection of Haughey's speeches that was published in 1986 as *The Spirit of the Nation*. He would have written many of the speeches. In the introduction, the advisor wrote: "Charles Haughey's political career and achievements are unmatched among his contemporaries."[61]

The book was quickly labelled 'The Thoughts of Chairman Charlie'. It was available at a special price of £20 from Fianna Fáil headquarters. At the annual Fianna Fáil dinner dance in December 1986 a leather-bound copy signed by Haughey and Mansergh was sold at auction for £800.

The tome generated strong reaction from political opponents. When Shane Ross, a senator for Trinity College, was asked in a questionnaire what he would do if the world were ending, his reply was to start reading *Spirit of the Nation*, as "then the end of the world would be a welcome relief". According to Ruairi Quinn, the book was "loyal servant of Ceaucescu sort of stuff".[62] Garret FitzGerald remarked: "It was an extraordinary act of sycophancy. It would have been remarkable even if Haughey was this outstanding character."[63]

While Mansergh said he had free reign on the material, he was not a disinterested author. He had had a ringside seat during most of the Haughey leadership. He was the Fianna Fáil leader's most loyal supporter. The task which Mansergh rates as Haughey's greatest achievement postdated the publication of *The Spirit of the Nation*. This was the imposition of fiscal rectitude on the economy in the late Eighties and early Nineties.

When Haughey was elected Fianna Fáil leader in December 1979 the national debt was emerging as a serious economic and political concern. The new Taoiseach correctly identified the problem. In January 1980 he made a special television address. "The figures which are just now becoming available to us show one thing very clearly. As a community we are living way beyond our means." However, Haughey's words were not matched by actions.

Throughout their period in opposition in the mid-1980s, Haughey had constantly questioned the wisdom of the government's hair-shirt economic policies. He backed lobby groups seeking additional spending in their respective areas.

The Fianna Fáil slogan in the 1987 general election implied increased rather than reduced public expenditure. 'Health cuts hurt the old, the poor and the handicapped,' was the message on the billboard posters around the country. Despite these sentiments the stark economic realities had in fact been recognised and accepted by Haughey and his advisory team. Haughey was listening to economists like Colm McCarthy of DKM Consultants in Dublin as well as the stockbroker and businessman, Dermot Desmond. Their message was clear: Ireland was broke and drastic action was required. Mansergh recalled: "By 1986, as in 1956, deep depression had set in, with the feeling that the rest of the world was passing us by, and we wondered if we were condemned forever to a mediocre economic performance."[64]

Fianna Fáil entered the 1987 general election with an offer of 'good government' but with no promise to increase spending. In fact, the party had decided to drop its opposition stance and was ready to adopt a hair-shirt economy policy, drawing on sentiments originally expressed in the 1982 *Way Forward* plan.

The U-turn was classic Fianna Fáil, another example of the populism and pragmatism identified by Mansergh as at the core of the party. Of course, opponents would consider the policy shift as cynical politics regardless how beneficial the end result. Mansergh observed:

> I always recall during an interregnum, when we were poised to make the transition from Opposition to Government, a front bench spokesperson being reprimanded for repeating a promise made a few days earlier during the election campaign. What was valid then, was not necessarily valid now.[65]

There had been significant internal discussion on what to do about the economic situation. In the budget introduced after the 1987 general election Fianna Fáil proposed even greater cutbacks in public spending than those favoured by the outgoing government led by Garret FitzGerald. But there was also a second strand to the Fianna Fáil economic policy. The plan to cut public spending was coupled with advocacy of a tripartite system of economic management involving the government, employer groups and the trade unions. The concept had been discussed at the National Economic and Social Council but had been little developed by the Fine Gael/Labour coalition. Mansergh believed a mistake had been made.

The negotiations with the trade unions, farmers and employers concluded in October 1987. The era of social partnership was born. Bertie Ahern was centrally involved in the deal, yet he credited Mansergh with convincing the Fianna Fáil political leadership of the merits of the approach:

> Mansergh had a hell of a lot of influence I think, on the change in policies of Fianna Fáil in the mid-Eighties. He certainly was involved in our evolving policies on the North and the economy. If you wanted to know anything it was Martin Mansergh you would talk to.[66]

The three-year deal with the unions, employers and farmers – entitled *The Programme for National Recovery* – set down certain economic targets to resolve the debt problem with a promise to share the benefits from any upturn in the Republic's economic fortunes. The social democrat in Mansergh was an enthusiastic proponent of the social partnership concept:

> In many ways, economically, the country has not looked back since things were taken decisively in hand at that period after 1987. I mean, I regard '87 as being as at least as important a turning point as the Whitaker White Paper in 1958.[67]

Haughey's shrewd economic management in the 1987-92 period stood in stark contrast to the reckless approach which characterised his first two periods as Taoiseach in the early 1980s. Several individuals including Mansergh were responsible for the changed stance.

Mansergh believed the 1987 economy policy platform was

one of the greatest achievements of Haughey's political career. This desire to credit Haughey remained a consistent feature of Mansergh's objective to position the fourth Fianna Fáil leader within the pantheon of great European politicians:

> In that contrast, and of course, no exact parallels can be drawn, he may have something in common with a number of other controversial European leaders of stature among his contemporaries. Everyone, not just the Government or Fianna Fáil, will have difficulty confronting the necessary task of disentangling strands of the legacy that have been deeply woven into the fabric of Irish life, the positive to be kept from the negative that must be discarded.[68]

The attempt to draw parallels between the 1987 recovery policies and the industrialisation strategy of the late 1950s is questionable. The latter heralded a fundamental reorientation of the State's economic outlook while the former was at its simplest a crude cost-cutting exercise. Nevertheless, the combination of public expenditure reductions, and nascent social partnership, precipitated an improvement in the economic situation after 1987. The policy was described by economists as 'expansionary fiscal contraction,'' in reference to the situation whereby economic growth started to increase when the government implemented its policy of cutting public spending.

Alongside the economic recovery, clandestine contacts with the Republican Movement were established under the new Haughey government. There were indications that a peace process could be developed to end the conflict in Northern Ireland. These twin issues – the economy and the North – dominated Haughey's political agenda although other matters were to once again threaten his leadership of Fianna Fáil. The motivation for another leadership challenge was rooted in a series of controversies made public in 1991 – all of which were associated with financial impropriety.

Controversy was never far away during the Haughey era but there was a difference between the events of 1982 and those matters which came into the public domain in 1991. The scandals of the early 1980s were largely associated with illegal telephone tapping and interference with judicial administration. These events indicated a pattern of abuse of power. However, many of the controversial matters that came into the public domain in 1991 were connected with the relationship between politics and business, and all involved money.

The sense that impropriety was widespread was first established when controversy developed in the late summer of 1991 around the sale of the State-owned Irish Sugar Company, latterly known as Greencore. A conflict of interest arose when a senior executive was discovered to have had a material interest in the sale; along with other managers at the company he shared in a £7m profit on a transaction involving no personal financial risk. The revelation was given political impetus, as Bernie Cahill, the chairman of Irish Sugar, was a close associate of Charles Haughey. When the first scandal was reported in the media, Mansergh was in Paris for a weeklong course on eighteenth-century history:

> I went out to Versailles, where I got soaked in a thunderstorm and had to seek shelter in the great doorway of a stable near the former Estates-General. I went in the course of the afternoon to the Petit-Trianon. With a vague sense of calm before the storm, having to go back to work in the morning, I lay in the grass musing on the peace of the hamlet, from which Queen Marie-Antoinette was summoned, as the Paris mob converged in the early October days of 1789 on the palace. When I arrived home to Dublin later that evening I bought a *Sunday Independent*, which contained the first details of the Greencore affair, as we faced into an autumn of unprecedented political turbulence, with new controversies, and affairs, or as some would prefer it, scandals, arising every week.[69]

In the autumn and winter months of 1991 the Irish public became familiar with the inner workings of companies such as

Telecom Éireann and Celtic Helicopters as well as the identities of businessmen like Dermot Desmond and Michael Smurfit. Shortly after the Irish Sugar revelation it emerged that another State-owned company, Telecom Éireann, had paid £9.4m for a property in Dublin despite the State Valuation Office having decided that the property was worth £6m. Businessman Michael Smurfit was chairman of Telecom but he also had an interest in the company indirectly involved in the property deal.[70]

In the Dáil Haughey was under continuous pressure from the opposition parties. There were allegations of a so-called 'golden circle' of influential business and political figures. Questions were asked about the site of a business campus in Blackrock in Co Dublin that had been purchased by University College Dublin. Pino Harris, a businessman associated with Fianna Fáil, had sold the site but it was unclear who instructed UCD to make the purchase. Paralleling these controversies were ongoing allegations of corruption in the beef industry. A central character in the latter investigation was Larry Goodman, a businessman who also had links with Haughey and Fianna Fáil.

The Irish Sugar and Telecom affairs, in particular, placed leading members of the business community under the spotlight. One of those involved in the Telecom affair was Dermot Desmond, a wealthy stockbroker who was also friendly with Haughey. There was further unease when it was revealed that confidential information about an Aer Lingus subsidiary had been given to a competitor, Celtic Helicopters, an enterprise owned by one of Haughey's sons. The information was obtained from Desmond who was acting for the Aer Lingus subsidiary. Desmond had – due to a 'postal error' – sent the documentation to the wrong company.

According to one writer: "The Irish Sugar, Telecom Éireann and Celtic Helicopters incidents each contributed to public unease, not just about business people but with politicians as well."[71]

There was great strain in Government Buildings where the daily work agenda was increasingly dominated by reacting to media and opposition questions about the latest revelation.

Mansergh was unimpressed as he stressed some years later:

> No matter how tenuous the connection, each new
> chapter was firmly pinned by media and opposition
> to a certain political culture, over which the then
> Taoiseach was alleged to preside. The period inspired
> extraordinary projections of fantasy that are often the
> substitute or compensation for the deficiencies of a
> less sensational reality … Many journalists and incl-
> uding others, have, I suspect, been deeply frustrated
> by their inability (to date) to track down an elusive
> Irish Watergate-style scandal, which they are
> convinced must exist.[72]

While the trust of Mansergh remained undiminished,
Haughey was running short of political friends. The loyalty of
his closest political allies – colleagues like Pádraig Flynn and
Máire Geoghegan-Quinn – had been tested over the decision to
enter coalition with the PDs in 1989. Moreover, the debacle that
had been the 1990 Presidential election campaign, and the
ministerial sacking of Fianna Fáil favourite Brian Lenihan, also
cost Haughey party support.

When the campaign of the 1990 Fianna Fáil presidential
candidate became embroiled in controversy, Mary Robinson, the
Labour Party candidate, was dramatically elected the Republic's
seventh Head of State. The contest had been billed as an epoch-
making battle between traditional Ireland represented by a long-
time Fianna Fáil minister and the modern outward-looking
Ireland represented by the liberal Trinity College lawyer.
Mansergh was drawn to a quotation from Daniel O'Connell,
"who towards the end of his life reprimanded the zealots of
Young Ireland: 'I shall stand by Old Ireland. And I have some
notion that Old Ireland will stand by me.'"[73]

Time, however, was not on the side of political figures
perceived as representing the values of Old Ireland. Lenihan
lost the presidential election in 1990 – less than 14 months later
Haughey himself would be out of office. Talk of his departure
increased with the scandals that emerged in late 1991.

At the start of the 1990s many backbench TDs believed Fianna Fáil would benefit from a change in leader. The allegations of unethical and inappropriate relations between politics and business convinced many Fianna Fáil deputies that they had to put distance between their party and the on-going revelations. It was against this background that in November 1991 Sean Power, a party backbencher from Kildare, tabled a motion of no confidence in Haughey.

This was the fourth direct challenge to his leadership in 10 years. But once again he saw off his opponents by 55 votes to 22. However, among the 22 votes against the leader were Albert Reynolds and Pádraig Flynn. They were both sacked as cabinet ministers for refusing to support Haughey in the confidence motion. The two politicians may have lost the vote in November 1991 but they were determined to return to end Haughey's tenure as Fianna Fáil leader.

Around this time, on a family trip to Stratford-upon-Avon, Mansergh mused upon the instability of power. An evening's entertainment at a performance of Shakespeare's *Julius Caesar* provoked obvious parallels: "The play stuck me as a good portrayal of the syndrome of seemingly indefinite leadership contrasted with the restlessness of subordinate ambition."[74] As Mansergh saw it – the victor in political battle while still alert to further threat may become somewhat contemptuous of the competence and capacity of his rivals while the latter group itself becomes impatient. The incumbent and the challenger – Haughey and Reynolds – were shaping up for further confrontation.

Mansergh described 1991 as an incredible year: "There was one blow after another. One wondered what's next?"[75] The answer to that question arrived in January 1992. The New Year started as the old one ended – with controversy. On an RTÉ television programme former Fianna Fáil minister Seán Doherty revealed that Haughey had been fully aware of the tapping of phones belonging to two political journalists – Bruce Arnold and Geraldine Kennedy – a decade earlier.

The revelation became a huge political issue. Doherty's allegation, if true, directly associated Haughey while Taoiseach with an illegal act. Mansergh described the Doherty statement as "astonishing." He recalled that when the original revelations became public in early 1983 Haughey had been "absolutely shattered" at the activities of his former Justice Minister. During the short life of the 1982 Fianna Fáil government, Mansergh had been "irritated by Arnold's well-written but tendentious pieces on Anglo-Irish relations" although he added, that there had "never been the slightest hint or sight by anyone of phone tapping or of the existence of transcripts".[76]

There were strong words of condemnation for the man seeking to bring down Haughey. The events of 1982 had been "a serious but temporary aberration from the longstanding traditions of the office, and the widespread concern about it was justified".[77]

In the intervening period Mansergh had discussed the events of 1982 with Doherty. During those conversations there had been no reference to the revelations made public for the first time in early 1992. The long-time advisor wrote that Haughey had "heroically beaten off the most determined assaults on his integrity and reputation".[78]

Doherty followed up his initial television intervention with a press conference. There was an industrial dispute at RTÉ, so the first Mansergh saw and hear of the latest Doherty allegations were on the main evening news at nine o'clock. He immediately rang Haughey at his north Dublin home but the Taoiseach was uncharacteristically subdued: "I found there was no fight in him whatsoever. But that didn't mean the fight had gone out of him."[79] The advisor departed from his South County Dublin home for Government Buildings where he worked on Haughey's defence until the small hours of the morning.

But no matter how Mansergh sought to portray the hero and the villain in the controversy, the reality was that this time Haughey was doomed. The Doherty disclosure precipitated the end of the Haughey years. Des O'Malley and his PD colleagues made it clear they would end the coalition government with Fianna Fáil if Haughey remained as leader. The prospect of a general election focused minds in Fianna Fáil. On 30 January 1992 Haughey announced his resignation as Taoiseach and leader of Fianna Fáil.

There was deep disappointment and tears among his political staff. Mansergh believed a good fight had been waged even if the end result was defeat:

> One of the pleasures and perils of being a political advisor is that you may get to fashion some of the weapons which your principals pick up to fight his or her political battles. I will always be intensely proud that for 10 years, but most especially in the autumn of 1991, I helped Charles Haughey to fight his political battles in the Dáil with some honour and effectiveness.[80]

Whatever about past controversies and future scandals there had been many good times since Mansergh arrived to work for Haughey in early 1981. Indeed, Haughey, Mansergh and Mara had in many ways provided Fianna Fáil with an intriguing triple act of political master, backroom advisor and media spokesman. "When Charles Haughey did something even his opponents were forced to applaud, he turned to PJ Mara and myself and said: 'And even the ranks of Tuscany could scarce forbear to cheer'." It was a quotation from Macaulay's *Lays of Ancient Rome*.[81] And the quotations were not just kept for keynote speeches:

> When he proudly regarded his Mitterrand-style grands projects like Government Buildings, Temple Bar or the Financial Services Centre, he would say grandly in the words of Sir Christopher Wren's epitaph: 'Si monumentum requiris circimspice', or if in a more self-deprecatory mood would speak of the 'new Bloomusalem!'[82]

When Haughey's political career ended in early 1992, he withdrew from public life. The retired politician gave few interviews and none on contemporary political matters. There were condolences and tributes for former colleagues such as

Neil Blaney and Brian Lenihan when they passed away. The IRA ceasefire in August 1994 was welcomed. But these public utterances were the exception as Haughey maintained his silence. However, his secret past eventually thrust him back into the public gaze.

In November 1996 the *Irish Independent* revealed details about matters raised during a court battle between members of the family that owned the supermarket chain, Dunnes Stores. Michael Lowry, a serving Fine Gael minister, was reported to have received payments from Ben Dunne, the chief executive of Dunnes Stores. There were tax and ethical implications related to the payments. Lowry resigned on 2 December 1996. The following day the *Irish Times* disclosed that a senior figure in Fianna Fáil had received over £1m from Ben Dunne. The country was talking about 'You Know Who' – an individual eventually named as Charles Haughey. The money was received from Dunne while Haughey was Taoiseach.

A tribunal of inquiry was established in February 1997. Haughey initially insisted that he had not benefited from Dunne's generosity. However, confronted with tribunal evidence he was eventually forced to accept that he had in fact received over £1.3m from the supermarket tycoon. "I accept that I have not co-operated with this Tribunal in a manner which would have been expected of me. I deeply regret that I have allowed this situation to arise," Haughey said in a statement to the tribunal in mid-July 1997.[83] When he gave public evidence it was a humiliating experience for the former Taoiseach.

The evidence provided some information about the sources of funds for Haughey's lifestyle. There was widespread public shock at the complexity of the arrangements that had succeeded for so long in keeping his financial affairs secret. Questions had long been asked but most in Fianna Fáil discounted the issue, accepting the story that Haughey, having made money in the 1960s, then profited from some wise investments.

Shortly after the revelations first became public, Mansergh said: "He attempted to keep his private life separate from his public life, so obviously I had no idea of the way things were being financed."[84] The Mansergh view was: his mentor's reputation may have fallen but his achievements remained. The long-time Haughey advisor refused to criticise him, a position he has maintained to this day.

The circle of people with any knowledge of Haughey's financial affairs was small. Money from businessmen was transferred though complicated and clandestine financial routes involving different currencies and crossing numerous national borders before ending up in accounts in the Cayman Islands. None of Haughey's political staff, including Mansergh, appeared to have known anything about their employer's secret financial affairs. Bertie Ahern, a close political colleague of Haughey's, explained the relationship between advisor and political master:

> What would Mansergh have said if he knew Haughey was up to this, that or the other? The fact is Mansergh wouldn't have known, he was dealing with policy. I would say Mansergh was never out to any of those functions with Haughey. While everybody else would be gone for dinner or for a jar, Mansergh would be in the National Library. People will say 'How could he not be there?' but he wouldn't be there, he wouldn't be there.

When it was put to Ahern that Mansergh's willingness to publicly defend Haughey was nonetheless surprising, Ahern remarked that:

> He will because he believes that Haughey actually did a good job. Only Mansergh knows how the peace process started under Haughey, and I think he's confined about what he can say about that. He knows but you'll never get it out of Mansergh.[85]

The loyalty to Haughey has been unflinching. When the manner in which Haughey financed his lifestyle became public many erstwhile supporters placed distance between themselves and the former Taoiseach. Mansergh, if anything, went in the other direction.

> Let me nail my colours quickly to the mast. I am
> proud to have worked with him; to have helped him
> fight his many political battles, and to have assisted
> him in a small way, helped him in a small way, so
> that he could be free to provide real and effective
> political leadership for over a decade.[86]

Nonetheless there has been some slight acknowledgement of
wrongdoing. Mansergh accepted there were potential dangers
of political leaders financing their lifestyles through private
donations. But the criticism was made in general terms without
specifically linking Haughey directly to the tangled story that
emerged at the tribunals of inquiry:

> Bertie Ahern has the right and the duty to lay down
> what financial practices are acceptable in the party
> that he leads ... to avoid any danger of abuse arising
> from being under a massive obligation, and to stake a
> clear distance from any deviation, if such occurred
> without people's knowledge, in the past.[87]

The advisor preferred to concentrate on the wider historical
narrative that may eventually be told about the career of his
former political boss. Mansergh in effect assumed the role of
defender of Haughey's political legacy. On several occasions
since 1997 he has defended Haughey in public, providing
reminders of – what he considered – were the lasting political
achievements from Haughey's time as a national politician:

> Even in those historical figures we admire, we do not
> have in any way to approve or condone all their
> actions or attitudes ... even if there were things about
> which we would be deeply unhappy, whatever may
> emerge, Charles Haughey's political achievements
> remain.[88]

Mansergh pointed to the things he believed would comprise
Haughey's legacy – improvements for the elderly; reform of the

judicial system; assistance for the arts; a successful Irish Presidency of the European Union in 1990; forging progress on Northern Ireland and the rejuvenation of the economy after 1987.

The public disgrace of Charles Haughey was likened to a "tragedy" that caused "great heart-wrenching". There has been much to admire in Mansergh's loyalty to his former boss but there has also been a touch of the naivety that Haughey himself identified in his advisor.

On occasion there has even been an element of 'protesting too much' to the advisor's defence of his former employer. Mansergh told a Fianna Fáil function in May 1997 that one of Haughey's faults:

> was great generosity; to constituents in distress; to charities of all descriptions. I will always remember the day of my father's funeral in Tipperary a little boy from the town coming up to the official car in the cortege and asking Charlie, 'Is that you?' The window rolled down. The little boy was given a fiver. That was the man.[89]

It was hardly an excessive fault, but the reality was that more often than not Haughey was a receiver rather than a giver of money. Moreover, when Mansergh told that anecdote in May 1997 only part of the hidden story of Haughey's financial affairs had been revealed. The former Taoiseach gave evidence at the tribunal of inquiry two months later. When Judge Brian McCracken's report was published in August 1997 the conclusion was damning:

> The Tribunal has been unable to accept much of the evidence of Mr Charles Haughey … It is quite unacceptable that a member of Dáil Éireann, and in particular a Cabinet Minister and Taoiseach, should be supported in his personal lifestyle by gifts made to him personally.[90]

Over the following five years more startling information

became public. Another tribunal of inquiry was established to determine the sources of Haughey's income during his years as leader of Fianna Fáil. It emerged that when he replaced Jack Lynch as party leader and Taoiseach in December 1979 there was an outstanding debt with AIB of almost IR£1.2m. When Mansergh joined the Haughey staff in January 1981 his boss was in effect a kept man funding his lavish lifestyle with other people's money.

Cumulatively, the evidence about Haughey unearthed by tribunal lawyers has been damning: he received millions from senior business figures while he benefited from money in secret offshore bank accounts. The Gandon mansion, the island off the coast of Co Kerry, the yacht, the expensive tailored shirts and the best of wines were all paid for with somebody else's money. What, if anything, these generous financial donors received in return for bankrolling Haughey has yet to be established. The former Taoiseach continued to insist that he had no involvement in the management of his personal financial affairs.

But the emergence of this information did little to diminish Mansergh's respect and near-devotion to the man he served for 11 years. He remained in contact with his old boss. The two men often speak by phone. Mansergh occasionally travels to Kinsealy for tea. In the most robust manner possible he defended Haughey in the summer of 2001:

> I would say, as a fact to be taken into consideration, that one of Haughey's first decisions when he became Taoiseach was to cancel the project to construct an official residence for the Taoiseach which would have cost at that time seven or eight million pounds and probably a million or two a year to run. Instead he had a place of his own, if you like, which was suitable enough as a Taoiseach's residence and he didn't bother the taxpayer with it. I think the point should be made that there had been a proposal that the Taoiseach's lifestyle, any Taoiseach's lifestyle, should be supported to a very substantial extent by the taxpayer and he turned it down.[91]

The defence of Haughey was not without a trace of the Mansergh wit. In a speech in 1998 on the value of historical commemorations he observed:

> Even personal memory can be weak, particularly when old men face accusations arising from their past, be it a Vichy official questioned about his role in the deportation of Jews, a lieutenant-colonel seeking to justify the events of Bloody Sunday, a Guinness boss quizzed over insider trading methods relative to a take-over (and who is the only known recoverer from Alzheimer's Disease), or even present or former political leaders around the world about controversial actions they may have authorised, meetings they may have held, or financial contributions they may have received.[92]

But from his reading of history, Mansergh may have seen Haughey's reputation determined. Writing about the Home Rule politician, Tim Healy, Mansergh observed, "Like many public figures, his curse was that his reputation was forever frozen at one moment in time, and nothing he could do could ever shake it off."[93]

Six

The Republican Belief

The first shots in the War of Independence were fired in Co Tipperary on 21 January 1919, two miles from the Mansergh family home at Grenane. Two police officers were escorting a cart carrying gelignite to a nearby quarry. As they moved along a windy narrow roadway the officers, both Catholics, were unaware that masked and armed IRA men were waiting for them behind the ditch.

Dan Breen led the republican group. "Here is our chance," Breen remarked to a colleague, "let us start the war soon, or the army will lose heart."[1] The sound of horse hoofs and the rumble of a heavy cart over the rough hilly road signalled the approach of the two officers. They were walking a little behind the cart, each with a rifle in his hand. The IRA men called on their foes to surrender but they held firm with their fingers on the triggers. "Quick and sure our volleys rang out. The aim was true. The two policemen were dead," Breen recalled.[2]

Nicholas Mansergh, a nine-year-old boy, heard the fatal shots. Many years later, in his book *The Unresolved Question*, Martin Mansergh's father wrote: "History was forged in sudden death on a Tipperary by-road as surely as ever it was in meetings at Downing Street or for that matter at the Mansion House in Dublin, where the Dáil met coincidentally but fortuitously for the first time that same day, 21 January 1919."[3]

The officers, one of whom was a widower with four children, lay dead on the ground as the IRA men made off with their rifles and the gelignite. Today, a memorial marks the place when the ambush took place. Every January an invited dignitary gives a commemoration address at the location. On a clear January morning in 1998, Martin Mansergh travelled the short distance from his home at Friarsfield to the memorial site at Soloheadbeg. It was an important moment for him. "This ceremony today is in a small way – and here I speak not politically but very personally – a symbolic act of reconciliation."[4]

Those attending had gathered – as Mansergh saw it – to pay tribute and keep alive the memory of a pivotal moment in Irish history. The particular poignancy for the Friarsfield resident was derived from the invitation itself as the idea for the Mansergh address had come from a relation of Dan Breen.

On that morning in January 1998, Mansergh quoted Seamus Robinson, another of the IRA men involved in the attack. "The action at Soloheadbeg was designed to set the ball rolling," Robinson had declared. Moreover, as Mansergh read his Irish history, the 1916 Easter Rising had been "a well-calculated prelude to a successful and organised guerrilla struggle, which began at Soloheadbeg."[5] There would be wider implications from the struggle for independence in Ireland. The conflict was a "watershed" for anti-imperialism within the British Empire. Mansergh observed that there were many countries around the world that acknowledged a debt to Ireland's sacrifice and example.

But he did acknowledge that people from all political and religious persuasions in the island had paid a price. Families like the Manserghs would have lived anxiously through the years of revolution in the knowledge that neighbours from a different political and religious persuasion would determine their futures.

Nicholas Mansergh, "an historical realist" according to his son, "recognised that political independence would simply not have happened without events … " like the Soloheadbeg ambush. The cost was also acknowledged by Nicholas Mansergh: "For the policemen who died at Soloheadbeg there was reserved the melancholy fate of having fallen on the wrong side of history … even successful national revolutions exact a price, the nature of which later generations find it hard to remember and contemporaries impossible to forget."[6]

One of the first public speeches made by Martin Mansergh on the topic of Northern Ireland was at a conference organised by the SDLP in June 1982. The final sentences of that address were an apt description of the task undertaken during the career of the Fianna Fáil advisor: "We are like a jigsaw, where the pieces do not appear to fit. The challenge is to put it together by rearranging them."[7] Over the following two decades, Mansergh was one of those individuals who sought to rearrange the jigsaw. His reading of history was from a constitutional republican perspective. Indeed, the Mansergh narrative was not the most accommodating for the unionist tradition, the tradition of his own family.

The Mansergh outlook is best summarised by Padraig Pearse's dictum: "Ireland unfree shall never be at peace" His father's writing on Ireland and nationalism had a profound influence. In his own view, a "broad anti-imperialist outlook" was inherited from his father. Mansergh saw himself as following in a democratic republican tradition. He was a passionate and committed republican but a non-violent one.

Seán Duignan – in his memoir of the 1992-94 Albert Reynolds-led governments – captured the Mansergh outlook:

> He was every whit as republican as portrayed by admirers and critics alike, although his insistence that he was unalterably constitutional made not a whit of difference to his detractors. They still painted him as a kind of Provisional IRA pawn. I remember him on one occasion lucidly, and without a trace of bitterness – he might have been talking of someone else – explaining to me how that reasoning was fundamentally erroneous.[8]

Mansergh accepted that views in the Republic towards the IRA campaign hardened over time as any initial justification in the 1969-70 period disappeared: "My impression is that a certain and understandable ambivalence at the beginning among a section of the population in the South gave way over time to a more decided rejection of methods of violence."[9]

Mansergh had long disagreed with the view that violence never had any political effect, but he was not convinced that the modern IRA campaign had any serious impact on the direction of British policy towards the North. "I see absolutely no evidence from our dealings with the British Government, or indeed its dealings with the anyone else, that it was materially swayed by bombs in the City of London."[10] He made his argument using the example of a hypothesised loyalist bombings in Dublin in 1994, which did not weaken the resolve of the Irish Government to make the peace process work.

History is the key to understanding Mansergh's republican outlook. Unlike the majority of those members of the party he has served, Mansergh drew together different strands of the Irish historical narrative to create an ideological position. In his opinion, there was little room for unionism as the political momentum, ebbing and flowing over the last 200 years, led in the direction of a united Ireland.

Two characteristics defined the Mansergh approach – uniting the different traditions and uniting the divided stands of Irish nationalism. From Irish history, Mansergh was aware of the progress achieved when the different traditions on the island were united in common cause. He considered the 1798 Rebellion as the start of the modern physical force tradition. It was given life – he argued – by a combination of draconian repression and the decision of the British-backed oligarchy in Ireland to prevent democratic reform. Expectations in Ireland were raised by the French Revolution – the ideas derived from which, made the *ancien régime* in Ireland even more unacceptable.

The 1798 Rebellion left the two traditions North and South more wary, more divided and ready to go their separate ways. This was a mistake, according to the Fianna Fáil advisor:

> Anyone who still cherishes the ideal of a united independent Ireland, has to find some way back to the beginning, to the United Irish project of uniting Protestant, Catholic and Dissenter under the common name of Irishman and indeed these days, Irish-woman.[11]

The historical figures admired by Mansergh not surprisingly came from the republican tradition. The names included the Co Tipperary Fenian Charles Kickham, the Home Rule leader Charles Stewart Parnell, the Easter 1916 rebel Padraig Pearse and Dr William Drennan, a founder of the United Irishmen. Indeed, Mansergh frequently quoted Drennan, whom he described as "the father of democracy in Ireland and of constitutional republicanism."[12] In 1794 Drennan remarked that: "the spirit of the North will again become the spirit of the nation." It was an observation that found its way into an Árd Fheis address delivered by Charles Haughey and provided the title for the book of his collected speeches.

Drennan – a medical doctor who worked in Belfast, Newry and Dublin – came from a Presbyterian background. Mansergh was drawn to the forbearance and magnanimity as recorded in some of the poetry written by Drennan:

Alas for poor Erin! that some still are seen
Who would dye the grass red in their hatred to green!
Yet oh! When you're up, and they down, let them live
Then, yield them that mercy which they did not give.

But the Presbyterian doctor was important for other purposes. Mansergh used Drennan's life story to illustrate his argument that the majority tradition in Northern Ireland was in the past composed of different national identities and had considered different political options. This was a theme to which Mansergh frequently referred much to the annoyance of unionist leaders who read their history in a different way.

The Mansergh political and philosophical outlook was not just concerned with uniting the different traditions. Perhaps an even greater emphasis was placed on harnessing the disparate forces of Irish nationalism. Again from the experience of history, Mansergh noted the national advances when the different components of Irish nationalism united in common cause, more often than not with the support of the Irish-America constituency.

The Fianna Fáil advisor had long been a keen student of the

New Departure of 1878, the policy that brought the Fenians and Irish-America to support the political strategy adopted by Charles Stewart Parnell. There was a twin track strategy – land reform and self-government. Parnell was among the political figures the Fianna Fáil advisor showered with plaudits. There was admiration for the "exceptional vigour of his leadership" which allowed the 19th-century nationalist leader to harness the support of those who might otherwise have been more wedded to revolutionary methods.[13]

The coalition allowed Parnell to make decisive breakthroughs on the land question, on the issue of Irish self-government as well as being the first national leader to mobilise the resources of Irish-America. Mansergh considered the 1878-86 period as one of national advance as all the elements within nationalism were united in common cause. The grouping eventually split but was revived in the 1918-21 period – behind the demand for national self-determination – another period of national advance, Mansergh argued.

Over a century later, the Fianna Fáil advisor sought to convince Charles Haughey of the benefit of replicating the Parnell strategy – uniting the different strands of nationalism on the island backed by Irish-American opinion. But in the 1980s the main obstacle to united political action by nationalists was the IRA's campaign of violence.

In many respects Mansergh's greatest service in his period as a political advisor was in helping to build the ideological bridge for militant republicanism to transform into a purely political and democratic force. Sinn Féin's Martin McGuinness recognised this contribution: "The big names in the peace process at the beginning were Gerry Adams, John Hume and Albert Reynolds but there is no doubt whatsoever that Martin Mansergh played a huge role."[14]

In working to achieve the ceasefire objective, Mansergh placed great trust in the principle of national self-determination as outlined in 1917 by the US President Woodrow Wilson. This was not a simple or trouble-free concept. Nationalists in Northern Ireland felt that their right to national self-determination had not been respected in 1920-21. The contemporary task was to get northern republicans to place more emphasis on national self-determination rather than on the blunt demand for British withdrawal. This meant ruling out the immediate creation of a united Ireland. The principle was central to the dialogue which opened with the Republican Movement in the late 1980s.

President Wilson coupled national self-determination with the principle of consent. All territorial settlements should be made in the interest of the populations involved. This position obviously created difficulties for the partition of Ireland. "Whether partition was necessary or right or not in 1920-21 is one question, on which there are still legitimately strong views. It is another question, how it is possible to deal with the issue at the level of principle over 70 years on."[15] Whatever about the injustices of history, Mansergh argued that contemporary reality had to be accepted.

Demanding the incorporation of territory outside the jurisdiction was not feasible on practical terms. It was also contrary to international law as expressed in the UN's Charter and Covenants. The guiding principles included an acceptance that territorial changes must take place with the fully expressed wishes of the people involved and that all disputes must be resolved by peaceful means with no resort to the threat or use of force. Those principles were elaborated upon in the 1993 Downing Street Declaration where the objective was "to work towards a new agreed Ireland based on justice and equality and respect for the democratic dignity, civil rights and religious liberties of both communities."[16]

Mansergh placed great store in the result of the 1918 Westminster Elections when Sinn Féin candidates won a majority of the seats on the island of Ireland. They adhered to the party's abstentionist policy refusing to travel to take their seats in London. Instead, the newly elected Sinn Féin MPs met in Dublin in January 1919, styling themselves as TDs and forming what became known as the first Dáil. The view was that the minority unionist population could not be allowed to block indefinitely self-government in the rest of Ireland.

According to Mansergh, this gathering provided the mandate

for the War of Independence. This analysis was based on comments from the Ceann Comhairle in the first Dáil who noted that war would be the consequence of the passing of the Declaration of Independence. The IRA Volunteers were fighting to establish the Irish national democracy that was the expressed will of the majority of people on the island but rejected by Britain. It would have been preferable to uphold the independence proclaimed by Dáil Éireann by peaceful means but in 1919 that was not a realistic option. In Mansergh's thinking, political violence throughout Irish history was nearly always produced by a combined result of "a failure of nerve by constitutional political leaders and with the equal constitutional inability of many British politicians ... "[17]

The 1921-22 Treaty debates and the issues of unity and status were topics Mansergh returned to frequently in conference addresses and published papers. The Sinn Féin aspiration was for an independent 32-county Republic. However, the Treaty negotiations diluted the status issue from republic to a dominion within the Commonwealth while the unity issue was resolved with the partition of the island as laid out in the Government of Ireland Act, 1920. In the absence of unionist intransigence a peaceful settlement would have been attainable, the Fianna Fáil advisor believed.

Mansergh rooted unionism in the 1800 Act of Union, which he described as, "one of the foundation stones of the unionist tradition ... [which provided] ... the principal *raison d'etre* of Northern Ireland."[18] He also argued that the Act of Union was born out of corruption and was an anti-democratic arrangement: "The Union of Parliaments of 1801 was a pact largely between landed elites of Britain and Ireland, in which the vast majority of the Irish people were neither asked nor involved"[19]

In his writings on Northern Ireland, and in the advice given to successive Fianna Fáil leaders, Mansergh argued that the root cause of the conflict was a historical wrong. Righting that wrong had to be the central objective of policy on Northern Ireland. From an examination of history, he described Ireland as the Achilles heel of the British Empire. The responsibility for this situation rested with the British:

> If the Irish question had been better handled and the demand for self-government accommodated earlier, by granting Home Rule in the 1880s, Ireland need have been no more disruptive for the Empire and later Commonwealth than say the evolution of Canada, Australia, and South Africa to Dominion Status.[20]

Mansergh argued that it was hard to comprehend the adamant rejection of the Home Rule compromise by unionism as it "would after all have combined a Nationalist desire for self-government with the unionist determination to retain Ireland in the Union."[21] The unionist stance only served to fuel the aspirations of nationalist Ireland. As Mansergh put it: "Instead of half a loaf, it was a third of one."[22]

There was little truck with the unionists who resisted the Home Rule proposals. Unionism was, according to Mansergh, a negative political philosophy: "It sought for as long as it could to block, frustrate or delay the weight of numbers, the democracy derived from demography ... "[23] Moreover, it was "an expression of a bundle of interests, by people who were convinced that the preservation of their vital interests depended on the establishment and maintenance of the Union."[24]

In the Mansergh view, this obstruction had a long history going back to the days of Daniel O'Connell. The consequences were far-reaching. "The obstruction of the development of a national democracy had many far-reaching consequences, more radical than intended, both for relationships within Ireland and between Ireland and Britain."[25]

No matter the scale of his involvement or the level of his achievements, the Co Tipperary man repeatedly antagonised the unionist tradition. He expressed regret that "some of those whose forebears came to this island nearly four hundred years ago still purport to regard most of it as 'a foreign country'."[26] And beyond the personal, he was disparaging about unionist figures: "The first leader of Irish Unionism was Captain Edward Saunderson from Cavan, sometimes nicknamed 'the Orange Parnell'. Even his biographer Alvin Jackson struggles to make him an interesting, let alone, an inspiring figure."[27]

The less-than-flattering compliments were returned from the unionist side. Leading unionists were critical in their assessment of the Fianna Fáil advisor. "He articulates the die-hard republican agenda in a posh English accent," Ken Maginnis observed in 1992.[28] In the period before the Good Friday Agreement, John Taylor dismissively remarked that Mansergh was "a man who knows very little about Northern Ireland … ."[29] Two years after the Agreement, David Trimble described him as a "well-known anti-unionist."[30] These views, of course, came from the leading political figures in the more politically moderate Ulster unionist Party. There were less comforting attitudes among the more hard-line sections of unionism.

Members of the Ulster Unionist Party also recorded their discomfort dealing with the Fianna Fáil advisor during the 1997-98 discussions that led to the Good Friday Agreement. An advisor to Taylor and Trimble, Steven King explained: "Some of our people would have preferred to deal with a genuine Catholic nationalist. They can't really understand quite where he comes from. You see the opposite with people like Eoghan Harris or Ruth Dudley Edwards who are seen as close to us. It's the same thing. If somebody has gone outside the tribe then there is an automatic distrust."[31]

Trimble had little time for those unionist families who shifted identity in response to the political changes at the time of the Anglo-Irish Treaty in 1921. There was nothing more offensive to the Ulster Unionist leader than terms such as 'former unionist' or 'ex-unionist'. He differed fundamentally from Mansergh on the core issues of national allegiance, identity and the constitutional status of Northern Ireland.

Mansergh started from a position that accepted that the North was not part of the Irish State and would only become so with the agreement and consent of both parts of the island concurrently. It was a doctrine of one nation, two jurisdictions. Therefore, unionism was not a separate national identity but rather a tradition within the Irish nation.

Trimble, however, was proud of his Britishness and was patriotic in respect of the emblems of Britain such as Poppy Day

Martin Mansergh with his father Nicholas and daughters Fiona and Lucy in the late 1970s.

Launch of Nicholas Mansergh's collected Irish papers in 1991, Diane Mansergh (centre) with Bertie Ahern and Martin Mansergh (right) and Noel Dorr and Professor Joe Lee (left).

Martin Mansergh with Charles Haughey, Leinster House 1981.

On helicopter to Killybegs, Co Donegal, February 1987. Martin Mansergh alongside PJ Mara with Charles Haughey in background.

Local elections, 1985. Charles Haughey press conference as Martin Mansergh watches on.

Launch of *Spirit of the Nation*, December 1986. From left: Martin Mansergh, Charles Haughey, Bertie Ahern (then Lord Mayor of Dublin) and Seán McBride.

Martin Mansergh with Charles Haughey in Government Buildings on the Fianna Fáil leader's last day in office, February 1992.

Forum for Peace and Reconciliation, Dublin Castle, November 1994. Martin Mansergh with Albert Reynolds.

St Patrick's Day in the White House, March 1994. Martin
Mansergh (far left) looking on with officials Paddy
Teahon and Dermot Gallagher as Albert Reynolds speaks
from the podium. Bill Clinton and Al Gore to the right.

Derek Speirs

Government Buildings, September 1997. Meeting with Sinn Féin
delegation as multi-party talks begin in Belfast.

Government Buildings, December 2001. Sitting at the cabinet table after the institutions established under the Good Friday Agreement are given legal effect.

Drumcondra, July 1997. Watching on as Joe Lennon, Government Press Secretary, records Bertie Ahern speaking on mobile phone.

Derek Speirs

Dinner at Friarsfield, Co Tipperary, with President Mary McAleese and her husband Martin, 2000.

In discussion with Ulster Unionist Ken Maginnis at a British–Irish Association meeting.

Martin and
Elizabeth
Mansergh.

The Advisor.

Derek Speirs

and the honours system. He was unwavering in his commitment to the United Kingdom. But the Fianna Fáil advisor had difficulty with the proposition that Northern Ireland was British or that the six counties were not Irish counties or Irish soil: "Politically and culturally, Northern Ireland is, as its very name suggests, at least as Irish as it is British … "[32]

This type of opinion, however, only further antagonised unionists. One of the most vocal critics of Mansergh was also one of Trimble's strongest supporters. Businessman John Laird – a member of the House of Lords with the title Lord Laird of Artigarvan – observed: "He's a tremendous disappointment; totally mono-minded and does not see things from anybody else's viewpoint. He skews history for his own viewpoint in my opinion. He's a negative force … "[33]

Laird heads the Ulster-Scots Agency that was established by the Good Friday Agreement as part of recognising linguistic diversity on the island of Ireland. Doubts have been expressed about the linguistic status of Ulster-Scots and whether it constitutes a language or merely a dialect of English or Scots. Moreover, as one writer noted, "In some instances the language is perceived as a unionist attempt to generate a language that is associated exclusively with British identities and traditions."[34] Mansergh adopted a less than sympathetic attitude observing that Ulster-Scots was "frankly not well defined".[35]

The two men exchanged terse letters after they met for lunch at the House of Lords in early 2001. Mansergh noted his dismay at the "politically confrontational approach" that he believed Laird had been adopting. He added that "Treating Ulster-Scots as a propaganda weapon to try and beat the Irish Government and the Republic over the head in order to impress unionist voters will go precisely nowhere."[36] In reply Laird accused Mansergh of "insensitivity towards the plight of the Ulster-Scots community in Ireland"; of making a "personal attack" on him and of not having "a basic understanding of why unionists are unionists".[37]

The latter was a criticism shared by many leading unionists. Laird explained: "His understanding of unionism is very skewed; very poor. He has a total lack of understanding of why unionists will not subscribe to a mono-cultural island and why we want to be recognised as a separate identity on the island."[38] The issue of identity was obviously related to political outlook, and Laird saw in Mansergh a set of "imperialistic aspirations to govern a section of the United Kingdom".[39]

Yet despite these differences Mansergh on several occasions aimed helpful comments in the direction of Trimble. In November 1998 the Fianna Fáil advisor observed that the Good Friday Agreement allowed space for those who wished to preserve the Union on the basis of a pluralist parliament for a pluralist people. The remark was made at a time when Trimble was in some difficulty with hard-line sections within his own party. It was gratefully received. Professor Paul Bew of Queens University observed: "At certain points Martin has been very helpful. Despite the fact that Martin is green, is green, is green, he has used language that has not been unhelpful."[40]

Nevertheless, Mansergh's view of the Northern unionist identity shaped his attitude to those from Southern unionist backgrounds. As within his own family, the partition of Ireland initially left many Southern unionists with divided national identities. But in Mansergh's opinion the Irish Republic assumed the position of heir to the diverse traditions that co-existed post-1921.

In the latter context, little sympathy was on offer for the campaign of the Reform Movement that sought national minority status for those citizens of the Republic who considered themselves as unionists. Mansergh rejected the lobby group's call that every Irish citizen should be entitled to British citizenship, in recognition of the pre-1921 position when the island of Ireland was part of the United Kingdom.

Correspondence with Robin Bury of the Reform Movement drew a sharp response from the Fianna Fáil advisor: "I am a busy person, and I would like to bring this lengthy correspondence to an end, as it is not leading anywhere."[41] Mansergh was sceptical of the wishes for a continuing British point of reference among the wider community in the Republic. In his view the successful integration of the ex-unionist community into the Irish State was one of its major achievements. Not that he was denying the Reform Movement its objectives: "Anyone is entitled to campaign for a reintegration of Ireland with the United Kingdom. The last unionist to stand in Cork South-West in the 1980s got the same sort of vote as the Natural Law Party."[42]

In the Mansergh historical narrative, unionism has been in decline for the last 200 years. "With the exception of the few from a Protestant background who came to articulate the cause of Nationalist Ireland, unionists (who also included some well-to-do Catholics) were throughout the century fighting a rearguard action against the erosion of their position in a more democratic age."[43] The battle for the 26 counties was lost in 1921 while – Mansergh argued – a different approach was in recent times undermining the logic of Northern Ireland.

The Fianna Fáil advisor saw the peace process in a wider historical context, beyond the post-1969 IRA campaign:

> The peace process has to resolve much more than the Troubles of the past twenty-five years. It has to address the whole legacy of history and the many unresolved problems inherited from the past. Those festering problems have contributed to the length and virulence of the Troubles...[44]

In lecture after lecture, Mansergh traced the conflict in the North back to the compromise of the 1921 Anglo-Irish Treaty, which "brought civil war in the South and sporadic violence leading to civil war in the North after a delay of fifty years".[45] While accepting that Southern nationalists and Northern unionists broadly achieved their objectives from the Treaty, Mansergh argued that the unequivocal losers were northern nationalists.

This community in the North had been guaranteed four safeguards from the Government of Ireland Act 1920 and the Anglo-Irish Treaty the following year. But during the 1920s all four safeguards were either dismantled or simply ignored. Proportional representation to protect the minority was dropped as extensive gerrymandering became the salient feature of electoral politics in the North; the Council of Ireland, intended to keep Ireland in economic and administrative terms as a single unity, was also dropped; the guarantee of non-discrimination in the Government of Ireland Act was ignored as "religious discrimination was the most marked characteristic of Stormont rule"; and the Boundary Commission, which would have allowed a few areas with a nationalist majority to join the South failed to deliver. [46] The combined effect of these failures was that nationalists were a minority in the Northern state, without any influence.

Northern nationalists were further betrayed by Free State policy towards the North that was, in Mansergh's words, both "inconsistent and ineffective". All of this served to generate sporadic violence up to the outbreak of the contemporary conflict. Thus, Mansergh argued, that to end the modern day IRA campaign would require the removal of the bitter left-overs of 1921. He noted:

> If there had been fairness and non-discrimination, and institutionalised North-South co-operation from the beginning, it is unlikely that the pressures which led to the Troubles 50 years later would ever have built up.[47]

When violence erupted in Northern Ireland in August 1969 the Mansergh family were staying at Barley Cove in west Cork where "every night those staying in the villas crowded round the television screen".[48] There were passionate discussions between Nicholas Mansergh and his children. "My father was convinced the IRA would be back. My brother and myself tried to explain to him that this was different. It was about civil rights, not old style Republicanism or Nationalism. We felt he knew more about the War of Independence than the spirit of the 1960s."[49] But events were to prove Nicholas Mansergh right. His historical perspective provided a more effective means for interpreting events than the contemporary insights of his sons.

Reassessing the period, Martin Mansergh later said the 1960s civil rights campaign gave way to violence because of two events in 1970, one in Britain and the other in the Irish Republic. The key event in Britain was the change of government from Labour to Conservative in 1970, which replaced "the initial reformist approach and sensitivity with a determination to restore order and to give clear backing to the Stormont regime."[50] Mansergh argued that this led a section of the nationalist community to abandon democratic protest for the traditional recourse to arms.

The 1969-70 Arms Crisis was identified as a defining event in the Irish Republic. The Fianna Fáil advisor considered those events as the moment when "the Irish Government, recoiling from giving any assistance for self-defence for fear of misuse, lost all restraining political influence over militant republicanism in the North, a situation that would continue for almost twenty years."[51]

Over that time all attempts to forge a compromise peace settlement between moderate unionists and moderate nationalists were largely unsuccessful. The missing ingredient for a peace strategy was the involvement of the Republican Movement. Through his involvement in secret contacts with the republican leadership from 1988 onwards, the Fianna Fáil advisor would make a significant contribution to the history of the island of Ireland.

Interestingly, despite the clandestine contacts, Mansergh was to the fore in establishing Fianna Fáil's position as the true holder of the ideals of republican icons like Tone and Pearse. "One of the fundamental fallacies both of republican fundamentalists aided and abetted by the revisionist school of history is to see the modern and mainly Northern-based Republican Movement as the sole legitimate heirs of 1916."[52]

As well as offering criticism of the republican view of Irish history, Mansergh was not prepared to easily let the Republican Movement claim ownership of the historical figures and events so central to Irish republican history. In this regard, a knowledge and grasp of Irish history placed the Fianna Fáil advisor in a strong position. He helped cement Fianna Fáil's linkage to republican history through involvement in the 1798 Commemoration Committee and also participation in other events including annual orations to old IRA figures. Little ground was ceded to Sinn Féin although in fact many senior republican figures believed Mansergh's constitutional republicanism could be more strongly linked with post-ceasefire Sinn Féin than with Fianna Fáil. The Sinn Féin National Chairman, Mitchel McLaughlin observed:

> There is within Fianna Fáil a very interesting dichotomy. There are people who describe themselves as republicans and they're not United Irelanders. But they are republicans in the sense that that's the political system in the South. That's not something that's spoken out loud. I actually think that Martin Mansergh did take a national perspective and did have a very clear sense that the current constitutional position would not hold … He was driven by the same sense of urgency to find an agreement as Sinn Féin.[53]

Unlike many of his party colleagues, Mansergh offered an intellectual attachment to the iconic figures from republican history. There have been several jostles with columnist Kevin Myers in the letters pages of the *Irish Times*. In August 2000 Mansergh took exception to a column on Padraig Pearse, penned by Myers. The defence of the man who led the 1916 Easter Rising was strident and did not pull punches in answering the question posed by Myers: what did Bertie Ahern and others see in Pearse?

Mansergh argued that Pearse was a co-founder of: "an independent democratic Irish State, the 1916 Proclamation which he largely drafted having an analogous role to the 1776 American Declaration of Independence." Indeed, according to Mansergh the foundation of the State dates from Easter 1916 as all the main political parties in Dáil Éireann today had some involvement in the rebellion.[54]

Critics of Pearse – and the violence that followed the failed Easter Rising in 1916 – were adopting too narrow a focus. In Mansergh's opinion, if there was bloodshed in Irish history it was because Britain refused to apply to Ireland the logic of the principle of 'government by consent'.

During his term as Taoiseach Bertie Ahern gave a portrait of Pearse pride-of-place on the wall in his office in Government Buildings. Yet, it was easy to understand why many people found the attachment to Pearse uncomfortable and unsavoury. The contemporary men of violence in the guise of the Provisional IRA had used Pearse and the men of 1916 to justify their actions. "Ireland unfree shall never be at peace" – spoken by Pearse in his graveside oration in 1913 of the republican O'Donovan Rossa – was for the IRA an endorsement of their campaign. It was on this basis that Myers hit back at the Fianna Fáil advisor:

> Let Mansergh sit in a classroom. What can he say to a student who supports the Real IRA and uses Pearse as a prop to defend himself against charges of being anti-democratic? If Pearse was prepared to push Redmond aside, what is wrong with pushing Bertie Ahern aside? Does Mansergh believe that bleating about the Belfast Agreement can blur the logical link between Pearse and the Provos, between the Provos and the Real IRA?[55]

But Mansergh was not prepared to let the contemporary men of violence lay claim to republican history. He was highly critical of the military republican tradition for its interpretation of Irish history – "the preposterous nonsense concocted of a pseudo-apostolic succession from Pearse to the Second Dáil to Sinn Féin to the IRA to the Provisional Army Council of the IRA, to Republican Sinn Féin."[56]

Not that all sections of the broad republican family were impressed with Mansergh. According to one radio station in nationalist West Belfast, he was 'The conscience of the Dublin Government', and his appearance at a meeting in the area in early 1998 was described in *An Phoblacht/republican News* with the headline: 'He came, he spoke, he didn't impress'.[57] Some weeks later Bernadette Devlin McAliskey, a critic of the multi-party talks that were underway in Belfast, went on the offensive:

His solution is essentially a 25-year strategy to release
the situation in the North from the tension of the past
25 years in hope that by not addressing the problem
over the period of the next 25 years, at the end of it
we might be able to engage in a rational discussion
with the unionists and, as Martin Mansergh has said,
'That discussion in 25 years time may or may not lead
to an united Ireland.' Now that is a perfectly valid
position for Martin Mansergh, but it is not a valid
position of the leadership of the Republican Movement.[58]

Mansergh disagreed. Moreover, there were harsh words for
the Republican Movement's long-standing failure to recognise
the institutions of the Irish Republic. He described as a

fiction that the true Government of Ireland is not that
elected by the people, but an entirely unknown and
unaccountable secret paramilitary junta, that has a
green book for a constitution containing all sorts of
sanctions in breach of fundamental human rights. All
of that has become an increasing embarrassment,
even for those involved.[59]

According to Fianna Fáil colleagues, public expression of
these criticisms during the peace process was curtailed, for very
good reason. One senior Irish Government official noted: "There
would be no one more critical of Sinn Féin than Mansergh but
that wasn't his task. His job was to bring them in." It was a
view shared by Bertie Ahern who relied heavily on Mansergh's
assessment of Sinn Féin positioning during the negotiation of
the Good Friday Agreement. "Mansergh would give advice on
whether we were getting a load of nonsense or whether the
concerns were real. He understands the military and the
political side and he is rarely wrong," one senior Fianna Fáil
colleague observed.

Mansergh drove the idea that the best objective for the
future was a unitary state achieved by agreement and consent

which embraced the whole island of Ireland. An internal settlement was not an option. He argued that the issue of Northern Ireland was not just the relationship between the two communities but between two countries. "In dealing with the North, they [the British Government] are dealing not so much with part of their own country, but with part of another country ... "[60] The secret contacts which in the 1980s started the peace process were about reconciling peacefully – in the absence of coercion or violence – those differing historical, political and constitutional aspirations.

Seven

Talking to the Provos

On 1 March 1981, Bobby Sands, an IRA prisoner in the Maze Prison in Northern Ireland, started a hunger strike aimed at securing political status for republican inmates. Martin Mansergh was only two months into his new job as advisor to Charles Haughey. The ramifications of the events played out in the Maze Prison were huge. Mansergh recalled: "It had a national and international impact different from anything else that occurred during a 25-year conflict. It put the spotlight on human rights and dignity in a particular situation, in a way that no armed action was capable of doing."[1]

The hunger strikes placed enormous strain on relations between the Fianna Fáil Government in Dublin and Margaret Thatcher's Conservative administration at Westminster. Thatcher adopted a hard-line policy, declaring that Sands was a "convicted criminal" with whom there would be no negotiation. She remained firm to that position. By the end of the hunger strikes in October 1981 ten republican prisoners were dead. Sands was the first to die after 66 days on hunger strike. News of his death on 5 May provoked riots across Northern Ireland. The following week – after the death of a second hunger striker – over 2,000 people descended on the British Embassy in Dublin.

According to Mansergh, the hunger strikes were "a turning-point in the Northern conflict as well as a catalyst for the greater politicisation of the Republican Movement. They struck a chord that the conflict in itself had not done."[2] This situation first manifested itself when Frank Maguire, the MP for

Fermanagh-South Tyrone, died on 5 March 1981. The Republican Movement was presented with an opportunity to tap public support for the hunger strike campaign. However, a Sands candidacy would clash with the traditional Sinn Féin policy of abstentionism in relation to electoral participation. There was also the added uncertainty related to the political repercussions of failing to win the by-election. But these concerns were eventually put aside. Sands took the Westminster seat on 9 April, beating his unionist opponent by just over 1,000 votes.

The success in the Fermanagh-South Tyrone by-election encouraged the Republican Movement to contest several constituencies in the general election in the Republic in June 1981. Two prisoner candidates were successfully elected to the Dáil while several others polled strongly. Their performance had a direct impact on the Fianna Fáil vote. Haughey's party fell short of an overall majority and was replaced in government by a Fine Gael/Labour coalition led by Garret FitzGerald.

The hunger strikes left a deep impression on Haughey's Northern Ireland policy, as Mansergh acknowledged: "From then on, he steered a more pronounced republican course, which became very evident back in Government in 1982."[3] There were, of course, other factors involved, particularly Haughey's failure to build a working relationship with Thatcher after the December 1980 Anglo-Irish Summit and the arrival and influence of the new political advisor, Martin Mansergh.

When Haughey was elected leader of Fianna Fáil in December 1979 there was some apprehension about his positioning in relation to Northern Ireland. His role in the Arms Crisis in 1969-70 remained unexplained. However, the initial movement by the new Taoiseach was positive. He first met with Thatcher in May 1980 and the two leaders reached agreement on "new and close political co-operation". But the Haughey-Thatcher relationship faltered over their differing perspectives on the North. According to the academic Paul Arthur, this "reflected a clash of nationalism personified in two conviction politicians: the 'born-again' nationalism of Margaret Thatcher and the more familiar, weary dirge of Irish victimhood rehearsed by Charles Haughey."[4]

Under Haughey the Fianna Fáil policy on Northern Ireland reverted to a form of republicanism not followed since the leadership of Eamon de Valera. Mansergh admitted that there was "a determination to hold the republican ground and not cede it to anyone else".[5] The advantage of this hardening position on Northern policy under Haughey became apparent in later years – "many of the elements of the ideological bridge, which would be of crucial importance in the peace process right up to the ceasefire, were built."[6]

This assessment from Mansergh, however, involved a strong element of retrospective justification for hard-line 'green' policies that at the time did little to advance peace in Northern Ireland. Indeed, in the short-term, this Fianna Fáil policy drove the party onto the political margins occupied by Sinn Féin and Ian Paisley's Democratic Unionist Party.

The 1981 hunger strikes lessened prospects for a serious policy initiative. In any event, Haughey was out of office by June 1981 and when he returned eight months later his stance on the Falklands War permanently soured any potential future relationship with the British Prime Minister. Moreover, there were other areas of difficulty with the British including Thatcher's stance on Europe and her opposition to increases in agriculture prices for European farmers.

As a consequence any hope of a political breakthrough on Northern Ireland was all but ended while Haughey was Taoiseach. Thatcher observed that: "no commitment exists for Her Majesty's Government to consult the Irish Government on matters affecting Northern Ireland".[7] It was only after the Fine Gael/Labour coalition government was elected in the Republic in November 1982 that there was real movement in Anglo-Irish relations. Garret Fitzgerald stressed the need for a 'constitutional crusade' to make the Republic more accommodating to the unionist tradition in the North. This policy was matched by the objective of marginalising Sinn Féin.

FitzGerald was particularly alarmed at the electoral rise of Sinn Féin to the detriment of the John Hume-led SDLP. In the aftermath of the hunger strikes Sinn Féin was an emerging political force in northern politics. In elections to a new Northern Assembly in October 1982 Sinn Féin abandoned its abstentionist policy in relation to contesting elections while continuing its traditional policy of not taking seats won. The party secured 10 per cent of the first preference vote while the SDLP garnered just under 19 per cent. This added weight to the assertion that Sinn Féin was displacing the SDLP as the main voice of northern nationalism. FitzGerald was one of those who believed that this could lead to more violence and much greater instability.

The electoral growth of Sinn Féin was, according to Mansergh, "a particular preoccupation of Garret Fitzgerald".[8] However, in truth Fianna Fáil was also closely watching the political emergence of Gerry Adams and his supporters. This was evident from the hardening stance adopted under the leadership of Haughey guided by advice from Mansergh. Fianna Fáil was not going to cede political ground in the Republic to Sinn Féin. Nevertheless, there was certainly a difference between Fianna Fáil and Fine Gael strategy for dealing with the Republican Movement – Mansergh and Fianna Fáil would ultimately attempt engagement, even in the absence of a ceasefire, while FitzGerald favoured marginalisation.

The Fine Gael Taoiseach moved on two fronts – seeking consensus between the various strands of constitutional nationalism on the island while also seeking greater political co-operation between the governments in London and Dublin. FitzGerald envisaged all the constitutional parties north and south of the border participating in round-table discussions to find a political accommodation. It was a variation on a suggestion for a constitutional council first proposed by the SDLP. The idea of the New Ireland Forum was born. Unionists quickly spurned invitations from the Dublin Government while the cross-community Alliance Party also decided not to become involved. What they feared – a forum for nationalists to promote the idea of a united Ireland – became in their absence that very thing, a forum dominated by constitutional nationalism.

The first public session of the New Ireland Forum took place on 30 May 1983. Haughey's traditional republican outlook was apparent from the beginning. The objective of a united Ireland was a core value for Fianna Fáil and the party delegation made it clear that this principle was not for negotiation. Haughey said the Fianna Fáil task at the Forum was "to construct a basic position, which can then be put to an all-round constitutional conference, convened by the Irish and British Governments as a prelude to British withdrawal".

Mansergh was the principal driver of the Fianna Fáil team at the Forum, producing material for the political delegates and ensuring all responses were consistent with party policy. Academic Paul Arthur observed: "Fianna Fáil's was the most disciplined delegation. They all followed the party line throughout, and three of their alternates uttered not a word during the entire proceedings of the forum's plenary sessions."[9] Among the other members of the Fianna Fáil secretariat was Veronica Guerin, who later earned a reputation as an investigative journalist before being murdered in 1996.

There was some expectation within the Irish Government that the Forum would weaken the nationalist position on the unitary state model as the principal means of reaching a political accommodation. Alternative options such as joint sovereignty were being pursued. But Mansergh had little time for what he considered a revisionist approach. As Arthur noted: "The new thinking illustrated the distance between Fianna Fáil and the other forum teams. With the introduction of options other than Irish unity, the traditional Fianna Fáil position had to be protected. The party's head of research, Dr Martin Mansergh, who played a key role throughout the forum exercise, was called into bat against the revisionists."[10]

The final report of the New Ireland Forum was published on 2 May 1984. While offering some accommodation to the unionist community, it was essentially a constitutional nationalist interpretation of the problems of – and solutions for – Northern Ireland. The report concluded: "The desire of nationalists is for a united Ireland in the form of a sovereign, independent Irish state."

The report examined three options – unitary state, joint authority and a federal arrangement. FitzGerald observed that the unitary state was "the ideal we would aspire to." However, Haughey argued that a unitary state was the only solution which would work – it was "not an option, it is the wish of the parties of the Forum ... Neither of these other two arrangements, federation or joint sovereignty, would bring peace and stability to the North."

The initial Fianna Fáil press statement welcomed the report but the party's response hardened by the time Haughey spoke to the media. "Early in the day we praised the report but over the day the response took a very deliberate line on the unitary state," one party official recalled.

The Thatcher Government in London showed little interest in the report of the New Ireland Forum. The Northern Secretary, Jim Prior, said the British Government was not particularly concerned about the recommendations. Yet in the aftermath of the Forum report, discussions got under way between London and Dublin. Some 18 months later these talks led to a significant development in policy on Northern Ireland.

The FitzGerald-led Government in Dublin sought to convince their British counterparts of the need for a joint political response to deal with the emerging threat of Sinn Féin. However, Thatcher was more focused on reacting to the Republican Movement with greater security measures, particularly along the border. She favoured the idea of joint security zones to facilitate the pursuit of republicans from the North into the Republic. This concentration on security was further increased when in October 1984 the IRA bombed the Grand Hotel in Brighton, the venue for the annual Conference Party conference. Five people were killed. Thatcher narrowly escaped injury.

The FitzGerald strategy was also driven by the desire to win greater Irish Government input into policy on Northern Ireland. He pressed the idea of joint authority – one of the suggestions from the New Ireland Forum report – at an Anglo-Irish summit at Chequers in November 1984. Thatcher was unreceptive and appeared to wreck any chances of political movement at a post-summit press conference. "I have made it quite clear that a united Ireland, that is out. A confederation of two states, that is out. Joint authority, that is out." The response was summed up as 'Out, out, out'.

Relations were strained but all was not lost. Over subsequent months officials on both sides of the Irish Sea made progress on what emerged in November 1985 as the Anglo-Irish Agreement (AIA). The agreement institutionalised the right of the Irish Government to be heard in relation to the concerns of the nationalist community in the North. It reaffirmed the long-standing British position – in place since 1920-21 – that if a majority of the citizens in Northern Ireland voted clearly for a united Ireland then legislation to give effect to that wish would be passed at Westminster. For republicans this was in effect a unionist veto but the principle of consent had been agreed by the two governments.

The possibility of a united Ireland was left open to be achieved should the majority in the North clearly favour such a course. Mansergh remarked: "What constituted 'clearly' voting for a united Ireland, and whether it meant something more than a simple majority, was left constructively ambiguous."[11] In subsequent years the principle of consent became central to secret discussions involving Mansergh and republican leaders.

The other innovation in the agreement was an intergovernmental conference jointly chaired by the Northern Ireland Secretary and the Minister for Foreign Affairs. The conference was to be serviced by British and Irish civil servants who would be based at Maryfield in Co Down. This was the organisational structure through which the Irish Government could raise views and make proposals. The agreement "ushered in an era of direct rule with a green tinge" – according to Bew and Gillespie who saw this new era symbolised by the permanent presence of Irish Government officials at Maryfield.

The subjects that could be raised at the conference included political matters, security and related matters, legal matters – including the administration of justice – and the promotion of cross-border co-operation. FitzGerald believed the AIA provided more than consultation but less than joint authority. He saw it as a mechanism that would ease concerns about political alienation among members of the nationalist community in the North while also reducing the ability of Sinn Féin to become the dominant voice for that community.

Mansergh's reaction was to reject the agreement. On the day it was signed the Fianna Fáil advisor was in Leinster House explaining to all who would listen in party's fifth floor offices why FitzGerald had got a bad deal. One of those present recalled: "Martin was singularly unimpressed with the agreement as was Haughey but they would have had different reasons for rejecting it. Mansergh was intellectually against it while Haughey's attitude was largely driven by the basic thing that if this was good for Garret then we have to oppose it." Mansergh's rejection of the AIA in 1985 was rooted in a constitutional concern that Article One of the agreement gave recognition to Northern Ireland.

The Dáil ratified the agreement by 80 votes to 75. Fianna Fáil voted against. Haughey told the Dáil:

> We are deeply concerned that by signing this agreement the Irish Government are acting in a manner contrary to the Constitution of Ireland by fully accepting British sovereignty over a part of the national territory and by purporting to give legitimacy to the British administration in Ireland.

A senior Fianna Fáil politician Brian Lenihan was sent to the United States to lobby against the deal. However, the Fianna Fáil stance was widely out of line with public opinion. An opinion poll for the *Irish Times* published on 23 November 1984 indicated overwhelming backing for the Agreement while Haughey was only carrying 52 per cent of his party's supporters for his policy.

The Fianna Fáil response to the AIA was damaging both internally and externally. Haughey confirmed the view of his opponents that he was a hard-line republican; the events of the 1970 arms crisis were recalled to further support this thesis. The warring factions within Fianna Fáil diverged in their response to the agreement. Des O'Malley and several supporters backed the AIA and ultimately this difference of opinion cemented their parting with Fianna Fáil. Mansergh later acknowledged the error made – "that opposition may have been costly in domestic political terms."[12]

But the Fianna Fáil opposition had more wide-ranging consequences. The party was isolated in the wider political world. Political friends in London and Washington were surprised. Kevin McNamara, who was the British Labour Party's spokesman on Northern Ireland for much of the 1980s, was not alone when he observed "I put the opposition down to domestic politics in Fianna Fáil."[13]

Moreover, the party had strange bedfellows in their opposition to the AIA – Sinn Féin and Ian Paisley's Democratic Unionist Party. Unionists were appalled at the arrangements. The AIA might not have been joint authority but the Republic was been given a say, however limited, in the internal affairs of Northern Ireland. Paisley and his supporters undertook a campaign of civil disobedience across the North. There was a real sense of betrayal by the British Prime Minister. Paisley told the congregation at his Belfast Church – "O God, in wrath take vengeance upon this wicked, treacherous, lying woman; take vengeance upon her, O Lord, and grant that we shall see a demonstration of thy power."[14]

Mansergh later accepted that the rationale for rejecting the AIA was ill-founded:

> Fianna Fáil mistook Article 1 of the Agreement as constituting *de jure* recognition of Northern Ireland and therefore incompatible with Articles Two and Three of the South's Constitution. The Supreme Court in 1990 took a different view. But there was little problem about embracing and working the institutional mechanisms of the Anglo-Irish Conference, either in opposition or on return to office.[15]

The Supreme Court's view was delivered in a case taken by two unionist brothers, Chris and Michael McGimpsey, in 1990. They argued that Article One of the Agreement contradicted

Articles Two and Three of the 1937 Irish Constitution. However, the Supreme Court in Dublin rejected their case noting that Articles Two and Three were a 'claim of legal right' over the 'national territory' – they were not merely 'aspirational' but rather a 'constitutional imperative' designed to achieve Irish unity. This interpretation meant that Article One of the AIA did not recognise the position of Northern Ireland within the United Kingdom. The judgement totally undermined any intellectual rigour behind the Fianna Fáil position although by the time the Supreme Court ruled in 1990 the party had already done a major policy reversal.

Haughey was elected Taoiseach after the February 1987 general election without any significant public change in Government policy on Northern Ireland. He accepted that the Anglo-Irish Agreement was an international accord that was binding on the governments in Dublin and London. The Fianna Fáil U-turn was typical of the populism that underpinned Haughey's tenure as party leader. Moreover, the original policy decision remained the biggest blemish on Mansergh's record on Northern Ireland policy. The unproductive battle over the agreement, however, coincided with a subtle – but highly significant – development sanctioned in private by Haughey.

Mansergh was one of a small group of individuals who believed that, after two decades of violence, time was running out for politics to take control of the situation:

> Had the violence continued much longer, some of the parties in this State would have become increasingly reluctant to sit round the table under any conditions with those they held responsible – a trend in opinion that had to be taken into account.[16]

There was a second issue to be considered – could the IRA be defeated by military means? Mansergh believed the answer was in the negative. "While the fortunes of war continually fluctuated, the overall situation was a prolonged military stalemate," Mansergh observed.[17] Tougher security measures and new extradition legislation followed atrocities such as the

1987 Enniskillen bombing or events like the Eksund shipment when the IRA attempted unsuccessfully to bring arms and ammunition into the Republic. But security legislation aside, in reality government policy had become that of containment. From the mid-1970s onwards the annual death toll settled at between eighty and one hundred a year. Northern Ireland had arrived at what was controversially described as 'an acceptable level of violence.'

In Mansergh's opinion this reality risked the possibility that at times of high tension the situation might get out of control and result in serious loss of life. He was convinced that notwithstanding the IRA's physical and material ability to carry on a long war – which he believed was not in doubt – the moral capacity to do so did not exist. Moreover, from the perspective of the Republican Movement, Mansergh argued, political objectives would not be advanced while violence continued. Indeed, they could even go backwards. He believed that loyalist and republican paramilitary violence represented a form of political veto. Violence could prolong the stalemate and frustrate the politicians, but it was not capable of advancing the causes of any group or community.

However, Mansergh's was a minority viewpoint in the 1980s. The orthodox political response to the conflict was based on the belief that marginalisation of the extremes would enlarge the middle ground from which a political settlement, and possibly peace, would eventually emerge. The Fianna Fáil advisor explained:

> The prevailing orthodoxy, based on a combination of the Arms Crisis experience and concern about the effects of the failed British attempts to negotiate bilaterally, was that there should be no contact of any kind between governments and spokespersons for paramilitaries for fear of giving them the impression that they were winning, and also as a means of demonstrating moral distance and indeed repugnance.[18]

In opposition during the mid-1990s, Mansergh was advising Haughey that this approach was doomed to failure: "Despite some brave attempts, that policy could only take us so far, and failed to provide a decisive breakthrough."[19]

Any decision to open talks with the Republican Movement involved a huge political gamble; the positive and negative consequences of such a fundamental shift in policy were enormous. There had been sporadic contact with the republican leadership although primarily on the British side. The London Government held discussions with the IRA in 1972 and 1975 while limited covert contact was maintained over the following years.[20] However, there was no direct line of political communication with the Government in Dublin apart from some limited contact at the time of the 1981 Hunger Strikes. Indeed, such was the strength of feeling about Sinn Féin that the FitzGerald-led Government adopted a policy of boycotting functions at which Sinn Féin representatives were attending.

There had long been a tetchiness in the relationship between Mansergh and the former Fine Gael leader. FitzGerald was Mansergh's political boss when he joined the civil service. While they both have fine academic minds, their divergence on political matters ran deep. Indeed, much of it was explained by FitzGerald's antagonistic attitude to Haughey, which obviously clashed with Mansergh's strong sense of loyalty. There was some annoyance at an article penned by Fitzgerald in August 1994 when speculation of an IRA ceasefire was growing. Mansergh noted that Fitzgerald:

> said that he was disturbed by reports that I was in direct contact with republicans. All of this presupposed that the paramilitaries could be militarily defeated or forced to stop by political developments or by public political exhortation from a distance.[21]

Given this, it is ironic that the former Labour Party advisor, Fergus Finlay, has observed

> I will always believe that it was a great tragedy that, for example, Garret FitzGerald and Martin Mansergh never had a chance to work together. The nature of adversarial politics makes that sort of relationship impossible – but it would have made history.[22]

Mansergh had arrived at the conclusion that contact with the leadership of the Republican Movement was necessary if the Northern conflict was ever going to be ended. "It is difficult to make omelettes without breaking eggs" was his repeated argument.[23] It was a view also shared by a Roman Catholic priest who would play a central role in creating the peace process in the 1980s and early 1990s.

Father Alex Reid was born in Co Tipperary but moved to Belfast in 1967. A member of the Redemptorist Order, he was based at the Clonard Monastery which bordered the nationalist Falls Road area and the loyalist Shankill. Reid had long sought an end to paramilitary violence. Driven by a desire "to get the situation off the streets and around the conference table" he first acted as mediator between feuding republican groups in the mid-1970s.[24] In this role as 'facilitator' Reid first met Gerry Adams. During the 1981 hunger strikes the Redemptorist priest was involved in attempts to find a settlement to the protests.

Reid believed that condemnation of the IRA was not enough. Republicans had to be engaged with so as to convince them that their campaign of violence could never achieve their ultimate aims. He helped to arrange meetings between republican leaders and the head of the Roman Catholic Church, Cardinal Tomás Ó Fiaich. But any hope for an end to the conflict appeared slim. The death toll continued to increase. By the mid-1980s almost 2,500 people had been killed in the Troubles in Northern Ireland.

Nevertheless, Reid persisted with his discussions with leading republicans, arguing that a united Ireland was only attainable through peaceful methods. Adams told him that political movement could come through the creation of a united nationalist position involving Sinn Féin, the SDLP and the main political parties in Dublin. "And if they could come together and agree on a common democratic strategy that would provide an alternative strategy that could credibly be sold to the IRA," Reid recalled.[25]

This was the type of strategy that Mansergh applauded Charles Stewart Parnell for achieving in the 1880s. It was a repeat of the 'New Departure' policy when constitutional politicians harnessed the support of those who believed physical force was in principle justified. Mansergh was to hear Reid argue that progress on ending republican violence could come if the Irish Government met with Sinn Féin to add credibility to the process.

There was little prospect of this thinking winning over the Fitzgerald-led Fine Gael/Labour coalition Government that was in power in Dublin between November 1982 and February 1987. As noted previously, Fitzgerald's principle motivation in the aftermath of the 1981 hunger strikes was to prevent a resurgent Sinn Féin supplanting the SDLP as the main nationalist party in Northern Ireland.

The IRA campaign continued but Reid interpreted what Adams was saying as pointing to the possibility of a historic breakthrough. The republican leadership, if offered the possibility of a purely political route for achieving their objective, were open to persuasion provided a strategy involving nationalist parties in the North and the Republic could be built. Reid recalled:

> So the problem then was, the Sinn Féin leadership could do nothing about developing such a strategy unless they were able to talk directly to the other parties. And the other parties at that time wouldn't speak to them unless the IRA stopped.[26]

In effect the peace process started with the Redemptorist priest in 1982. Numerous attempts were made to get the SDLP and senior politicians in the Republic to talk with Sinn Féin. But for a variety of reasons none of these attempts were successful in establishing the first contact. The process was stillborn until 1986 when Reid himself seized the initiative.

The Clonard-based priest first put pen to paper: "I decided this was the last throw of the dice, that I would put it all on paper so that the opportunity that was there to end the armed struggle would be known and on paper..."[27] The 15-page typed letter was sent to John Hume in May 1986 and to Charles Haughey in November of the same year. The SDLP leader responded immediately and, the day after receiving the correspondence, travelled to Belfast.

Reid spoke to the journalist Tim Pat Coogan who helped to arrange a meeting with the then opposition leader, Charles Haughey. The three men met at Haughey's Kinsealy home in North County Dublin. The Fianna Fáil leader listened to Reid outline a scenario detailing how the IRA could be persuaded to call a ceasefire. Reid wanted Haughey to meet Adams who he considered was prepared to re-direct the Republican Movement into the political arena.

In his quiet low-key manner, Reid argued that the Adams-led republican leadership could be convinced to lay down their arms, but that this could only come about through face-to-face discussion. Talks had to be aimed, in the first instance, at ending the isolation of the Republican Movement. Adams and his supporters had to be shown that a broad constitutional and nationalist family existed which they could join to pursue the objective of a united Ireland. But this would only happen when the IRA no longer felt that it was out on its own.

Haughey listened but his instinct was not to meet Adams while the IRA campaign continued. However, at a subsequent meeting the Fianna Fáil leader introduced Reid to his party's Head of Research. The Redemptorist priest had never heard of Mansergh, let alone met him. "I remember saying to him [Haughey] later, 'Is it alright what I say to him?' And he said: 'You can say to him what you'd say to me.'"[28] Haughey still remains reticent about his role in the early days of what became the Northern Ireland peace process: "I don't want to say too much about the peace process. It's a very crowded stage. What's the saying? 'Success has many fathers.'"[29]

Reid has been equally silent. The normally tight-lipped priest never fully explained how the peace process began, but for this book he spoke extensively about the secret contacts that led to the IRA ceasefire in August 1994. The first meeting with Mansergh remained one of his most vivid recollections from his involvement in the peace process. It was a key moment, according to Reid:

> What does the Bible say, 'There was a man sent by God'; I thought 'Cometh the hour, cometh the man.' Martin was the ideal person for conducting a debate with the Republican Movement, which aimed at talking the gun out of Irish politics. You wonder if it would have succeeded without him.[30]

After Haughey introduced the priest and political advisor, the two men left the Fianna Fáil leader and moved into another room in his Abbeyville home. There, Reid explained the contents of the letter he had sent to Haughey, and his belief that there was "an opportunity of getting a ceasefire."[31] Reid recalled:

> I'd say I did more of the talking that morning. You had a sense that he was with you and that he supported the whole idea, and that he was prepared to work at it. After taking four or five years to get to that stage – all the going around the corners and meeting yourself coming back – it was a terrific boost to be linked in with somebody who was in Martin's position. And you always knew that if you could persuade Martin about whatever the argument was, he would get the go-ahead – you could put the kettle on.[32]

The Mansergh-Reid-Adams connection was crucial to the development of the peace process. The Redemptorist priest facilitated communications between Adams and Mansergh. He would meet them separately. In Dublin, the coffee shop in the National Gallery of Ireland and the Mont Clare Hotel became regular meeting places. After Albert Reynolds replaced Haughey and the process entered deeper negotiations in the 1992-94 period, Reid would become a regular figure around Government Buildings in Dublin.

The Fianna Fáil advisor was described in coded messages as 'the man' while in documents typed up by Reid the letter 'M' was used. Reid himself was simply known as 'the priest'. Seán Duignan later wrote:

> There was the man Reynolds referred to only as 'the priest'. Slightly built, almost wraith-like, he would 'appear' and invariably make a bee-line for Mansergh's room ... I knew from the way Reynolds referred to him that he was a vital link to Sinn Féin and the IRA.[33]

Reid would type up the contents of these discussions and pass the document on to the other side, generally with some personal commentary about positions and possibilities. When Mansergh was given the documents, he was reading material with significant republican fingerprints, as he himself admitted:

> The IRA were kept informed of the state of the dialogue, though it was not always clear if a particular written message had come from the IRA or Sinn Féin, as from time to time we received both, or indeed whether it always strictly mattered. My working assumption was that one was always dealing with the one movement, in which people had different roles at particular times.[34]

It was a slow process, particularly on the republican side. Sometimes up to 12 weeks would pass before a response was provided. As each new version of what emerged as a joint-position paper was exchanged, Adams continued to argue with Reid that face-to-face dialogue would speed up the entire process. With the exception of two meetings in 1988, Haughey was unwilling to sanction direct contracts, although from the middle of 1992 his successor approved regular meetings between Adams and Mansergh.

Reid was clearly driven by a conviction about the pastoral responsibility of his church to intervene directly in the conflict. Through Reid – and his Redemptorist colleague, Fr Gerry Reynolds – the Sinn Féin leadership entered discussions from 1988 with Mansergh and also John Hume, leader of the SDLP. The provision of a southern political perspective from Fianna Fáil to Sinn Féin was hugely significant. Indeed, it is probable that there would have been no peace process without this input from Dublin.

A great deal of the commentary on the 1988-94 period has concentrated on the Hume-Adams dialogue to the detriment of the Mansergh-Adams exchanges. The ideas expounded by Hume were influential and certainly provided part of the framework for the settlements that followed. The SDLP leader was drawing on a philosophical outlook developed over the previous two decades. He wanted movement away from the republican fixation of uniting territory so as to concentrate efforts on uniting the people on the island. The parallel contacts with Mansergh followed similar subjects. However, Mansergh offered the Republican Movement an additional, vital ingredient that was not available from their talks with Hume – the embrace of government.

When Fianna Fáil returned to power in 1987, direct contact was made with Sinn Féin. Two secret meetings were held between representatives of the two parties in 1988. Mansergh – along with Fianna Fáil colleagues Dermot Ahern and Richie Healy – met with Adams and two other senior republicans – Pat Doherty and Mitchel McLaughlin – in Dundalk.

It was a high-risk strategy. Haughey told Ahern if the Co Louth meeting was made public those attending would be disowned. There was no official sanction. No government fingerprints would be evident. Ahern replied:

> You said to me I'd be on my own but yet Mansergh will be with me. Surely if anything comes out people will say Haughey must have known what was happening because Martin Mansergh was part of it?' His

response to me was: 'We'll be able to get over that one.[35]

The former Fine Gael minister Austin Deasy later asked Haughey in the Dáil if the Government was in contact with Sinn Féin. Haughey gave an ambiguous reply that no member of the Government had any contact. Mansergh made the subtle although not very credible distinction – "The Government *per se* was not involved, but the party of Government was."[36]

There was some unease in the Fianna Fáil delegation about the contacts, especially as republican violence continued. It was only a few months since the Enniskillen bombing on Remembrance Day in November 1987. Large numbers of Protestants had gathered in the Co Fermanagh town to remember their dead at an annual parade and religious service. An IRA bomb was concealed in a community hall behind the crowd. Without any warning the bomb exploded. A wall was demolished and tonnes of rubble and masonry crashed down. Eleven people were killed and more than sixty injured.

The attack was a disaster for the IRA. As television pictures were transmitted the world saw the awful scenes and also heard the forgiving words of a local man, Gordon Wilson. In a poignant radio interview, he told of being trapped in the debris holding his daughter's hand. They talked for while before Marie Wilson said to her father: "Daddy, I love you very much". Then there was silence. Wilson said afterwards "She was a great wee lassie. She was a pet, and she's dead. But I bear no ill will. I bear no grudge."

Mansergh believed the 1987 Remembrance Day bomb in Enniskillen was the catalyst for the peace process. The horror of Enniskillen forced the military and constitutional wings of Irish republicanism to re-examine their positions. When asked when the peace process began, Mansergh mentioned the Enniskillen bomb, and the "horror, futility and unacceptability of violence. From that day, time was running out for the paramilitary campaigns … "[37]

The only person told about Mansergh's new responsibility was his wife, Liz. She was fully supportive. Any doubts they had were not related to personal safety, but rather the morality underpinning the contacts. As Mansergh observed: "If you believed they were leading nowhere, well then the moral justification would disappear."[38]

The only time the couple questioned the secret contacts was when the IRA bombed a shopping district at Warrington in Lancashire in March 1993. Two children were killed, 3-year-old Jonathan Ball who was shopping for a Mother's Day present and 12-year-old Tim Parry who had planned to buy a new pair of football shorts. The level of condemnation matched the outrage which had followed the 1987 IRA bombing in Enniskillen. The Manserghs were left to ponder the value of talking to people who were linked to such terrible deeds.

However, the Fianna Fáil advisor believed the Republican Movement was on the cusp of a historic decision that would only be facilitated by governmental coaxing from Dublin. Relations had developed and a considerable trust existed. The operation of a stop-go policy would not assist the developing peace process.

Nevertheless, there was no certainty about what could be achieved when the first face-to-face contacts were made in 1988. The first meeting between the Fianna Fáil delegation and the republican leadership took place on a Monday morning at the Redemptorist monastery in Dundalk. In a wooden panelled room the representatives of Sinn Féin and Fianna Fáil, in effect the Irish Government, sat on either side of a long table.

Fr Reid did the introductions. He said: "I'll be leaving you in a minute but I'd just like you to pause a moment for a short prayer to help you in your deliberations." Dermot Ahern later said: "I remember during the prayer I felt it was very eerie in the way it was being done, but I was very conscious that it was a momentous occasion because it was obviously top secret."[39]

The meeting lasted for two hours. The atmosphere was cordial and business-like. "There was no raising of the voice and certainly no harshness, no bullying and no heckling. People were trying to get a dialogue off the ground," Mansergh recalled.[40]

Adams and Mansergh did most of the talking. The Fianna

Fáil advisor impressed the Sinn Féin team who had become familiar with his writings through their contacts-by-proxy over the previous months. They quickly came to accept his background as the quality of his contribution indicated a resolve to make the process succeed.

Mitchel McLaughlin remarked: "Here was someone who had a very clear sense of the possibilities of what could emerge from the process. Someone who was very strategically located within the political establishment."[41] Adams was impressed: "I had previously only been aware of him in a general, vague way. I found him to be very matter of fact and straightforward."[42]

The Fianna Fáil delegation was particularly interested in the comments made by Adams. He was almost 40 years of age and all he had experienced in his life was violence. Now the Sinn Féin President wanted to ensure there was peace for his children and his children's children. Mansergh said:

> The point was made that northern nationalists were alienated from Dublin. They claimed that if British troops were stationed in Dundalk the popular reaction would be the same as in the north. They needed an alternative political strategy, if violence were to stop. The view was expressed that the Anglo-Irish Agreement was not worth the candle, as the cost of the provocation of unionists was not commensurate with any substantial gain. We naturally stressed the total unacceptability of violence to the people of the south, and pointed out that it was the single most potent divisive factor weakening Irish nationalism, with northern nationalists, nationalists north and south, and the Irish-American community all divided on the question of the legitimacy of violence, thus preventing combination for electoral or other purposes.[43]

Mansergh met with Adams on two occasions in the first half of 1988. The discussions were free ranging without any agenda. What struck Mansergh was the ideological nature of the conversations, which went to the very core of Irish republicanism. While Sinn Féin had ended its abstentionist policy in relation to taking seats in Dáil Éireann in 1986, republicans were still uncomfortable about giving recognition to the parliament of a Republic, that they did not even consider a republic at all. Moreover, their argument about the British as a colonial power occupying and exploiting Northern Ireland was harder to make in the aftermath of the AIA. They also failed to encompass within their thinking the expressed wishes of the unionist community. There was an inability to accept the British identity favoured by unionists and their desire to remain within the United Kingdom.

Mansergh's early discussions with the Republican Movement were based on carving out common ground and convincing Adams and his colleagues that a continuation of violence did not represent the most effective way to achieve their ultimate aim. The first tentative steps, which would lead to the August 1994 IRA ceasefire, were being taken.

The first face-to-face meetings were hugely significant for the Republican Movement as Reid explained:

> It was a big thing for Sinn Féin to say they had met representatives of Fianna Fáil, in brackets the Irish Government. That created credibility with the military side of their movement, that they were actually being taken seriously and engaging at the highest level … [44]

The early contacts also served to tease out definitions of key concepts such as self-determination and consent. Much of the peace process was about finding a common language that could accommodate the objectives of various participants.

The Anglo-Irish Agreement in 1985 provided the Republican Movement with both linguistic and theoretical challenges. The agreement showed that the British Government was prepared to acknowledge the legitimacy of Irish nationalism. Both Mansergh and Hume argued that the British were now neutral participants in the Irish question. But republicans were still using a language lumbered by history. They talked about the partitionist parliament at Leinster House, about British imperialism and about the necessity for a fixed timetable for British withdrawal. Mitchel McLaughlin recalled the language learning-curve faced by the Republican Movement:

> That was a challenge particularly for Sinn Féin. One of the early benefits was the advice we were being given by Martin Mansergh about how certain words and language was charged in a very political way.[45]

The dialogue with the IRA spawned almost six years of debate on these fundamental principles. Mansergh observed:

> The ideological issues underlying conflict were for the first time being directly addressed and debated, such issues as whether Britain still had a strategic interest in Ireland or was politically neutral, the divisive and weakening effect of armed struggle or nationalism, and the conditions under which Irish unity could be achieved in future.[46]

The 1988 discussions ended without any apparent movement. In fact both Hume and Fianna Fáil had separately arrived at the same conclusion. The IRA was not yet prepared to call a ceasefire. It was clear to those involved that the principle republican objective with the dialogue was to win political credibility and to end their isolation. Nonetheless, while there was as yet no agreement, a dialogue of sorts had started. The very fact that the different components of Irish nationalism were communicating was in itself significant.

Despite the ending of the formal contact, secret channels of communications between the various strands of nationalism in Ireland were kept open by the relentless activity of Reid. The Mansergh-Adams dialogue continued in secret without the knowledge of other key participants. John Hume was keeping officials in Iveagh House briefed about his contacts with Adams, but neither the SDLP leader nor the Department of Foreign Affairs were told about the Mansergh-Adams exchanges.

There was one immediate stumbling block in their discussions – the Anglo-Irish Agreement, that ironically both Fianna Fáil and Sinn Féin had rejected when it was originally signed. In government Mansergh and Haughey had changed their stance. However, for the republican leadership the agreement still presented a difficulty given their belief that it copper-fastened the unionist veto. Reid recalled Mansergh bringing up the 1985 deal: "He often said, 'We're a sovereign government, we have international obligations and we are bound by the Anglo-Irish Agreement.'"[47] The efforts to overcome this issue delayed the process, according to the Redemptorist priest.

The secret dialogue was given a considerable boost with the appointment of Peter Brooke as Northern Secretary. Brooke came from an Anglo-Irish background but carried no political baggage in relation to the North. He told Mansergh about a distant relation, the eighteenth-century poet Charlotte Brooke, who introduced the word 'Fenian' into the English language.

Brooke raised eyebrows with his prediction that governments eventually end up talking to those they regarded as terrorists. There was further interest from nationalists – and considerable anger from unionists – when the Northern Secretary, in the context of the end of the Cold War, observed that Britain had no selfish strategic or economic interest in remaining in Northern Ireland. It was a key statement that enormously assisted the clandestine discussions with Adams.

Mansergh believed the declaration removed a huge historical barrier:

> That 'selfish strategic interest' was the reason for Henry II's invasion of Ireland in 1171, for the brutal repression of Elizabeth's reign, when the Spanish threat was at its greatest, and the colonial settlements first in Munster, which failed, then in Ulster. It was responsible for the civil wars and the Cromwellian conquest, for the battle between two English kings for control in 1690-1, for the Act of Union, as I have said, and for the determination on the part of many in the

British establishment to hold onto Northern Ireland from the late 1940s to 1990, through the Cold War period ... Today, there is no strategic threat that can be used to justify Britain holding onto any part of Ireland.[48]

The idea for some form of declaration to define this nascent conceptual framework was made by Reid. He was convinced agreement would facilitate an IRA ceasefire. However, Mansergh was urging caution, as the Redemptorist priest recalled:

I remember one day walking along the beach in Killiney, this is one of my vivid memories of the time 1987 to 1990. We were talking about putting together this nationalist strategy. And he said 'Look, we have to be careful because if we put together a strategy that is supported by all the nationalist parties, we're going to frighten the unionists – actually, I think he said 'It would terrify them more than the IRA would terrify them'.[49]

In his contacts with Adams, Mansergh argued that violence was unnecessary. The Sinn Féin President said that the people of Ireland had a right to national self-determination. But the Fianna Fáil advisor indicated that self-determination had to be coupled with the principle of consent. The unionist position had to be recognised. Adams considered this a re-statement of the unionist veto over the achievement of a united Ireland, the ultimate expression of national self-determination. He argued that the British had to become persuaders for this position and that they had to set a timetable for their withdrawal.

While the various ideas on a way forward were developing, Hume made the next move. On 6 October 1991 the Derry politician sat at his desk and wrote in longhand on lined white paper an important input into what was eventually – after extensive re-drafting – to become the Downing Street Declaration.

The Hume document sought to reflect as well as reconcile the divergent political positions. Set in an Anglo-Irish context, the draft drew on the Hume-Adams discussions as well as the dialogue between Adams and Mansergh. It sought to re-orientate the traditional republican view of the British position and to make the governments in Dublin and London more central to decision-making on the future of Northern Ireland. It stressed a different view from the traditional Sinn Féin analysis that Britain was the imperial power in Northern Ireland. Hume argued that Britain had no selfish strategic, economic or political interest in remaining in Northern Ireland. Peter Brooke had said so. However, there could be no change without the agreement of the people of Northern Ireland – a principle Mansergh argued was set in stone by the Haughey Government. In other words, self-determination had to be firmly linked with the principle of consent.

The draft document was a long way from the republican objective of a united Ireland achieved through British withdrawal. However, it contained new language and concepts, and most importantly included unionists within the framework of nationalist thinking, something that Sinn Féin had been unable – and unwilling – to previously countenance. The document also contained the commitment that an IRA ceasefire would be followed by a conference convened by the Government in Dublin. In fact, Haughey had already promised that if there was a ceasefire he would reconvene the New Ireland Forum. The key difference with the Forum, which met during the FitzGerald coalition, would be the participation of Sinn Féin.

In mid-October 1991 Hume brought his white lined paper to a meeting with Haughey in Dublin. Haughey listened to the SDLP leader's contention that the principles in his document would address republican concerns and produce an IRA ceasefire. The Taoiseach asked Mansergh to examine the document and to assess the possibilities.

The text, in what became known as the Hume-Adams document, paralleled – but was not the same as – the content of the exchanges between Sinn Féin and the Government in Dublin. Over the following two years a confusing process of osmosis occurred. In a sense Hume-Adams was an input into an overall document – known in the private exchanges as

"Dublin's proposals" – which was directed by Mansergh.

It was a task well-suited to the Fianna Fáil advisor. His skills as a wordsmith were widely recognised, plus nobody associated with the Irish Government was so familiar with republican thinking. Sinn Féin had come to respect Mansergh's commitment to building a peace process and appreciated the quality of his contributions.

The Sinn Féin National Chairman, Mitchel McLaughlin recalled:

> He recognises – and this is where he would be closer to Sinn Féin – that a united Ireland is a political option to be determined by the people of Ireland in the exercise of self-determination. They may decide to go for a united Ireland – and they probably will – but it is not a principle, the principle is self-determination. Martin Mansergh understands that totally.[50]

Mansergh worked on the document developing the themes and the ideas. The contents were infused with the language of diplomacy and the thinking of Government. The objective was to draw together the different strands of Irish nationalism. However, Haughey also wanted to involve the unionist community. Dialogue was sought with the leader of the Ulster Unionist Party, Jim Molyneaux. An intermediary was identified. Mansergh travelled to London to meet Enoch Powell, the former unionist MP who was a confidant of Molyneaux. Their two private meetings were described as "long and animated" but ultimately proved to be unproductive.

The Taoiseach raised the possibility of a joint initiative in December 1991 when he met John Major who had just replaced Margaret Thatcher as British Prime Minister. He told Major that the text might offer a breakthrough. However, Haughey himself was out of a job early in 1992.

He was succeeded as Fianna Fáil leader and Taoiseach by Albert Reynolds, a businessman-turned-politician who had served in all of Haughey's cabinets until he turned leadership challenger several months previously. Reynolds promised a fresh start with new faces at all levels within the party. Mansergh – as a Head of Research within Fianna Fáil and Special Advisor to the Taoiseach – served at the pleasure of the party leader. He was the leading member of the *ancien régime,* having served as Haughey's advisor for 11 years. His departure was expected when Reynolds took control.

Eight

Ceasefire

One of Charles Haughey's final tasks as Taoiseach was to brief his successor on the embryonic peace process. The psychological barrier of talking with the republican leadership had been broken in 1988. But, in the intervening period, progress had been slow. Haughey's role was vital – and has still not been rewarded with due recognition – but as he departed power he was not to take credit for bringing about a lasting peace.

Indeed, during his 12 years as leader of Fianna Fáil, and four terms as Taoiseach, Haughey had never succeed in overcoming the great distrust with which he was viewed in Northern Ireland. To most unionists he was simply a no-go area, largely because of the unexplained events associated with his involvement in the 1970 Arms Crisis. Moreover, his handling of the 1981 hunger strikes disappointed many within the nationalist community and, as a result, they also approached him with deep suspicion.

Albert Reynolds carried none of that baggage. The Longford politician had said little of note about Northern Ireland during a ministerial career dominated by economic portfolios. However, he had had a long personal interest in the North. Reynolds attended the 1970 Arms Trial and through his business interests had developed contacts on both sides of the border. As a Government minister he was involved in north-south economic co-operation. Moreover, in private, Reynolds had made known his preference for a more pragmatic response to the Anglo-Irish Agreement which would have seen him on the opposite side of the internal Fianna Fáil divide to Mansergh. "He was sometimes praised by the then Taoiseach Garret FitzGerald, no doubt, to annoy Charles Haughey," Mansergh recalled.[1]

So when Haughey informed Reynolds about the secret contacts with the Republican Movement the incoming Taoiseach immediately saw the possibilities. He also realised the importance of Mansergh so as to ensure continuity between the two administrations.

One of the first tasks of the new Fianna Fáil leader was to persuade the man long identified as a Haughey aide to remain on the payroll. Mansergh was surprised when asked to stay on as Special Advisor, and admitted: "There was little track record to inform expectations when he became Taoiseach."[2] Indeed, no one could have predicted the twists and turns that would be associated with Reynolds's tenure as Taoiseach. But there was little need for persuasion. Mansergh had the ability to separate the issues from the individual.

The Fianna Fáil advisor opened a 1996 biographical article on Reynolds with the ancient Greek phrase: "The fox knows many things. The hedgehog knows one big thing."[3] If Haughey had been a fox, Reynolds was a hedgehog. From the moment he assumed the leadership of Fianna Fáil, and was elected Taoiseach, Reynolds had one objective – persuading the IRA to end its campaign of violence. His single-mindedness was an ideal compliment to the precise historical analysis presented by Mansergh. Neither man agreed with the methods of the IRA.

One newspaper in 1994 quoted 'a long-time associate' as saying that "Martin Mansergh has infused a sense of history into Albert Reynolds."[4] The view was somewhat harsh on the Taoiseach's appreciation of Northern policy, although there was no denying his reliance on Mansergh for the analytical and historical framework for the task to be undertaken. This was evident from the very start of their working relationship.

On the day of the Fianna Fáil leadership election, Reynolds asked for clarification on some facts about Northern Ireland. The main question put was: What was the counterpart to

Articles Two and Three? Mansergh replied that in a strict legal sense the answer was the Act of Union but that the 1800 legislation was probably too far in the past and also too confrontational. He suggested the real counterpart was the Government of Ireland Act, 1920 as it created Northern Ireland, the *de jure* legitimacy of which was challenged by the 1937 Irish Constitution.

Reynolds took the advice and told his first media conference that consideration would be given to changing Articles Two and Three if the British Government would alter or repeal the Government of Ireland Act, 1920. The incoming Taoiseach was seeking a balanced constitutional accommodation. It was a sophisticated historical and political analysis provided by his new advisor. The comments were received with interest within republican circles but caused some surprise among the Dublin media. Reynolds was a self-made man who had made money from promoting dancehall events in the 1960s and later from a dog food company. There was an element of media snobbery in the coverage he attracted.

The change in leadership brought much upheaval in Fianna Fáil and also within the party's relationship with their coalition partners, the Progressive Democrats. Reynolds was true to his word in altering the political and official personnel who worked for Fianna Fáil. Many Haughey supporters were demoted from cabinet while backroom staff like PJ Mara quickly departed. Mansergh was in an unusual position, a Haughey loyalist retained by the man who had led the charge against his former boss. The loyalty to Fianna Fáil impressed Reynolds who believed that Mansergh's involvement in the various leadership heaves had been honourable. But the new Taoiseach was primarily motivated by the possibility of creating a peace process, and Mansergh was central to that task.

Seán Duignan, who joined the Reynolds team as Press Secretary in early 1992, observed that the Taoiseach "clearly regarded Mansergh as his most valuable adviser. I soon noticed that, although they might not always see eye to eye on issues such as the economy or whatever, they seemed to think almost as one on Northern Ireland."[5]

In terms of working-style, Reynolds was more direct than Haughey. He was impatient to get things done. Mansergh remarked:

> No doubt, the huge number of deals that he negotiated and the type of poker-playing that was often involved in the process influenced his approach to the more complex task of political negotiation and deal-making subsequently.[6]

If Mansergh had admired Fianna Fáil for its pragmatism, he was now working for the party's ultimate pragmatist. The advisor knew as much. He observed of Reynolds: "His understanding of republicanism was always a pragmatic one. He did not believe that IRA violence in the North ever made sense, nor was he consciously influenced by revisionism either."[7]

The change of leadership was very evident in the handling of the developing peace process, as Mansergh quickly discovered. Reynolds picked up the threads of the proposed initiative that had been discussed by Haughey and John Major at the end of 1991. Along with having no personal baggage or track record on Northern Ireland policy, Reynolds came to the subject with another advantage. He already had a good working relationship with his counterpart at 10 Downing Street. They had met previously at European Union Council meetings when Reynolds was Minister for Finance and Major was British Chancellor of the Exchequer. The Taoiseach sought to convince Major that a deal could be done. Much of this belief was based on political intuition and the feedback being provided by Mansergh.

Mansergh was one of the several behind-the-scenes individuals who had a significant influence over the direction of the peace process. The longer the contact with the Republican Movement continued, the more the small group expanded. Ultimately, there were a handful of key figures in the Irish and British governments who worked tirelessly to achieve the 1994 ceasefire and four years later, the Good Friday Agreement. On the Dublin side they included civil servants such as Noel Dorr,

Dermot Nally, Paddy Teahon, Tim Dalton, Dermot Gallagher and Seán Ó hUiginn.

These key officials drawn from the Department of Foreign Affairs and the Department of Taoiseach – along with their political masters – were the core group that drove the peace process in Dublin. A former Foreign Affairs official observed that during the 1992-94 period: "you could gauge someone's importance to the Process by looking at the speed dials on the fax. Mansergh's personal button was there, well smudged from use, as was the Embassy Washington, the Embassy London, the US Embassy Dublin, the SDLP and the Tánaiste's office in Leinster House."[8]

Mansergh developed close working relations with two officials from the Department of Foreign Affairs, Dermot Gallagher and Seán Ó hUiginn. Gallagher was Ireland's Ambassador in Washington between 1991 and 1997. While in the American capital he built an influential network of contacts in Washington that were important at key moments in the peace process. He was centrally involved in the negotiations leading to the Good Friday Agreement.

Ó hUiginn had headed up the Anglo-Irish division at Iveagh House during the 1990s. He was one of the main drafters of what became the Framework Documents in 1994. The British and unionist politicians saw him as a green bogeyman. Known as the "Prince of Darkness", he had – according to Mansergh – "an enormous understanding of constitutional nationalism" in Northern Ireland.[9] There was deep respect for him from the Fianna Fáil advisor. Ó hUiginn – who replaced Gallagher in Washington in 1997 – was the subject of mistaken identity in the Irish Edition of the *Sunday Times* at the end of 1999. The article provoked Mansergh to write to the newspaper:

It is ironic that in the same column in which Niall O'Dowd is called 'a bit of a thick' for mistakenly calling Wolfe Tone a northern Protestant, the ambass-ador in Washington, Seán Ó hUiginn, is confused with the former secretary of the department of the Taoiseach, Padraig Ó hUiginn, both distinguished and celebrated public servants. Might I suggest, as a new year's resolution, that casting stones should be left to those who never make inadvertent factual slips?[10]

The Irish Government – and in particular the Department of Foreign Affairs – had close links with the SDLP. There was an official policy of non-contact with Sinn Féin representatives while the IRA continued its campaign of violence. One former diplomat recalled that "such was the quarantine on SF that every week a Third Sec [junior diplomat] would have to go down to the GPO in O'Connell Street to buy their newspaper, *An Phoblacht/Republican News*, rather than have the Department subscribe to it."[11] Set against this background, the idea of the Taoiseach's Special Advisor liasing with leading republicans left senior diplomats aghast. However, Mansergh's status as a political advisor, as opposed to a civil servant, made the contacts somewhat easier to accept.

The Fianna Fáil advisor had good relations with the senior British officials who worked on the developing peace process, including Robin Butler, the British Cabinet Secretary and Sir John Chilcott, permanent under-secretary at the Northern Ireland Office. Chilcott was "far-sighted and imaginative", while Thomas was "tough-minded but unfailingly courteous. Both were resourceful."[12]

The British were impressed with Mansergh and rated him highly even if they differed fundamentally with his ideological position on Northern Ireland. "Clever and rather dangerous," was the assessment of Sir Patrick Mayhew who added, "He is very adroit at the manipulation of nuances in expression, which was really the stuff of those enormously tedious talks, as inevitably they had to be given the sensitivities involved."[13] On more than one occasion John Major raised with the Taoiseach, what the British saw as the hard-line republican line being adopted by the Irish Government advisor. When Reynolds was asked to consider replacing Mansergh, Major was told not to pursue the issue.

Bertie Ahern was aware of the British fascination with Mansergh. The Fianna Fáil leader said:

> I'd say the Tories were deeply suspicious of him because he didn't fit in to what they would have expected. When Tony Blair got in, they all knew who Mansergh was. I remember in opposition talking to Tony Blair, and Mansergh would be with me, and Tony Blair would even say: 'Is that guy Mansergh?' They knew of him, of his position and of his influence.[14]

British officials and politicians were intrigued to be facing an English-born, public school educated, Oxford University graduate. They could not work out how – what one called 'one of our own' – came to be working for Fianna Fáil, and advocating an intellectually based brand of constitutional republicanism. Bertie Ahern was aware of the British uncertainty over Mansergh's background:

> I think that's what spooks a lot of people, not least the Brits. The credentials are very different. It took them a long time to figure him out. I would love to see the 30-year papers about what they thought of Mansergh, and I have no doubt that there is a lot of British intelligence on Mansergh. I have no doubt about that. I hope I live long enough to see the papers released.[15]

Interestingly, Mansergh spoke himself about the operations of British intelligence in Ireland. These clandestine agencies had, Mansergh claimed, "circulated black literature about the Lynch Government, and there may well have been efforts to assist destabilisation of the Haughey Government in 1982".[16]

Mansergh succeeded in winning over his British counterparts with what one official described as his "engaging sense of humour". In truth, they were happy to deal with the polite and courteous Fianna Fáil advisor, who notwithstanding his passionately held political beliefs offered a sharp contrast with several mandarins in the Department of Foreign Affairs with whom they constantly clashed.

British journalists writing about Northern Ireland found

Mansergh a good sounding board on Irish Government policy. Dean Godson, an Assistant Editor at the *Daily Telegraph* newspaper in London, saw evidence of Mansergh's worth for the Irish administration: "There is absolutely nobody comparable in the British system and that's greatly to the British system's disadvantage. There is huge respect for his abilities."[17]

A decade after Mansergh first applied those abilities to starting the peace process, the Government in Dublin was led by Albert Reynolds, a politician prepared to gamble his Government on securing an IRA ceasefire. Seán Duignan recalled the atmosphere in Government Buildings where only a small circle of people knew about the strategy:

> I was becoming increasingly aware of comings and goings around the Taoiseach's department. Mansergh would disappear at intervals for a day or a two at a time – it was considered indelicate to refer to his absences...[18]

The republican leadership was interested in news that Reynolds was prepared to take risks for peace by progressing the draft declaration. Individuals like Gerry Adams and Martin McGuinness were attracted to the idea of the coming together of the two strands of northern nationalism with the Government in Dublin. The movement from armed to unarmed struggle would create an all-Ireland nationalist strategy. Critics would later refer to it as the Pan-Nationalist Front.

Work continued throughout 1992 on developing what would become a joint declaration. The Government in Dublin lengthened the document given by Haughey in his final months in office to Major. The draft was embellished with the language of diplomacy. But the essence and structure remained. The revised document was sent back to the two Northern leaders for comment. All these discussions and contacts were undertaken under a cloak of secrecy. Reynolds recalled:

> I knew enough about the Republican Movement to know that a leak would make them break off all

communications. The only way to do it was to keep the whole thing close. I said to Martin, 'If there's a leak it's either you or me.' Both of us realised the dangers of a leak and the damage it would do. We had to get the confidence of the Republican Movement.[19]

There were signs of progress with republican acceptance of – and use of – the diplomatic language included in the Mansergh text. The first Sinn Féin response came in February 1992. Reid was the conduit, meeting with Mansergh in Dublin:

They rewrote the document, accepting a lot of it, maybe 75 per cent but then there were one or two paragraphs. They reworded the whole thing and it went back to Dublin and Martin tried to adapt whatever they had objected to. That's where he was great. He would never say 'take it or leave it'. He would get the thing and try to reword it in a way that met their concerns and, at the same time, within the parameters of what the Irish Government was free to do.[20]

The draft declaration was based on principles endorsed by the three stands of Irish nationalism which – the participants believed – could convince the IRA to pursue its objectives by purely political means. While republicans considered the unpublished document a basis for peace, it was obvious that the principles would be problematic – and most probably unacceptable – to the British Government.

The republicans wanted a British commitment to become persuaders for Irish unity. They also wanted an agreed timeframe for British withdrawal linked to the self-determination concept in the declaration. The Conservative Government was being asked to become more than merely neutral bystander on Northern Ireland. John Major's majority in the House of Commons was dependent upon support from the Ulster Unionist Party. So given the parliamentary arithmetic at

Westminster, the republican ethos in the draft declaration was always going to be problematic, even leaving aside the long-standing Tory association with the unionist cause. It was a shift in thinking that Irish Government officials knew would never wash with the British.

Mansergh was adamant that the principles of consent and self-determination were central to any agreement on the declaration. The Irish Government was not prepared to accept anything at variance with the Anglo-Irish Agreement. There were legal obligations entered into under the 1985 accord; they were enshrined in international law and so they had to be honoured. The Fianna Fáil advisor had moved a long way since 1985 when he urged rejection of the deal done between Garret FitzGerald and Margaret Thatcher.

The document Mansergh was now drafting on Northern Ireland was laced with a republican ethos. He admitted:

> The initial draft went to the outer limits of what was acceptable. Even when difficulties of communications were partially overcome – and in the circumstances they were difficult enough just among republicans themselves – the whole initiative was understandably treated with extreme caution on both sides.[21]

Towards the end of 1992 the Fianna Fáil/Progressive Democrat coalition collapsed. News was relayed to Mansergh that should a Fine Gael-led administration assume office in the Republic, then the declaration, and with it any peace process, would be stillborn. The leadership of the Republican Movement could have expected a much less tolerant approach from Fine Gael. The party's leader John Bruton would have had great difficulty with the idea of contact continuing without an IRA ceasefire being called. When the possibility of Fianna Fáil forming a government with the Labour Party was first mooted, Mansergh saw a route to ensuring that the progress achieved during the secret discussions over the previous five years would not be lost.

Reynolds soon found himself Taoiseach in a government

involving Fianna Fáil and the Labour Party. Work on the draft declaration continued with the Labour Party advisor Fergus Finlay joining the team of officials looking to end the IRA campaign. Finlay was told about the secret contacts but given no details. There were several discussions within the Labour camp on the merits of the Reynolds-Mansergh approach. They were aware that should news of the contacts become public, it would meet with universal criticism from the opposition benches as Fine Gael and the PDs rounded on the Government. However, as the killings continued in the North, Dick Spring decided to give the emerging process time.

Mansergh remained the main contact point, with Fr Reid continuing to act as the intermediary for the dialogue with the Republican Movement. As the possibility of a saleable strategy became more likely, Reynolds sanctioned direct contact between his advisor and the republican leadership. The meetings – generally between Mansergh and Adams – took place in the Redemptorist monastery in Dundalk. In contrast to 1988, Fr Reid remained in the room. He had previously believed it was better to leave the participants to themselves but later came to accept that this approach was wrong.

The presence of a third party helped to reduce any tension and also served, he believed, as a reminder of the task being undertaken. Martin McGuinness would often accompany Adams. The atmosphere was good; the talking would last for several hours and Reid would frequently leave to placate an impatient cook who saw uneaten meals going cold. "They got on very well and understood each other. There was no soft-peddling of positions," Reid recalled.[22]

The principal difficulty revolved around the concept of self-determination which was defined in paragraph four of the draft declaration. Those involved in the contacts recalled that the definition was contested more than any other issue in the document. Sinn Féin would quote the United Nations Charter on the rights of nations to self-determination. However, Mansergh – while accepting that the Irish people had the right to self-determination – argued that they were also free to decide just how that self-determination would be exercised. That definition was problematic for Sinn Féin as it involved acceptance of the need of unionist consent for any political movement. But the participants were moving closer to agreement on core principles which – with British involvement – would end the IRA campaign.

In April 1993 Adams and his colleagues stressed the importance they placed on the mechanics of what would happen after publication of a joint declaration; they made it clear that when talks would start and how they would operate were as important as the content in any declaration. They were keen to tie down the practical details of what exactly would happen after a ceasefire. Talks with the British Government were vital to convincing the IRA of the value of an alternative strategy. However, the Dublin administration was still unsure how the British would respond to the draft document. Reid recalled Mansergh's view at that time: "Martin used to use the expression that we have stretched our position like a bit of elastic – way out to the very point that if it went any further it would break."[23]

In May 1993 Reid met with Mansergh in Government Buildings. He had reached the conclusion that Sinn Féin was agreed in principle to the latest draft document. "I think this thing is okay," he told the Fianna Fáil advisor who immediately brought him into see Reynolds in the Taoiseach's office.[24] The dialogue over the wording was over. The next step was to convince the British to come on board. Later that day, Reid became uneasy about his assessment. "I may have put them [Sinn Féin] in a position where they were going to take responsibility for something which they really hadn't got the okay for. It was a valid interpretation of what they were saying … "[25] Uncertain about what he had told Mansergh and Reynolds, Reid returned to the advisor's office who calmed him down. "The dye is cast. Let's go," Mansergh said.[26]

It was against this backdrop in the middle of 1993 that Reynolds argued that the British could be bounced into accepting the latest draft. The Taoiseach wanted to meet the British Prime Minister in secret to hand over the document so as to emphasise the importance he personally attached to it. The idea caused consternation with the Labour Party as Fergus Finlay explained in his political memoir:

> Early in 1993, he conceived a plan involving flying to London without any further ado, under the pretext of taking in a West End show, and presenting himself at 10 Downing Street – catching John Major on the hop, and persuading him to adopt this document in its entirety.[27]

The Labour Party leader, Dick Spring, was not impressed with the idea. When the two men met, Spring argued that the British Government would have no choice but to reject the draft. Indeed, when Major was informed about the idea of a secret meeting he rejected it:

> It would never stay secret, and of course it would immediately arouse all sorts of suspicions – conspiracy theories, never far away from the Irish question, would absolutely abound. All hell would break loose. So I said, 'Come off it, Albert, we can't do that.'[28]

Reynolds and Mansergh were convinced that if the British signed up to the draft declaration, then it was probable that a cessation would be forthcoming from the IRA. Mansergh knew that the IRA Army Council had seen the document and had reacted positively. But not every one shared this assessment.

The Taoiseach was talked out of his idea of a secret meeting with Major although the draft was eventually presented to the British Government in June 1993 as an Irish Government document. Reynolds handed it over to the British official Robin Butler at Baldonnell Airdrome in Co Kildare.

The British were fully aware of the talks between Dublin and republicans. They were very uneasy about the document, especially given that it required them to become persuaders for Irish unity and to adopt a timetable for withdrawal from Northern Ireland. These proposals were unacceptable. Mansergh recalled:

To say they handled it with kid gloves would be something of an understatement. They were prepared to discuss but not negotiate it, and on several occasions in the autumn of 1993 many of them would have preferred to put it aside.[29]

The view in London was that the document was a nationalist manifesto. "Far from being a breakthrough, they still showed little comprehension of what might be acceptable to the British Government, let alone the unionist majority – to whom they offered virtually nothing," John Major wrote in his autobiography.[30]

But the prospect of achieving an IRA ceasefire continued to motivate Mansergh and his colleagues on the Irish side. The two governments agreed to redraft the document with a view to agreeing a joint Anglo-Irish Declaration. The process had now moved beyond the Mansergh-Adams dialogue and the other northern nationalist contacts. Over the following months discussions continued on what London considered a Dublin document covered with significant republican fingerprints.

The fragile process then hit a number of diplomatic crises. The first difficulty came in late September 1993 when Hume and Adams announced that their discussions were at an end and that they were giving the Government in Dublin a report containing their conclusions.

The two leaders of nationalism in Northern Ireland were unaware of the state of the negotiations between the two Governments. Their public announcement may have been an attempt to speed up acceptance of their draft text and bring about the ceasefire they both believed could be achieved. But the revelation of the behind-the-scenes contacts was greeted with mixed public and media response. The campaign of violence was still underway.

To add to the controversy, Hume departed on a trade mission to the United States. He was gone for a fortnight, leaving confusion over the status and content of a document that the Dublin Government said it had not received. "I have rarely seen the Taoiseach or Mansergh so upset," Seán Duignan wrote in his personal diary on 27 September 1993.[31] Mansergh acknowledged that "the stakes were raised dramatically" but he stopped short of criticising Hume for his action.

The reaction to revelations about the Hume-Adams contacts illustrated the dangerous undertaking Mansergh was engaged in. He had gained a reputation for discretion and an ability to maintain confidentiality. But in late November 1993, the BBC *Panorama* television programme claimed that Mansergh was acting as a contact between the Dublin Government and the leadership of the Republican Movement. Reynolds had told the Dáil the previous June that any contact with Sinn Féin was conditional on a definitive rejection of violence by republicans for achieving their political objectives.

The PD leader Mary Harney said she wanted to ask a direct question – had his advisor met either Sinn Féin or the IRA? Reynolds gave a non-committal answer: "I do not propose to go into details of the wide ranging contacts that I have … and the communication that exists … as have always existed … in trying to get information as to the situation that exists in relation to violence in Northern Ireland."[32] The Taoiseach declined to answer the content of the media reports while he sought to shift the policy criteria from no-ceasefire, no-contact to no-ceasefire, no place at the negotiation table.

The following year, in July 1994, the RTÉ *Prime Time* programme claimed that Mansergh had crossed the border to met senior republicans "in what is understood to be a series of informal but important meetings." The Dublin Government would not confirm the reports. The impression had been allowed to develop that arm's length links with Sinn Féin had been maintained. However, direct contact between the senior advisor to the Taoiseach and the Sinn Féin leadership was a different proposition. A Government spokesman said "All contacts involve community intermediaries as has been pointed out by the Taoiseach on several occasions." But the spokesman refused to say whether Sinn Féin constituted "community intermediaries".

In fact, Reynolds had sanctioned meetings between Mansergh and Adams. When he became Taoiseach in early

1992 he had had no knowledge of the background contacts or of the meetings with the republican leadership back in 1988. He was aware of the risks involved in approving direct contact:

> In a sense the violence made the risk greater to take but nevertheless things were so bad that not to have taken it would have been a failure of leadership. Martin would often remind me of the risks especially as we didn't know where the whole process would end.[33]

Mansergh added:

> All of us were conscious that in politics the dividing line between success and debacle is often a very thin one and that we had to be ready, if necessary, to sacrifice our jobs and perhaps even put ourselves at risk.[34]

Towards the end of 1993 the Taoiseach continued to talk of a pre-Christmas breakthrough. However, the mood on the British side was becoming increasingly pessimistic. They wanted the idea of a joint declaration dropped. The revelation of the Hume-Adams document caused considerable disquiet within unionist and loyalist communities in Northern Ireland. Major was under pressure from the Ulster Unionist Party at Westminster. He was constantly reminded that his Government was in a minority position in the House of Commons, dependant for survival on the support of Ulster Unionist MPs.

To counter this potential problem the Irish Government started communication with the loyalist paramilitary groups. Mansergh recommend that they use Roy Magee as an intermediary. Magee was a clergyman whose parish in East Belfast covered the UDA and UVF strongholds. The Reynolds Government sought to reassure the loyalists that they wanted peace for its own sake. At a meeting in Dublin Magee presented a set of political principles including the right to pursue constitutional change by peaceful means and the right to free political thought. Mansergh believed that the principles dealt with the concerns of loyalists and they were subsequently incorporated into the Draft Declaration. However, the principles were in fact points that the loyalists wanted to offer as comfort to nationalists. The misunderstanding only emerged after the joint declaration was published.

The Irish Government briefed several parties in the North including the Alliance Party on the discussions that were underway. It was a policy that paid dividends in building support for the initiative. The Church of Ireland Archbishop of Armagh Robin Eames was told about the content of the document. The Ulster Unionists would not meet Reynolds or Mansergh so Eames was used to assess their potential response to the emerging initiative. Indeed, Eames helped draft what became the sections in the declaration on creating greater trust between North and South. He also discussed the plan with Downing Street, telling the British that there was a desire among the unionist/Protestant population in the North for peace so long as there were no major concessions of principle.

There were few positive developments in the late autumn and early winter months of 1993. The disagreement with the British continued. Relations were increasingly acrimonious. When Reynolds met Major at a EU summit at the end of October he agreed to create some public distance from Hume and Adams. Despite these reassurances the British were still uneasy about the value of the declaration. But Reynolds was not prepared to abandon the initiative. Mansergh was providing consistent feedback from his republican contacts to the effect that a deal was possible. The British were told that if they opted out, the Irish would progress alone and publish the document as a Dublin-inspired initiative. Political brinkmanship was developed to a fine art.

While these discussions were underway the IRA campaign continued at a relentless pace. The death toll in October 1993 was the highest in any month since October 1976. Twenty-seven people lost their lives in October 1993. Ten people were left dead, and another 57 injured, when an IRA bomb exploded in a fish shop on the Shankill Road in Belfast. The IRA said the attack was intended to kill members of the Ulster Defence

Association who, they claimed, were meeting in a room above the shop. The bombing was recalled in the book *Lost Lives*:

> The attack caused widespread horror, particularly since two children and four women were among the casualties of the explosion, which took place when the Shankill Road was thronged with shoppers on a Saturday afternoon.[35]

Moreover, there was widespread condemnation of Gerry Adams when he helped to carry the coffin of Thomas Begley, the republican activist who had died in the Shankill bomb explosion.

There was another setback to the peace process when the IRA bombed the City of London causing millions of pounds in damages to the financial heart of the British capital. There were harsh words for the republican leadership but also within Government Buildings in Dublin. Seán Duignan recalled:

> This incident produced the only division of opinion on the process that I observed between the Taoiseach and his chief adviser. Mansergh did not believe, then or subsequently, that the British Government was materially swayed by the London bombing. Reynolds, however, suspected the British were deeply shaken – the IRA had hit the same district a year previously – and that the vulnerability of London to such attacks was a factor in terms of subsequent developments.[36]

During November and the early part of December 1993, intensive discussions were undertaken at official level. Mansergh and other senior Irish Government advisors met with their British counterparts to try to complete the draft document. Fergus Finlay recalled: "Martin was erudite, and constantly amazed the British side with his analytical approach to the context of our negotiations."[37]

On 19 November 1993 the *Irish Press* newspaper published a front-page exclusive revealing the contents of an Irish Government position paper which called on the British to acknowledge 'the full legitimacy and value of the goal of Irish unity by agreement' in return for changes to Articles Two and Three of the Irish Constitution. The document proposed a greater role for the Republic in policy on the North through joint North-South administrative bodies with executive powers. There was great anger within the very limited Government circle that had access to the position paper. "Reynolds and Mansergh were appalled – they regarded the leak as almost criminally irresponsible," Duignan said.[38]

The leaked position paper was, however, the least of the worries. Several more critical difficulties emerged. On 26 November Sir Robin Butler travelled to Dublin to table an alternative British document to that which had been under discussion. There was consternation in Dublin with Reynolds threatening to end the process.

Mansergh believed the British approach would not win republican endorsement particularly as the concept of self-determination was now being confined to Northern Ireland. The discussions over the preceding weeks had already diluted the nationalist thrust in the document sent to the British the previous June. As it was, republicans had approached the June 1993 document with some trepidation. Self-determination had to be based on an all-Ireland basis or the opportunity for peace would be wasted. The two documents were irreconcilable. The Taoiseach spoke of a 'breach of faith'.

To make matters worse, Butler was also to inform Reynolds of a story which would appear in that week's edition of the *Observer* newspaper. The exclusive story would reveal that the British had had secret contacts with the IRA. The contacts dated back to 1990 and they showed the British willing to hold face-to-face meetings with republicans on foot of a two-week IRA ceasefire. Unionists were to feel betrayed while in Dublin there was considerable anger. Reynolds and Mansergh – already annoyed over the new British document – reacted with fury to the news that Butler conveyed.

During the discussions on the joint declaration the British had refused to move from the position that there had to be a permanent end to violence before they would enter talks with Sinn Féin. The only positive from the *Observer* disclosure was that it was evidence that the British were serious about dealing with Sinn Féin if a ceasefire was called. Nevertheless, there was anger in Dublin. In his diaries Seán Duignan wrote: "...Taoiseach has 40-minute chat with Major – No dice, John; you double-dealed on links with Provos; you never told us, plus your communication through Sir Robin Butler on Friday was a disaster."[39]

Mansergh recalled:

> It was clearly a matter of deep embarrassment to them. The embarrassment was that they had told us nothing about it. I was told afterwards by a senior British official that the reason for the contacts was that the British Government wanted to check out for themselves what John Hume was saying to them. John Hume is the type of person who likes to take a fairly optimistic assessment, and I think each Government wanted their own direct contact with Sinn Féin so that they could form their own independent judgement.[40]

The written record of the secret contacts between the IRA and the British Government provided some evidence of the principles underpinning the latter's negotiating stance. The British were not prepared to 'join the ranks of persuaders' for Irish unity. What the Irish Government wanted to achieve with the joint declaration was a British position of neutrality on the future political and constitutional position of Northern Ireland. Crucially for the process, this objective was subsequently achieved.

Amid all the revelations and recriminations, plans for an Anglo-Irish summit on 3 December were in doubt. While it did eventually proceed at Dublin Castle there were bad-tempered clashes between Reynolds and Major. The Taoiseach accused Major of bad faith. They met in private session with Reynolds expressing his anger in undiplomatic language. Outside ministers, advisors and officials waited to see whether or not trust could be restored. When the two leaders re-emerged the British draft was not mentioned and discussions restarted on the Irish paper. The British withdrew their document. The final deal would be a compromise version of what Mansergh had drafted the previous June.

There was more toing and froing between officials and a further meeting between Reynolds and Major at an EU Summit. A deal was eventually reached on 'an agreed framework for peace'. On 15 December 1993 at 10 Downing Street the Joint Declaration was agreed. There were still doubts on the British side as Mansergh was all too aware but they "finally became convinced that they had to take hold of the peace initiative, if the moral high ground were not to be lost, regardless of whether it in fact brought peace, about which they were highly sceptical".[41]

Nevertheless there was a sense of accomplishment at Downing Street. John Mayor served champagne. Amid the celebrations Seán Duignan spoke to his governmental colleague. "I remarked to Martin Mansergh that the occasion had all the strained *bonhomie* of a shotgun wedding reception, but Mansergh said it was their natural (British) reserve."[42] The English-born Irishman was well qualified to read the mood.

Later Mansergh and Finlay worked in the British cabinet room:

> Martin Mansergh approached me with a script he had prepared for Albert's speech at the press conference, saying that it needed some rhetorical flourishes at the end, and would I mind giving a hand? So I sat at the British cabinet table in 10 Downing Street, and wrote a few paragraphs for the Taoiseach on Cabinet Office paper.[43]

The 1993 Downing Street Declaration, as it became known, provided another key foundation for the peace process. Mansergh considered it one of the highlights of the process. The original objective had been to bring republicans in from the wilderness. However, the end result was a diplomatic document that sought to encompass the views of the various participants in the Northern problem. There was widespread acceptance of the principles expressed in the document, although the DUP and Sinn Féin withheld their support.

The two governments had led the negotiations, but most of the language in the final policy document was Mansergh's. The text was both novel and complex; and it encompassed much of the language and thoughts that the Fianna Fáil advisor had been developing over the previous decade. Paul Bew and Gordon Gillespie have written that: "the Downing Street Declaration proved to be a document of considerable originality and sophistication."[44] Fergus Finlay observed: "The document was quite vague on the subject of Northern Ireland. I had a long discussion with Martin Mansergh in the course of the negotiations, and while he was giving nothing away, he spoke strongly about the need for a flexible approach."[45]

Despite the less-than-welcoming response from the republican leadership, Mansergh believed the Downing Street Declaration (DSD) was the blueprint for an end to violence. The document was based on the twin principles of self-determination and consent. These were the twin issues that had consumed so much of the time in the contacts between Mansergh and Adams over the previous years. The Republican Movement had started from a simple majoritarian theory of national determination but came to accept a more sophisticated definition. In a key section, the Downing Street Declaration noted: "It is for the people of the island of Ireland alone, by agreement between the two parts respectively, to exercise their right of self-determination on the basis of consent, freely and concurrently given, North and South, to bring about a united Ireland, if that is their wish."

Moreover, the British conceded the Irish people's right to self-determination but only in the context of the Irish Government accepting that Irish unity required the backing of a majority of people in Northern Ireland. The text contained compromises by all sides. The British gave the commitment to "encourage, facilitate and enable" agreement among the Irish people. The Irish Government accepted "that the democratic right of self-determination by the people of Ireland as a whole must be achieved and exercised with and subject to the agreement and consent of a majority of the people of Northern Ireland."

The notion of an agreed Ireland was a step away from the simple majoritarianism that had long set a majority in the North against a majority on the island as a whole. In essence, Irish nationalism was acknowledging that for unity to be achieved, the participation and agreement of the unionist people was essential. No longer was the objective a united Ireland, now it was an agreed Ireland.

As Mansergh knew, the principles in the declaration were a gamble designed to achieve an IRA ceasefire. Republicans had compromised on the principles contained in the June 1993 document. The Downing Street Declaration required further compromise. The concept of self-determination was qualified as an exercise to be undertaken by the people of Northern Ireland and the Republic but to be expressed separately. The language of Irish republicanism was being rewritten and one of the principle authors was Martin Mansergh.

The Fianna Fáil advisor understood the compromises and great leap in thinking that was now required from Gerry Adams and his supporters:

> In a sense Sinn Féin leaders were riding two horses at the same time in trying to reassure the wider leadership that this was still consistent with core demands. But they probably realised that, in practice, it was heading in the direction of a negotiated political settlement that would, certainly for the time being, fall considerably short of Irish unity.[46]

The Declaration permitted those parties that committed to permanently end the use of, or support for, paramilitary violence entry "in due course" to the political process. During the negotiations the British had sought a three-month quarantine period but the Irish Government rejected the idea. Reynolds wanted Sinn Féin included in normal political life as soon as possible. Mansergh knew that anything short of this commitment was unacceptable to the republican leadership.

Over the following months, Sinn Féin made repeated requests for clarification on the DSD. Reynolds had no difficulty clarifying the content but he was unwilling to start negotiations. Mansergh was in almost daily contact with leading republican figures. During this period the IRA maintained its campaign of violence including on the British mainland. In early 1994 IRA incendiary devices detonated in Oxford Street while mortar bombs were launched at Heathrow airport. While the devices did not explode the message about the IRA capability was obvious.

Not only was Sinn Féin seeking clarification of the declaration but the party also wanted immediate direct talks with the British Government. Gerry Adams told his party's 1994 Árd Fheis that the DSD was a significant departure in the attitude of the British Government towards Ireland but, he added, "One also has to ask, does anyone really expect the IRA to cease its activities so that British civil servants can discuss with Sinn Féin the surrender of IRA weapons after we have been 'decontaminated'?[47]

Mansergh urged the Republican Movement not to become caught up in short-term considerations but rather to make a strategic decision based on the long-term future of the people of the island. The Downing Street Declaration as a democratic framework provided a genuine political alternative to violence. There were more benefits on offer from a peace strategy. Rejection of the document would be a mistake not dissimilar to that made by Fianna Fáil over the Anglo-Irish Agreement in 1985. Tenuous distinctions should not be allowed to distract from the real fact that the Declaration had emerged from the June 1993 document known as 'Dublin's proposals'.

A three-day IRA ceasefire was announced at Easter 1994 to demonstrate that the organisation was sincere about the peace process. Major described the move as a cynical public relations exercise. There was some disappointment in Dublin that the IRA had not offered to go further but there was hope that more was to follow. Mansergh was fully aware of the intensive dialogue that was underway within the Republican Movement. The value of an unarmed strategy was being promoted by the Adams-McGuinness leadership axis. Mansergh was advising patience with the IRA despite the months that had passed since the Downing Street Declaration was published.

The Government in Dublin sought to reassure republicans and let them know that an end to violence would bring much goodwill and many advantages. Early signals were sent out in the form of what were described as 'confidence building measures'. The controversial Section 31 broadcasting ban in the Republic was lifted in January 1994. For two decades members of Sinn Féin and the IRA had not been heard on Irish radio and television. More importantly, the Clinton Administration in Washington ignored British opposition to the granting of a US visa to Gerry Adams.

Bill Clinton had been elected US President in November 1992 with the support of a key group of Irish-Americans. They sought to move US policy on Northern Ireland further up the agenda of the new administration. As the peace process moved closer towards an IRA ceasefire, they helped to redirect US policy on the North closer towards the views and attitudes of the Dublin Government.

Moreover, Clinton – who had been a student at Oxford University – had had a bad experience with the Conservative Government in London which had made clear its preference for the election of his Republican Party opponent during the 1992 presidential contest.

The appointment of Jean Kennedy-Smith in 1993 also contributed to the shift in transatlantic relations. A member of the influential Kennedy clan, she turned her residence at the Phoenix Park into a meeting place for all sides in the nascent peace process. Moreover, a powerful supporter of the Clinton administration was now in Dublin and the US President was indebted to the Kennedys for their help in securing the endorsement of the Irish-America lobby in the 1992 elections.

The arrival of Kennedy-Smith lessened the influence of the US Embassy in London over American policy on Northern Ireland. Raymond Seitz was US Ambassador in London between 1991 and 1994. He was incensed at the central role Kennedy-Smith was playing and also her none-too-private association with leading members of the Republican Movement.

In his memoirs Seitz later described Kennedy-Smith as "too shallow to understand the past and too naive to anticipate the future". His comments were scathing of his counterpart in Dublin; she was "an ardent IRA apologist," according to Seitz,[48] who was not alone in his views. Several staff members at the US embassy in Dublin dissented from Kennedy Smith's support for the Adams visa in early 1994 and made Washington aware of their concerns.

Several key US agencies advised President Clinton to refuse the visa application – Adams was associated with a group still engaged in violence while the British Government was totally against the idea. But Clinton and his immediate staff were also listening to other people, including the US Ambassador in Dublin, an Irish-American publisher Niall O'Dowd and Irish officials in Dublin and Washington. In early February 1994 Washington approved the entry to the US of the Sinn Féin leader. John Mayor spoke of his "astonishment and annoyance" at the decision.

Mansergh considered the American involvement to be highly significant. There was again the parallel with the unity of Irish-American opinion for the New Departure advocated by Parnell in 1876. On the Adams visa, Mansergh said: "While it did not produce immediate results, it made an important contribution to the eventual ceasefire."[49]

The lifting of Section 31 and approval for the Adams visa were presented to the republican leadership as evidence of the benefits that would accrue should they move towards exclusively political action. Adams and his colleagues were also given assurances that an IRA ceasefire would bring movement on the early release of prisoners and that they would be invited to a meeting at Government Building within seven days of an announcement of a complete end of violence. In December 1993 Dick Spring, the Labour Party leader and Tánaiste, raised the issue of decommissioning of IRA weapons, although the subject was not greatly progressed in public or in private at that stage when all efforts were directed at getting a ceasefire. However, the problematic subject was to return.

Mansergh had long argued that the Troubles started in the

1968-69 period because of frustration within the nationalist community in the North at their treatment as second-class citizens. He said: "While Northern Ireland was in formal terms a democracy, in reality it was no such thing, as the rights of the minority were disregarded."[50]

The Fianna Fáil advisor believed that by the summer months of 1994 the situation had been fundamentally transformed from that which prevailed in 1969, especially from a republican perspective. The different strands of Irish nationalism were uniting – only the absence of an IRA ceasefire was preventing the first public appearance of Reynolds, Hume and Adams. The Republic was re-engaged in the North in a comprehensive way not experienced since 1922. Ironically this process had been assisted by the Anglo-Irish Agreement; the deal that Mansergh had contested when it was unveiled in 1985. The other matter that had changed the political situation in 1994 was the active involvement of the United States.

Mansergh was well-versed by now in the thinking within republicanism, but as the summer months of 1994 arrived, the IRA violence continued. There was increasing scepticism about the ability of the IRA to deliver a ceasefire. Reynolds warned that without movement by the end of the summer he would draw conclusions and act accordingly. Mansergh drafted a letter to that effect, which Reynolds then sent to Sinn Féin. The idea of a limited ceasefire was rejected. A conditional ceasefire would prevent the development of confidence or trust. Sinn Féin was told that there would be no place for the party without a commitment to a lasting peace.

Over the previous months the face-to-face dialogue was undertaken on the understanding that the Irish Government advisor was speaking with the leadership of Sinn Féin. As speculation about the ceasefire continued the talks took on a new dimension with Mansergh meeting the leadership of the Provisional IRA.

Mansergh held secret talks with republican leaders in early July. The atmosphere in private was more positive than their public positioning. Martin McGuinness spoke about the early release of prisoners and the need for demilitarisation to convince the republican grassroots of the benefits of a ceasefire. "He and I met in all sorts of out of the way places. The meetings were lengthy and they seemed to go on forever. I think Martin had the right approach and certainly from my point of view he was the right person to be dealing with at that time," McGuinness recalled.[51]

By now Mansergh was familiar enough with his republican contacts to accurately read between the lines. He was encouraged at what he was hearing:

> I found them in a very, very practical-orientated mood, and essentially that the decision had been made. I'm not saying in formal terms, but just mentally the decision had been made, and it was a question of choreographing the next few weeks.[52]

In July 1994, Sinn Féin met in Letterkenny to decide its attitude to the Downing Street Declaration. Media reports indicated that a breakthrough was likely at the Co Donegal conference. But Mansergh was better informed on the mood within republicanism. He knew from republican sources that they viewed the DSD as part of a wider process, but not as a solution. The republican leadership was unhappy with what they considered 'negative and contradictory elements' within the DSD. In their view it did not measure up to June 1993 document. Moreover, any decision would only be taken when the possibility of a split in the movement had been overcome.

Mansergh's sources told him that the Letterkenny debate would appear to point towards a rejection of the DSD but the messages had to be read in terms of a wider debate within Sinn Féin and the IRA. Crucially, Mansergh was told about a briefing that Adams had given to the IRA just before Sinn Féin's conference in Letterkenny.

Fergus Finlay continued to be impressed by the quality of his colleague's intelligence: "I attended a meeting in London, with Martin and Seán Ó hUiginn, at which we warned the British Government in advance that the vibes from the Árd Fheis would be very negative. Martin asked the British to try to avoid "rebarbative comment" on the outcome (I had to look up the word when we got home – it means offensive), and assured them that a great deal of work was still going on to try to secure a ceasefire."[53] In fact Sinn Féin rejected the DSD at the party's Letterkenny conference, but Mansergh now knew that a decision had effectively been made on a ceasefire.

There was one further twist when in early August 1994 Sinn Féin sought a visa to allow the veteran republican Joe Cahill explain developments to supporters in the US. The importance of the Cahill visa was stressed to Mansergh and the Government in Dublin. This was not about propaganda but rather about convincing republican supporters in the US that the ceasefire was not a surrender to the British or a sell-out on their aims. Cahill, who was in his seventies, had twice been deported from the US after attempting to illegally enter the country. His involvement with the IRA was life-long. He was sentenced to death in the 1940s for the murder of a policeman and in the 1970s had been arrested on board a boat containing guns destined for the IRA.

Most key US officials were on holidays when the issue of the Cahill visa emerged. Once again Jean Kennedy-Smith was involved. Reynolds eventually spoke with Clinton who was on vacation at Martha's Vineyard in Massachusetts. Reynolds later recalled their conversation: "The President said to me – 'Did you read this man's CV?' And I said: 'No, I didn't have to because I don't expect the IRA to be producing saints anyway'."

However, the Taoiseach has one final card to play in convincing Clinton to go against all the advice available to him. Some days previously Mansergh had been given the text of the proposed ceasefire announcement from the IRA. He read the start of the statement to the US President who responded: "Okay, we'll take another chance. But I never want to hear from you again if this one doesn't run – goodbye."[54]

In August 1994 the process entered its most crucial stage. The final pieces in the ceasefire jigsaw were being put in place. The Cahill visa was issued. A delegation from the US arrived in Ireland lead by Congressman Bruce Morrison. The same message was being repeatedly put to the Republican Movement

– a complete cessation of IRA violence was required. The groundwork had been painstakingly laid but the participants were rewarded on 31 August 1994 when the IRA ended its campaign of violence. Reynolds was attending a meeting of the Fianna Fáil parliamentary party in Leinster House when he was given the news that the IRA had issued its statement. The statement read:

> Recognising the potential of the current situation and in order to enhance the democratic peace process and underline our definitive commitment to its success the leadership of Óglaigh na hÉireann have decided that as of midnight, Wednesday, 31 August, there will be a complete cessation of military operations. All our units have been instructed accordingly …

The justifications for an end to violence were clear. The Hume-Adams dialogue had created a unity within northern nationalism. By means of the Mansergh contacts the Government in Dublin had re-engaged in a comprehensive way with the North not evident since 1922. This coming together of the various strands of nationalism in Ireland also had the support of the US Administration, which pledged to guarantee fair play. Republican thinking on a ceasefire had considered these three developments and, as Mansergh argued, the situation was vastly different from the 1968-69 period.

The IRA announcement did not use the word 'permanent' for ideological reasons although other phrases were included to convey the republican commitment to the ceasefire. The British – and most unionists – were dubious about the IRA's intentions. They believed that the ceasefire was a tactical device.

Patrick Mayhew, who was Northern Ireland Secretary at the time, recalled that the IRA ceasefire:

> rather took us by surprise. A very welcome surprise, indeed. It would have been very dangerous and very wrong to have accepted it at face value without testing it, and thereafter treat Sinn Féin and the IRA

as if they were people who were forever done with violence; we needed to be reassured about that.[55]

The analysis was entirely different in Dublin. Mansergh was happy that the statement included the words: 'a complete cessation of violence' and 'a definitive commitment to the success of the democratic peace process'. The Fianna Fáil advisor believed the IRA commitment to a 'permanent ceasefire' was achieved in early September when Martin McGuinness said 'the ceasefire will hold in all circumstances.'

As Mansergh saw it, "complete plus definitive equals permanent."[56] He drew a historical linkage with the ceasefire statement from the anti-Treaty side at the end of the Civil War when Eamon de Valera declared: "the war, so far as we are concerned, is finished." Moreover, Mansergh argued that the August 1994 IRA ceasefire was much more explicit than either that in 1923 or the one declared in 1962 when republicans ended their border campaign.

Nine

Peacemakers

Within six days of the first IRA ceasefire announcement, Albert Reynolds hosted John Hume and Gerry Adams at Government Buildings in Dublin. Martin Mansergh attended the historic meeting, later recalling: "I was privileged to be the note-taker."[1] Unionists and loyalists were uncomfortable with the images of what they viewed as a Pan-Nationalist Front. But Reynolds was intent on drowning republicans with democracy and sought to draw them in as close as possible.

The promise to enter discussions with Sinn Féin was honoured by the Irish Government when the Forum for Peace and Reconciliation was convened at the end of October. Meeting at Dublin Castle, the Forum provided immediate access for Sinn Féin to a democratic body where many of the issues central to the developing peace process could be discussed.

For Mansergh, the modern physical force tradition in Ireland had been born with the 1798 Rebellion. Now the causes that had spurred the recourse to violence – a blockage to participation in the democratic process and draconian repression – were gone: it was possible to draw "a line under the 200-year-old physical force tradition in Irish politics."[2]

This idea was developed in two speeches written for Reynolds in the days after the IRA ceasefire announcement – the first was delivered at the opening of a commemorative site in Co Wexford where the 1798 Rebellion began and the second was for the Annual Liam Lynch Commemoration near Fermoy in Co Cork.

Lynch had been a leading republican in the War of Independence in the Munster area and had opposed the Anglo-Irish Treaty settlement. This apparently came as news to Dick Spring who asked the Fianna Fáil advisor somewhat to his "incredulity (but perhaps it was just his sense of humour): 'And who was Liam Lynch?'"[3] When Mansergh was a young boy his father had pointed out the place on the Knockmealdown Mountains where Lynch died.

> I remember talking to the Tánaiste Mr Spring in the Taoiseach's outer office, and he had a somewhat quizzical expression on his face, no doubt wondering about the appropriateness of these occasions, to the times that were in it, as I explained to him the historical background to these functions. But in fact, while honouring the past, the Taoiseach was also consciously drawing a line under it.[4]

Reynolds's speech at the Liam Lynch Commemoration was interesting in light of the extent to which post-ceasefire disputes over the decommissioning of IRA weapons delayed the advancement of the peace process. The script was quintessential Mansergh – running historical associations in parallel with contemporary developments. Just as Fianna Fáil had been brought in from the political wilderness by W.T. Cosgrave in the 1920s, Mansergh argued that the same approach had now to be applied to the Republican Movement. In his speech Reynolds observed:

> The Civil War was never resumed. Demilitarisation was successful. Prisoners were released. Republicans in due course participated in the political process, and were able to fulfil in government in the 1930s the political programme which would establish beyond doubt the compete sovereignty of the Irish State with a republican Constitution and form of government. It could be said that the Irish public liked republican politics much better, when they were dissociated from military action. At this distance in time, it is

easier to acknowledge that credit is due to W.T. Cosgrave for quickly including the participation of the newly formed Fianna Fáil Party in democratic politics in the Dáil, but also for allowing them to put their own presentation on what that involved. In the last few months, since the Declaration, I too have sought to bring Sinn Féin and the communities they represent fully into democratic politics.

While Mansergh and Reynolds may have wanted to allow the Republican Movement 'put their own presentation' on the ceasefire, and their entry into democratic politics, such an approach was not easily achieved. The decommissioning of weapons had emerged as a major stumbling block to progress.

There was no tradition of decommissioning in the history of republican uprisings. Since the 1798 rebellion the phrase 'the pike in the thatch' had conveyed the futility of pressurising for a voluntary surrender of arms. From the family holding at Friarsfield in Co Tipperary, Mansergh had some personal knowledge of the long-held republican attitudes towards decommissioning:

> ... unbeknownst to my forebears, who would have belonged to the gentry, guns were buried under a monkey puzzle tree near the house after the Fenian Rising in 1867, a spot near a plantation down the fields was used as an arms dump some time from the early to mid-20th century, because opened up, it left a large gaping hole in the ground around 1970.[5]

The Government in Dublin argued that requiring the IRA to hand over weapons before multiparty talks started was not a sensible precondition. In fact, during the 1993-94 period the idea of achieving a broad political settlement had been abandoned as too complicated. Instead, priority in the Mansergh contacts with the Republican Movement was given to ending violence. The order was peace first, with detailed negotiations leading towards a political settlement, second. The strategy meant that issues such as the disposal of weapons were sidestepped and left to accompany the eventual political settlement.

But there was a different view in London. The British Government – already concerned about the lack of the word 'permanent' in the ceasefire declaration – wanted the hand-over of arms to commence before Sinn Féin joined political talks. While a meeting between Sinn Féin and British civil servants did take place in early December 1994 there was a huge gulf in trust between the two sides despite the IRA ceasefire. Patrick Mayhew said: "Decommissioning was immediately an issue. People who retain control over weapons and who may use them for political purposes, don't have to actually use them to benefit from their influence."[6]

Decommissioning was not a new precondition but an unresolved issue that lurked in the background as attempts to get a ceasefire were undertaken. In December 1993 Dick Spring had spoken of the need for the disposal of weapons while Reynolds had warned Sinn Féin that the arms issue would have to be dealt with expeditiously once peace had been established. Mansergh had raised the subject of arms when he met with the leadership of the Provisional IRA in the lead-in to the August 1994 ceasefire. One of those present at the meeting recalled: "The question of arms was brought up but he was given a blank 'No', and when the IRA says no, that's the end of discussion on the subject." A choice was made: the leading figures in Dublin were prepared to park the arms issue so as to consolidate the IRA ceasefire.

While the decommissioning standoff was emerging as a serious issue to political movement, Government officials were negotiating what became the Framework Documents, which set out the political, legal and constitutional way forward. On 11 November 1994 Mansergh was co-chairing a meeting with Sir John Chilcot, the permanent undersecretary at the Northern Ireland Office, when news reached him that Harry Whelehan had been appointed as President of the High Court. The move precipitated the collapse of the Fianna Fáil/Labour Government, the detail of which will be discussed in a later chapter.

Albert Reynolds had led two administrations in the February 1992 to November 1994 period. The IRA had ended its campaign of violence on 31 August 1994 but this mattered little in the context of personality differences and policy clashes within the Fianna Fáil/Labour coalition. When his Government collapsed, Reynolds resigned as leader of Fianna Fáil and as Taoiseach.

On 15 December 1994 a new coalition administration took office in the Republic comprising Fine Gael, Labour and Democratic Left. The Fine Gael leader John Bruton led the three-party Government. In opposition he had displayed a more hostile attitude towards Sinn Féin than shown by the Reynolds administration. Moreover, Bruton was entering a process that had been underway for several years and which in the weeks after the August ceasefire announcement had entered its most delicate stage yet. Important personal and political relationships had developed with a great deal of trust existing between those involved. The learning curve facing the incoming Taoiseach was steep.

But he was wise to that reality. Prior to his election as Taoiseach, Bruton sought advice on a number of issues from Garret FitzGerald, his former party leader. FitzGerald suggested the retention of Mansergh as an advisor in Government Buildings. "I believed it would not be unhelpful to ask him to stay," FitzGerald recalled.[7]

Bruton had had his first real conversation with the Fianna Fáil advisor some years previously at the McGill Summer School. Mansergh impressed him. The Fine Gael leader believed Mansergh brought a rigorous historical approach to his job. But there were fundamental differences between the two men. Bruton admitted: "I don't agree with his republicanism. I think it's an introspective ideology that leads nowhere particularly useful. But I respect the sincerity with which he cleaves to this error."[8]

But the Fine Gael leader was prepared to set aside these differences given the important role Mansergh played as a contact with the Republican Movement. "I didn't want to throw aside what Albert Reynolds had done. And I felt that one way of ensuring continuity would be to have some continuity of personnel." Bruton wanted to "preserve informal contacts" with the IRA and the fact that Mansergh operated outside normal civil service channels was considered important.

The incoming Taoiseach raised the prospect of Mansergh remaining as advisor on Northern Ireland. However, the offer was declined as Mansergh believed his political home was with Fianna Fáil; to work for their political rivals would have involved a personal compromise he was unwilling to make.

When news of the decision reached Gerry Adams his reaction was extremely negative. One of the selling points for the peace process and ending the IRA campaign had been the political stability in the Republic. The Fianna Fáil/Labour coalition took office in 1992 with a huge parliamentary majority and the prospect of several successive terms in government. The argument obviously came unstuck with the political controversy in late 1994. But not only was the Government gone but Sinn Féin's main point of contact since the late 1980s had declined the opportunity to remain with the new coalition administration. "Gerry Adams was very upset with Martin's decision. He was furious with him," one individual close to the Adams-Mansergh contracts recalled.

Mansergh continued his work as Head of Research to Fianna Fáil under the party's new leader, Bertie Ahern. However, as part of the transition of power to the new Rainbow coalition, he provided Bruton with a confidential briefing on the peace process.

They met on 13 December 1994. Bruton kept a written note of the content of their discussions, which can be revealed here for the first time. Mansergh advised that there was a serious lack of personnel in the Department of the Taoiseach to deal with policy on the North. He made a number of suggestions on personnel from the Department of Foreign Affairs whose transfer would address the issue. One name mentioned was Seán Ó hUiginn. He also said that the relationship between Dick Spring and Patrick Mayhew was difficult which made it even more important to develop relations with John Major.

Bruton was informed of a number of 'symbolic gestures'

planned to consolidate and progress the peace process – eight or nine prisoners would be released in December with several more in January and emergency legislation would be lifted. Work on recasting Articles Two and Three was progressing and a new text was available which included the consent principle. Mansergh advised against issuing public invitations to unionist politicians as it only placed them under pressure and would cause difficulties should they decline.

The following is a summary of the Bruton-Mansergh meeting derived from the written note recorded in December 1994 by the Fine Gael leader:

> The distinction between peace and Sinn Féin ideology should not be forced. Too quick a move on arms could break the Sinn Féin leadership. It was psychological. They might surrender them to the Irish Government but don't use the term 'surrender'. They don't contest the process of decommissioning. There was little real disagreement on the shape of a political settlement. Adams agreed that a united Ireland was impossible without unionist support. Fifty per cent plus one was not enough. The talks-arms deadlock might be broken by the loyalists moving on arms first. Archbishop Eames was an important conduit to Molyneaux. The Framework Document was a Department of Foreign Affairs operation. A good formula had been worked out for solving the constitutional problem involving Section 75 of the Government of Ireland Act and that the papers were with the Attorney General. The Department of Foreign Affairs were planning to move Padraig Ó hUiginn but that was not a good idea.[9]

There was another crucial aspect to the conversation as recollected by the former Fine Gael leader:

He also told me that there was a clear understanding that there would be decommissioning, that that was understood by Sinn Féin but that too quick a move on decommissioning could break the leadership of Sinn Féin. But there was no question that decommissioning was part of the deal. Now he cautioned against the use of the term 'surrender of weapons' which is entirely understandable. He speculated about the possibility that the weapons might be disposed of to the satisfaction of the Irish Government, rather than in any way having anything to do with the British Government. But it was made quite clear by him to me at our meeting on 13 December 1994 that the understanding was on the part of Sinn Féin that in the context of the ceasefire there would be decommissioning by the IRA.[10]

By the end of 1994, decommissioning dominated the peace process agenda, and it would remain an apparently insurmountable obstacle for several years. The British continued to insist that there had to be some movement on arms before Sinn Féin could enter political talks. But the republican leadership wanted early movement into inclusive negotiations with no tests or obstacles in the way – the IRA had delivered a ceasefire, so now the British had to engage in talks.

However, the British Government moved with caution treating the IRA ceasefire with scepticism. In a speech in the United States in March 1995, the Northern Secretary Patrick Mayhew set down conditions republicans had to meet before joining the talks table – "the actual decommissioning of some arms as a tangible confidence-building measure."

There was also unhappiness in Dublin with the slow movement. Now in opposition Fianna Fáil could be more open in its criticism of the British. The party hierarchy was annoyed with the Major Government for failing to open ministerial talks with Sinn Féin. The need for decommissioning was not a prerequisite for entry to talks according to Fianna Fáil, which was content that the IRA ceasefire was a complete cessation.

Mansergh said in October 1995: "Fianna Fáil, neither in government nor in opposition, considered it realistic to insist on decommissioning as a precondition for talks."[11] There was an acceptance that any stipulation on arms as a precondition for access to the talks table would have "killed off the peace process" in the months prior to the August 1994 ceasefire.[12] Twelve months later when the IRA ceasefire had been ended, he observed:

> We need to recognise with lucidity that overemphasis on the decommissioning issue has played a key role in stalling the peace process. I know of no other peace negotiations in the world, where prior disarmament has been a requirement of parties coming to the table … The disposal of weapons must be negotiated, not simply peremptorily demanded.[13]

But while Mansergh and Fianna Fáil protested at the overemphasis on decommissioning, the Bruton-led coalition was dealing with the reality of an issue left unresolved in August 1994. Bruton recalled: "I believe that Fianna Fáil knew perfectly well – because Martin Mansergh was their advisor in opposition – that decommissioning was part of the deal, so any criticism that they may say of me for raising the issue were insincere."[14]

Having admired the peace process strategy whilst in opposition, Bruton as Taoiseach started to revise his assessment. There were radically different interpretations about whether or not decommissioning was part of the August 1994 ceasefire deal. "Sinn Féin said they thought resolving the arms question was not on the screen at all; Dick Spring clearly understood that it was; and the British Government understood that arms were part of the deal," Bruton said.[15] The Fine Gael Taoiseach added: "In retrospect it is clear to me that the previous Government's strategy left me with a situation where homework that they should have done before the ceasefire had not been done."[16]

Bruton also questioned the rigour of the deal done with the IRA in August 1994: "There are questions to be asked about the thoroughness with which the understanding was reached. Who was it that failed to ask questions what should have been asked?"[17]

There was much Fianna Fáil criticism of Bruton's handling of the peace process. The Ulster Unionist leadership in Belfast was closer in its thinking on decommissioning to Fine Gael than Fianna Fáil. A senior unionist advisor Steven King observed the Fianna Fáil criticism at first hand: "Some of that would stem from a slight snobbery within Fianna Fáil, and perhaps even with Martin, that they knew how to handle republicanism, and Bruton and Fine Gael were just not from the right sort of mindset to really deal with the peace process. It was a bit of the green card, wasn't it?"[18]

When Mansergh moved with Fianna Fáil from government to opposition a letter from 10 Downing Street was received. John Major wrote to the Fianna Fáil advisor that he had

> worked with single-minded devotion to move things forward, and enormous credit rightly belongs to you for what has so far been achieved. Thank you for the friendly and open manner in which you have always dealt with all of us. Your sense of humour and your profound historical knowledge have been invaluable assets.[19]

But having returned to opposition for the first time since 1987, Mansergh as a Fianna Fáil advisor had mixed views of the stance being pursued by the Conservative Government. There was some praise for Major for arguably putting the Irish question as high on the British agenda as any prime minister since Lloyd George, Asquith and Gladstone. Indeed, Mansergh placed the stumbling block within the London administration on the ground in the North. "With some exceptions ... the British political system has rarely shown much flair in handling people and affairs on this side of the water. I do not see much evidence even now that this situation has greatly improved."[20]

Bertie Ahern's speeches on the peace process – mostly written by Mansergh – were at that time laced with a strong nationalistic tone. They looked back over twentieth century Anglo-Irish history, citing times when the British walked away from pledges and shifted goal posts.

In the annual Fianna Fáil leader's address at Arbour Hill in April 1995, Ahern observed: "General Sir John Maxwell, when he ordered the executions of the 1916 leaders, was acting according to a certain disastrous military logic. We will not allow a similar style of political or lawyers' logic to wreck the peace process. It is difficult to conceive what rational political purpose is served, even from the British point of view, by singling out Sinn Féin and making political martyrs of them."

Mansergh was now adopting a higher profile. Until the IRA called its first ceasefire in August 1994 he was unknown to the wider public. The profile was fairly straightforward – he had edited a volume of the speeches of Charles Haughey, he was a Haughey loyalist and he was a nationalist with a green tinge. There was also some surprise when Reynolds asked him to remain as an advisor in early 1992. So when the IRA ceasefire was announced the media scrambled to publish a decent profile of this *éminence grise*. Few succeeded in moving beyond the basic biographical details, almost all concentrated on his Church of Ireland and Oxford University background.

However, in the aftermath of the August 1994 ceasefire his public profile dramatically increased. The wider community was getting to know a little more about the man who was so central to the creation of the peace process. He was accepting invitations to public meetings and writing articles and reviews for newspapers and academic journals. The themes were relatively narrow – the peace process and a defence of nationalism.

In an address to the Parnell Society, Mansergh let the frustrations with the slow pace of the political process come into the open:

> Our experience of the Anglo-Irish Agreement and the peace process has too often been that the main aim seems to be to slow down and dilute the dynamic for change and to reduce progress to a slow motion. The

reason or pretext cited is nearly always the unionists. Even with a new agreement, enormous inertia and, in places, hostility will have to be overcome to turn the promises of equality and parity of esteem in the Joint Framework Document into reality.

The Fianna Fáil advisor continued to argue that the IRA had not been given sufficient credit for the August 1994 ceasefire. And there was huge impatience with the delaying tactics of the British. But this was no surprise to Mansergh who observed that the British Government was merely persisting with a policy which went back as far as the Act of Union and the Treaty of Limerick – fine promises on paper were not always delivered. The reason or pretext cited by the British was nearly always the unionists, according to Mansergh.

He believed that the response of the unionist community was irrational and argued that the peace process had brought them great benefits:

> The Irish Government have been instrumental in getting the violence, which the unionists saw as directed against their community, halted for good. The halt in violence enables Northern Ireland to breath again and to recover economically.[21]

There were other reasons why the unionist response had failed to acknowledge the benefits from the peace process. Mansergh observed how the unionist community had been given a commitment that the Republic had no policy of coercion, either physically or politically. The constitutional future of Northern Ireland would be vested with the people there.

But there was annoyance with some sections of unionism: "There are those like the elderly Orangeman on television recently who seem to believe that parity of esteem and civil and religious liberty mean the right of the Orange Order to march through Catholic areas, just as 200 years ago civil and religious liberty meant in practice the penal laws."[22]

Although now a political advisor to an opposition party,

Mansergh was in almost daily communication with his republican contacts. They were telling him about the precarious position of the IRA ceasefire without a start to inclusive talks. The Sinn Féin publicity officer Rita O'Hare was one of those in regular contact with Mansergh. They had worked closely at the Forum for Peace and Reconciliation at Dublin Castle. O'Hare remarked: "Martin knew what could be done and he had an understanding of what couldn't be done. That's why he was so well placed."[23]

One of those taking heed of Mansergh's insights into republican thinking was Peter Temple-Morris, a Conservative MP with a strong interest in the North. He recalled meeting Ahern and Mansergh during the summer of 1995 when he was advised of the possibility that violence could return. "Martin was very strong about that," Temple-Morris recalled.[24] That bleak assessment came true when on 9 February 1996 the IRA ended its ceasefire. A massive bomb was detonated in Canary Wharf in the City of London. Two people were killed, millions of pounds in damage was caused. The peace process appeared to be finished. Republicans had had no expectation of entry into all-party talks. Now it appeared they had decided to pursue their objectives by other means.

Mansergh was at a conference in England when he heard news of the bombing. Canary Wharf made a huge impression on the Fianna Fáil advisor, according one of his counterparts on the unionist side. Senior Ulster Unionist advisor, Steven King observed: "Canary Wharf had a profound impact on his thinking. I think he had convinced himself that Sinn Féin was utterly sincere. Canary Wharf came as a real shock to Martin. I think since then he has been a little more wary of the Republican Movement."[25]

The Canary Wharf bombing happened just days after publication of the report of the International Decommissioning Commission, the body vested with responsibility for ending the stalemate on the arms issue. The Commission had been established the previous autumn although not without tension within the Irish Government.

In his autobiography, John Major observed that the differences "in Dublin led to some strange episodes."[26] He recalled how senior officials from the Department of the Taoiseach agreed terms of reference for the International Commission but then "a posse of officials from other departments arrived in hot pursuit, and spent the next day unpicking all that had been agreed."[27]

Relations between the Taoiseach and senior Iveagh House officials had become very tense, in particular, the relationship between Bruton and Seán Ó hUiginn. The latter remained the leading departmental contact with Sinn Féin and was the official who Mansergh had recommended to the Fine Gael leader as an advisor in late 1994. But there were other more serious problems. The differences between the Government's two most senior political figures – Bruton and Spring – were also clearly obvious to their British counterparts.

The International Commission offered a glimmer of hope on decommissioning. Chaired by George Mitchell, the US politician and Clinton confidant, the Commission proposed that arms be decommissioned during political talks, a compromise between the British demand for prior decommissioning and the republican argument that the process start at the end of negotiations. But in the absence of an IRA ceasefire there was no place for Sinn Féin at the talks table. In any event the Republican Movement had given up on both Bruton and Major.

The peace process remained on hold until the summer of 1997 when elections in Britain and the Republic led to changes of government with Tony Blair and Bertie Ahern taking office in their respective countries. The political landscape was changed. The New Labour Government with Mo Mowlam as Northern Secretary agreed to Sinn Féin's entry into talks without any precondition on decommissioning. The talks would convene in September and Sinn Féin would be welcomed to the table six weeks after a renewed IRA ceasefire.

In the Republic, Mansergh was back in Government Buildings as Special Advisor to Bertie Ahern, the third Fianna Fáil Taoiseach who employed him in this influential position. Mansergh spent the early weeks of the new coalition working with republican contacts to obtain a second ceasefire. Ahern had told the new British Prime Minister he needed a month to get the peace process back on track. Following intense behind-the-scenes diplomacy, Mansergh got the result the new Government desperately wanted.

The key move was a new British attitude on the arms issue. The Labour Government conceded that Sinn Féin could participate in talks without any decommissioning of IRA weapons provided the party accepted the principles enshrined in a report on decommissioning written by Senator George Mitchell and published in January 1996.

The Mitchell report said that those parties involved in all-party negotiations should affirm their commitment to democratic and exclusively peaceful means for resolving political issues. It also suggested that consideration be given to some decommissioning during the process of all-party negotiations, rather than before or after.

John Major's Conservative Government had in fact accepted the Mitchell Report but there was no progress in the absence of an IRA ceasefire. The outgoing Northern Secretary, Patrick Mayhew, acknowledged the necessity for the shift in British Government policy:

> We moved a long way from an initial, very simple and hard position. We did so because we came to accept – or, at any rate, believed that we ought to show that we accepted – that people in the IRA were not going to make what would seem to them to be a surrender. We came to realise that this was part of their philosophy, but of course we were all the time asking ourselves, and being told, 'you're being taken for a ride'.[28]

Any progress in the last months of Conservative rule was always going to be difficult given the level of distrust that existed between London and the republican leadership. Moreover, Major was dependant upon Ulster Unionist members at Westminster for his majority in the House of Commons. The situation changed in May 1997. Tony Blair had a commanding parliamentary majority so the Ulster Unionists were deprived of the influence the numbers game at Westminster had provided during the previous few years. The restoration of the IRA ceasefire – and republican acceptance of the Mitchell Principles – were now the main obstacles to Sinn Féin's involvement in the talks process.

The day before the second IRA ceasefire was announced Ahern was in his office in Government Buildings meeting Niall O'Dowd, the influential publisher of the New York-based *Irish Voice* newspaper. Mansergh burst into the room interrupting the meeting. In his hand he had the document Ahern had been waiting for – a statement in the name of Adams and McGuinness. The two Sinn Féin leaders said they had gone to the IRA and they expected the paramilitary organisation to announce a new ceasefire. Ahern thumped his fist in the air. The IRA declared its second ceasefire on 18 July 1997. Not long afterwards, one international publication observed that "According to a leading Dublin political observer 'you couldn't fit an envelope' between the views of Martin Mansergh and those of Sinn Féin President Gerry Adams."[29] There was some truth in the assessment with the republican leadership moving nearer to acceptance of constitutional action as the means to achieving their political aspirations.

Mansergh was impressed by the attitude displayed by the Blair Government, which he considered a decisive factor in the progress made in the summer of 1997. Not that there were no difficulties. The IRA shot dead two police officers in Lurgan on 16 June at a time when Sinn Féin representatives were in discussions with British officials. The Orange Order's annual marching season caused further problems especially the British decision to force the controversial Drumcree parade down the nationalist Garvaghy Road in Portadown.

The reaction of the British Government to the marching season "leant somewhat towards the unionist side," according to Mansergh who believed, the prospects for another ceasefire were "touch and go."[30] The British viewed the Irish Government opposition to marches through Catholic areas as unhelpful. But the response was important, Mansergh said, in convincing republicans "that there had indeed been a change of Government, not just a change in personnel at the top in Dublin."[31]

The multi-party talks process had actually commenced in June 1996 but without the participation of Sinn Féin who remained excluded while the IRA was off-ceasefire. George Mitchell, Bill Clinton's economic advisor on Northern Ireland, had been given the unenviable task of chairing the talks. He also subsequently headed the international body on decommissioning, which also involved the Finnish politician Harri Holkeri and John de Chastelain, a Canadian general.

The talks were divided into three interlocking strands. The first strand concerned the parties in Northern Ireland. The second dealt with the relationship between the North and the Government in Dublin. The third stand addressed relations between the governments in Dublin and London. However, the first phase of the talks process was undermined by rows over rules and procedures. Set against that background, the absence of Sinn Féin and the IRA's renewed violent campaign, little of substance was achieved before the Westminster elections in May 1997.

The change of governments in London and Dublin – along with the second IRA ceasefire – injected fresh momentum into the process when the talks reconvened in September 1997 at the Castle Buildings complex within the Stormont estate. The characterless venue consisted of modified civil servant offices, described by one participant as "the original sick building." This was where the participants were to spend the next seven months. The negotiations were serious but most of those involved did not talk directly to each other. When the Ulster Unionists wanted to address Sinn Féin they made their comments to Mitchell.

When the talks first started in 1996 the unionist parties had attempted to remove Mitchell as chairman who they perceived as favouring the nationalist side. Unsuccessful at this, they then tried to downgrade his role. But as time was to prove, the talks participants were fortunate in having the American Senator as their chairman. Mitchell considered carefully the contributions from all sides. His training as a judge was useful in dealing with the strained relations between the parties. Patience was his most salient quality. Nevertheless, the delegations continued to operate in the same building but without any interaction. They talked through the chairman and avoided each other in the canteen. Progress was painstakingly slow.

Following the June 1997 general election Mansergh continued his contact with the leadership of the Republican Movement. Over the following months secret meetings with republican leaders became a regular feature of his weekly routine. Once Sinn Féin joined the talks in September 1997 the secret discussions centred on the constitutional, institutional and political issues that would eventually comprise the Good Friday Agreement. Mansergh worked alongside senior civil servants Paddy Teahon, Tim Dalton and Dermot Gallagher, the latter swapping responsibilities with Seán Ó hUiginn in Iveagh House.

These secret talks went on for several months before Good Friday in 1998 but there was never a leak. Few notes were taken as the two sides pored over draft texts teasing out ideas, seeking movement in positions and arguing over interpretation of words and sentences. One Irish participant recalled: "They were tough negotiations and hard things were said. But we all knew they were probably the most important negotiations since the Treaty in 1920."

The delegations met regularly in places such as Dundalk, Ballymacscallen and Belfast. The Irish personnel would make their way to an agreed meeting place from where they would be collected and taken to what was known as "the teach" in west Belfast or another republican stronghold. Security sources in the Republic were increasingly expressing concern for the personal safety of the Taoiseach's Special Advisor on Northern Ireland.

Information was conveyed to Bertie Ahern that Mansergh was under threat from loyalist paramilitaries. "He was a target. We know he was watched," one senior Fianna Fáil source confirmed. Loyalists would for security reasons have had difficulty attacking a senior politician from the Republic while the civil service members of the talks delegation were relatively unknown figures. However, since the August 1994 IRA cease-fire Mansergh had emerged from the background to become a public figure who was well-known to all involved in the peace process.

The Irish civil servants were advised not to travel in their own cars; indeed they generally had a driver when going north. Moreover, the Sinn Féin delegation travelled by car but never in the same vehicle nor by the same route. Mansergh, however, had a set routine leaving Government Buildings by foot for Connolly Station from where he would take the train to Dundalk or Belfast. The train allowed him to read and get work done.

Ahern was advised of the dangers involved. "We had two stand-up fights with him in the six months leading up to the Good Friday Agreement to get him to stop taking the bloody train," a senior Fianna Fáil source recalled. One Government official remembered a row when Mansergh was bluntly told: "These guys need only walk onto the train when it's stopped at the station in Portadown. They know what you look like."

It eventually took the intervention of Martin McGuinness to convince Mansergh to alter his travelling routine. Sinn Féin's Chief Negotiator was increasingly exasperated with the Fianna Fáil advisor:

> I told him that I had a very deep concern about the way he was travelling back and forward from Dublin to Belfast at a time when the loyalists were involved in killing … I think he was probably fed up listening to me telling him that.[32]

During the peace process it was not just Sinn Féin representatives who were bemused by the train-travelling Irish Government advisor. When Mansergh met the political representatives of the Irish National Liberation Army in 1996 to assess the possibility of that group calling a ceasefire, he arrived in Portlaoise by train. Gerry Ruddy of the Irish Republican Socialist Party, who was present at the meeting, recalled:

"Because he came by public transport he would be checking his watch and working out the time it would take him to get to the train station."[33]

All of these contacts were undertaken in secret. Mansergh has great admiration for the risks taken by John Hume in opening dialogue with republicans in the late 1980s. He was appalled at the negative media commentary heaped upon the SDLP leader when news of his meetings with Gerry Adams first emerged. However, Mansergh also put his safety at risk. Personal danger was present from the time he accepted Haughey's request to meet with the republican leadership in 1988. But the face-to-face contact was crucial to the success of the peace process as Mansergh explained:

> To enable people to be willing to make critical strategic decisions for their movements – which carried far greater risks for them – a relationship of trust had to be created, and ultimately that was virtually impossible to do at a distance.[34]

His family were aware of the dangers inherent in the secret discussions but there was full support. The motivation was another example of the value of public duty that first prompted Mansergh to enter the public service in the 1970s and would for two decades drive his desire to contest a general election to be elected to serve the people in Dáil Éireann. But the peace process contacts brought great personal risk.

Mansergh was fully aware of the thin dividing line in politics between success and failure. However, the contacts with the Republican Movement brought more than normal political risk. If they were made public the political fall-out would most likely have seen him lose his job. There was also huge personal risk and there was no way of determining the safety factor.

The full extent of his involvement in the peace process was not discussed in any detail: even close family members were unaware of the specifics of the additional responsibilities that had been taken on board. Mansergh recalled: "In December

1993, when potentially actionable reports started to appear in the British tabloid press about meetings with the IRA and the UVF leaders north of the border, I recall going home at the weekend to Tipperary and being comforted to be told that, regardless of their truth or otherwise, everyone was behind me."[35]

On several occasions, Mansergh expressed concern about media coverage of the peace process. He said that it was not always conducive to a positive outcome to have the media camped outside the talks venue, "waiting to see who has moved a millimetre" during negotiations. He also highlighted media misinformation – "alive and well" in some quarters. At a media conference in February 2000 Mansergh cited two separate reports in the British media over the previous seven days relating to Sinn Féin and the IRA, which contained "not a scintilla of truth."[36]

The benefit of Mansergh's contacts with the republican leadership was evident when the multi-party talks recommenced in September 1997 with Sinn Féin's participation for the first time. The Ahern Government was fully aware of the sensitivities and specific pressures within republicanism. However, Mansergh was able to advise the Taoiseach when Sinn Féin was in genuine trouble over certain issues as opposed to when the party was simply adopting positions for its own political advantage. He had a unique read on the leadership of the Republican Movement.

Dermot Gallagher, a senior Irish foreign diplomat who became involved in the talks around that time, recalled:

> Martin had a particular status with the Republican Movement. He was one of the first to engage intellectually with them and they clearly took him very seriously. Even at the end when they might have been dealing closely with Paddy Teahon or Tim Dalton or myself they always had a particular deep respect for Martin.[37]

There was some political posturing by unionists after the

arrival of Sinn Féin at Castle Buildings in September 1997.
Relationships were still non-existent as was obvious to all
participants at the talks venue in Stormont. Despite the fact that
the representatives of unionism and republicanism were not
directly talking to each other, the very fact that they were under
the one roof was a significant advance. But the pace of
discussions was painstakingly slow. All sides were watching
their patch.

The structure of the talks continued to be based on the three
stranded approach which had been devised for the
unsuccessful multi-party talks in the early 1990s. The main
decision within Strand One concerned the structure of the new
administration to be formed in North; the type of assembly and
the workings of an executive that would emerge from its
membership. Strand Two dealing with relationships between
North and South was concerned with how powerful any North-
South ministerial bodies would be and the changes in the
Republic's Constitution. The least contentious part of the talks –
Strand Three – centred on East-West relations, that is, the
relationship between England, Scotland, Wales, Northern
Ireland and the Republic.

Unionists were keen to see a dilution of the Republic's
constitutional claim to the North. During the talks in 1992 –
held in the absence of Sinn Féin – the Dublin Government had
resisted suggestions that changes should be made to Articles
Two and Three of the Irish Constitution. Indeed, in November
1997 Mansergh said the question of deleting Articles Two and
Three, "simply does not exist". The comments provoked angry
responses from unionists who viewed the controversial clauses
with anger given their explicit claim of jurisdiction over
Northern Ireland.

The Deputy Leader of the Ulster Unionists John Taylor
dismissively said: Mansergh was "a man who knows very little
about Northern Ireland ... [and] ... That has become quite clear
in recent months and if he said that the question of Articles
Two and Three is a question that does not exist, it underlines
how little he understands about the reality of what is
happening at the talks at Stormont."[38] Despite Mansergh's

public comments on Article Two and Three, in private the Fianna Fáil-led Government accepted that change was inevitable. A continuation of the status quo would not assist in the attainment of a deal with Trimble and his colleagues.

To make matters worse, in terms of unionist reaction, Mansergh made his comments at a debate in West Belfast on the subject of the need for a nationalist consensus. The UUP leadership made their disquiet known at a subsequent meeting with the Dublin Government. "There is not yet within the Irish Government a realisation of the need for change and without that there will be no progress," Trimble told reporters.[39]

The Ulster Unionist leader dryly added that he considered it inappropriate that Mansergh should attend political rallies and involve himself in party political activities. Trimble was neglecting the fact that Mansergh was not a civil servant but an advisor to Fianna Fáil, the main party in the Republic's Government. But within the wider unionist community there was an increasing awareness of the sharpness of the Irish Government advisor. The unionist-leaning *Belfast News Letter* newspaper wrote: "There are some capable people at the Northern Ireland Office, but if their brains are Land Rovers, solid and reliable, then Mansergh's is a Porsche."[40]

The talks were initially due to conclude at the end of May 1998. However, towards the end of March George Mitchell set an Easter week deadline – midnight on Thursday, 9 April 1998. The decision was aimed at focusing minds and moving the delegations into serious negotiations. Moreover, sticking to the May timetable would have had the uncomfortable proposition of holding a referendum on the agreement at the height of the Orange Order marching season.

Mitchell wanted continuous negotiations from Monday 30 March until the Easter Thursday deadline. The game plan outlined by the American Senator was to have a first draft ready by Friday 3 April; reactions and responses from the delegations would be sought over that weekend with a second draft being completed for Monday 6 April. What would follow, Mitchell hoped, would be intense negotiations leading to a final deal by his cut-off point. The negotiations – which had started

22 months, previously – came down to a game of poker as the deadline came closer. All sides were refusing to show their hand. Bluff became a new weapon.

Mansergh's main area of responsibility was dealing with the constitutional changes that were under consideration. In many respects, a balanced constitutional agreement was at the heart of the talks process because from the constitutional arrangement flowed the institutional, human rights and equality issues. Mansergh was drawing on the historical work of his father in rewriting the terms of the Act of Union of 1801, the Government of Ireland Act of 1920, the Anglo-Irish Treaty of 1921 and, most particularly, the 1937 Irish Constitution.

The Irish Government was prepared to rewrite Articles Two and Three of the Irish Constitution so as to secure a deal. However, finding a suitable form of words was not easy, as the changes meant the removal of the Irish territorial claim to Northern Ireland. This was difficult for northern republicans to accept. At one meeting Bairbre de Brun of Sinn Féin made known her deep unhappiness with the proposals while Gerry Adams forcefully told Mansergh the changes were "totally unacceptable". One senior Irish Government official recalled: "A week before Good Friday it seemed distinctly possible that Sinn Féin would not accept the formula on Articles Two and Three. Martin could be very, very tough with them. He wasn't above raising his voice. I recall there were quite tough discussions."

Mansergh started from the position that Articles Two and Three were not an end in themselves but rather a means to facilitate a united Ireland. He reached a judgement that the achievement of that objective was better facilitated by changing the wording rather than through a preservation of the status quo.

The Irish Constitution drew a distinction between the Nation and the State. Mansergh argued that maintaining the integrity of a 32-county nation was a more important objective than a jurisdiction claim for the entire island. The wording also had to guarantee northern nationalists their membership of the Irish nation.

Moreover, he argued that the controversial articles contested the legitimacy rather than the legality of Northern Ireland, the latter having been conceded in 1925 with the Boundary Commission agreement. However, a political decision had been taken to deny the legitimacy of the North after the removal of the safeguards for nationalists, including proportional representation and non-discrimination, contained in the 1920 Government of Ireland Act. Given that those safeguards would be reinstated Mansergh argued that the political imperative for denying legitimacy would be removed, thereby allowing for changes to Articles Two and Three.

The new Article Two would create a clear link between nation and territory: "It is the entitlement and birthright of every person born in the island of Ireland which includes its islands and seas, to be part of the Irish nation." The proposed wording would strengthen the birthright of northern nationalists to Irish citizenship.

A new British Northern Ireland Constitution Act was drafted to supersede all previous legislation. Mansergh would later write: "The Act of Union may still be on the British statute book ... but it is now a dead letter as far as determining the future of Northern Ireland is concerned."[41] The British were being removed from the equation; sovereignty was being transferred from the Westminster parliament to the people of Northern Ireland acting with the people of the Republic.

The Irish Government was not conceding any explicit constitutional recognition for Northern Ireland but the new Article Three contained an acknowledgement of the North's existence. The territorial claim was being removed and the principle of consent enshrined as the means for one day peacefully establishing a united Ireland.

The Ulster Unionists met with the Irish Government to discuss the proposed text of the reworded Articles Two and Three of the Irish Constitution. Afterwards John Taylor told the media the Irish side was refusing to reveal the final text. Not so, countered the PD minister, Liz O'Donnell – "they are aware of the outline of the text." In fact, Mansergh – the primary draftsperson of the amendments – was present at a meeting with a UUP delegation when an outline of the proposed changes was given. But Taylor and his colleagues wanted to see the exact wording.

There was also unease within Fianna Fáil at the proposed constitutional changes. The party's republicanism was often underdeveloped and motivated more by chest thumping than serious intellectual rigour. Nevertheless, the aspiration of a united Ireland was one of the few objectives that provided party cohesion. Towards the end of March 1994, as the talks process entered its final decisive stage, Mansergh accompanied the Taoiseach and David Andrews, the Foreign Minister, to a meeting with Fianna Fáil backbench TDs. The trio wanted to calm unease over the proposed changes to Articles Two and Three. They spent two-and-a-half hours briefing party members on all aspects of the talks process but the constitutional changes were of most interest.

The Taoiseach later noted the involvement of his advisor in getting Fianna Fáil support for the constitutional changes, in the context of the Good Friday negotiations, pointing to:

> ... your mastery of the historical sweep and dimensions of the whole area and your acute sense of strategy and of what was politically possible. The latter sense and your outstanding drafting skills were vital in working out the package of constitutional amendments that was able to command such enthusiastic and widespread support in Fianna Fáil and, I believe, in the country at large.[42]

The Irish Government wanted powerful cross-border bodies to emerge from the negotiations. These bodies had to be underpinned by real links between a new assembly in the North and the Government in the Republic. This would only be achieved if the North-South dimension was enshrined in legislation passed at Westminster: anything less left open the prospect of unionists operating the northern institutional dimension but choosing not to work the cross-border bodies.

Mansergh placed great emphasis on these bodies seeing them as one step closer to the objective of a united Ireland. But the unionists were unhappy with the idea of substantial North-South co-operation. They feared that the cross-border structures would become the embryo government of a united Ireland. But as one media commentator noted: "Crudely put, if nationalists were going to agree to an Assembly, and tolerate a dilution of Articles Two and Three they would require a strong and vibrant North-South council with executive powers. Through this body, the Republic would be inextricably involved in the North's life."[43]

As the 9 April deadline approached discussions on the three strands continued. Officials from Dublin and London continued to work on a joint paper on cross-border co-operation. Mitchell promised to have a draft agreement with the talks participants by Friday 3 April so that they could consider the contents over the weekend ahead of the final few days of negotiations. However, the two governments had difficulty reaching agreement. Mitchell only received the Strand Two document on Sunday evening. Independent cross-border bodies were proposed with the objective of implementing decisions of a North-South Ministerial Council. The list of areas for co-operation was significant.

The outline of how the North-South Ministerial Council would operate was accompanied by a series of Annexes listing the areas of co-operation as well as allowing for the establishment of cross-border implementation bodies. More-over, the legal status for the Council and the related bodies was derived from Dublin and London thereby bypassing the new assembly in Northern Ireland.

The US Talks Chairman predicted that the Ulster Unionists would balk at the contents in Strand Two. The assessment proved correct. David Trimble and his colleagues were furious. John Taylor remarked that he "wouldn't touch this paper with a 40-foot barge pole." There was the real possibility that the Ulster Unionists would withdraw from the talks. However, any dilution of the draft to appease unionists risked antagonising Sinn Féin.

Mansergh spoke with the Taoiseach. The advisor recalled the choice facing Ahern:

Was he going to stick out for a maximalist North-South dimension, in which case the likelihood was that the negotiations would break down and the Irish Government principally would be blamed? Or was he going to accept a more realistic position?[44]

Events at Castle Buildings were complicated by a family bereavement. Ahern's mother Julia died in Dublin on Monday, 6 April. He left for her funeral mass the following day but returned to Belfast before the burial on Wednesday. By now, round-the-clock meetings were taking place between the delegations. It seemed that the Irish Government was going to dig in over Strand Two and the contents that had been agreed with the British. But when Ahern returned to Stormont on Wednesday evening a crucial meeting was held between himself, Blair and Trimble.

The British Prime Minister set out the position – unless Strand Two was revisited the talks would be over and the Irish Government would be blamed. The result of the meeting was a re-negotiation of Strand Two. The number and power of the cross-border bodies were reduced significantly. Ahern had compromised. But Trimble considered the concessions a climb down. His advisor Steven King later wrote: "As David gleefully reported to me immediately after the meeting, 'I have just witnessed the ritual humiliation of an Irish Prime Minister.'"[45]

Indeed, King retained the lasting impression that: "The end result was that Ahern backed down. The feeling we had, was that Ahern did his own thing and that Martin would have preferred to have held to a more rigid line on North-South bodies."[46] However, Mansergh believed there would have been the same unionist reaction, regardless of whatever structures and authority was proposed for cross-border co-operation.

In the main, Mansergh was not directly involved in the face-to-face negotiations at Castle Buildings. The talks were driven by politicians from the various participating parties, and also by the two governments. Mansergh's role was as a reference point for the Taoiseach who continuously checked and rechecked every sentence of every proposal with his political colleagues and advisory staff. Ahern explained the role played by his Special Advisor on Northern Ireland during the Good Friday negotiations:

> The thing about a fellow like Martin Mansergh is that when he's around it's a help because he'd be there keeping the parts together. It'd be important to check back, to be able to come back and talk to somebody, particularly in the kind of battle that was going on during that week when the discussions weren't just between myself and Tony Blair.[47]

The talks were nearing end-game. Mitchell and his staff held the master copy of the emerging deal. It was stored on a computer disc and was constantly being updated. Although the discussions continued, on several occasions it appeared that the process would break down.

With the Irish Government's acceptance of a diluted Strand Two a deal was concluded on cross-border bodies but there was still no agreement on Stand One, and the assembly and administration that would run Northern Ireland. Trimble and his colleagues initially favoured a government through a committee system – avoiding a cabinet would ensure they did not have to sit around the same table as Sinn Féin ministers.

The SDLP wanted an inclusive executive whose membership was drawn from a directly-elected assembly. As the midnight deadline neared, Trimble eventually agreed to move towards the SDLP position. Mansergh recalled John Hume and his party colleagues rushing into the offices of the Irish Government. There were hugs all round. A deal was now looking more likely.

As the negotiations at Castle Buildings entered their final hours, Ian Paisley and about 150 of his Democratic Unionist Party supporters arrived at Stormont. Paisley had boycotted the talks process. An impromptu press conference was interrupted by heckles from loyalists. Their shouting and chanting could be heard inside Castle Buildings. Members of the various delegations watched the scenes on television screens in their office complex.

Throughout the night there was much moving between the offices of the various delegations, but still unionists and republicans were not involved in direct communications. More and more people were arriving at the talks complex. These new arrivals were dubbed "Talks Tourists" by the Women's Coalition. The participants were nearing exhaustion as the negotiations entered Good Friday, 10 April 1998. The midnight deadline imposed by Mitchell passed but there were still several outstanding issues.

There were key interventions at various stages during the night from Bill Clinton. The US President was kept briefed on the details of the talks. He spoke by phone separately with Adams and Trimble, offering reassurance and encouragement. The participants were edging towards a deal but Sinn Féin had outstanding concerns.

In the early hours of Good Friday morning – to the dismay of officials from the two governments – Sinn Féin produced a list of outstanding issues on which they wanted clarification. Around this time Paul Bew, the Queens University academic and Trimble confidante, arrived at Castle Buildings having been told by members of the Ulster Unionist delegation that a deal was close. Bew lost his way inside the complex and found himself in the offices of the Irish delegation where despondency was the dominant mood. Mansergh was worse for wear. Bew recalled: "Exhaustion had taken over. Martin was a crumpled wreck, lying beside the window, utterly exhausted, as crumpled as you'll ever see him."[48]

Despite the exhaustion there was more work to be done to prevent the process collapsing. Ahern recalled the Sinn Féin intervention:

> I remember at one stage in those discussions when Sinn Féin came up with, as they are brilliant at doing, another 80 points that they wanted clarification on. Martin Mansergh would be the guy to go to, to say 'How do we answer all of these?'[49]

The release of paramilitary prisoners continued to cause

problems for Sinn Féin. A deal was eventually agreed which envisaged all prisoners being released within two years. References to decommissioning in the draft text also had to be changed to accommodate Sinn Féin concerns. The Republican Movement was not prepared to accept prior decommissioning as a precondition for joining the new executive. A compromise was agreed whereby the obligation of decommissioning was shared by all participants. The parties including Sinn Féin would use their best efforts to convince others to decommission arms. Decommissioning and participation in government were linked, one was dependent on the other.

An extraordinary night, to end an extraordinary week, appeared to be concluding in success as the dawn broke on Good Friday morning. But members of the Ulster Unionists were unhappy with what they considered as serious concessions to Sinn Féin. The UUP had started from a position that republicans would only be allowed to join the executive after the IRA decommissioned. What the draft agreement proposed was a long way from that original position. The deal allowed for Sinn Féin ministers without a start to decommissioning. Shortly after eight o'clock in the morning Trimble and his colleagues met to discuss the problem. The other participants were fully aware of the delicate position the process had reached.

Everyone was tired and on edge. Few had had sleep. There had been almost 36 hours of continuous meetings. So much had been achieved but it was still not clear whether or not a deal was going to be done. Martin McGuinness recalled the scene:

> I ran into Martin Mansergh some time towards the middle of the day. There were intense debates and discussions taking place within the Ulster Unionist negotiating team. I said to Martin, 'What's wrong now, what's the problem?' Mansergh replied: 'It's you, Martin – the fact that you're going to be in government.'[50]

Blair eventually wrote a side-letter to Trimble promising a

review of the participation rules in the event of any group not abiding by the democratic process. There were mixed views within the Ulster Unionist negotiating team. Ken Maginnis argued for acceptance – it was time to compromise. But the lack of prior decommissioning was too much for Jeffrey Donaldson, another member of the delegation, who left Castle Buildings. Trimble telephoned George Mitchell who turned to his staff and said: "They're ready to do business." It was 4.45 p.m. on Good Friday afternoon.

The Talks Chairman called all the participants together and at five o'clock on 10 April 1998, Mitchell declared:

> I am pleased to announce that the two governments and the political parties of Northern Ireland have rea-ched agreement. The Agreement proposes changes in the Irish Constitution and British constitutional law to enshrine the principle that it is the people of Northern Ireland who will decide, democratically, their own future.

The Good Friday Agreement proposed a balanced constit-utional settlement. The principle of consent was central to future relations on the island while national self-determination would be exercised North and South separately but concurr-ently, and without British interference. The Irish Government agreed to recommend a constitutional amendment to change Articles Two and Three. Mansergh was the principal author of the new wording.

The new Article Two stated:

> It is the entitlement of every person born in the island of Ireland, which includes its islands and seas, to be part of the Irish nation. That is also the entitlement of all persons qualified in accordance with law to be citizens of Ireland. Furthermore, the Irish nation cherishes its special affinity with people of Irish ancestry living abroad who share its cultural identity and heritage.

The new Article Three stated:

> It is the firm will of the Irish nation, in harmony and friendship, to unite all the people who share the territory of the island of Ireland, in all the diversity of their identities and traditions, recognising that a united Ireland shall be brought about only by peaceful means with the consent of a majority of the people, democratically expressed, in both juris-dictions of the island. Until then, the laws enacted by the Parliament established by this Constitution shall have the like area and extent of application as the laws enacted by the Parliament that existed immed-iately before the coming into operation of this Con-stitution.

The new wording was a formula that all sides involved in the talks were able to live with and more importantly, could sell to their respective constituents. Mansergh also achieved an-other objective. Previously when the Irish and British govern-ments had reached agreements different preambles were used for their respective texts. For example, in the 1985 Anglo-Irish Agreement the preamble to the British text read:

> Agreement between the Government of the United Kingdom of Great Britain and Northern Ireland and the Government of the Republic of Ireland

Whereas the preamble to the Irish text read:

> Agreement between the Government of Ireland and the Government of the United Kingdom[51]

In the negotiations on constitutional change, Mansergh was determined that this anomaly would be ended so that the two States would use a single designation respectively for each other. This objective was achieved with the Good Friday Agreement.

On the institutional side the agreement proposed a 108-

member assembly, which would work with the Government in Dublin in a North-South Ministerial Council to progress co-operation on numerous areas of mutual interest. A new policing service representative of the wider community would be established. Arrangements for decommissioning of para-military arms and a commitment to demilitarisation were included in the deal. The governments also agreed to an early release programme for prisoners convicted of terrorist offences. Mansergh noted the historical precedent for the release of prisoners. The British had approved a number of amnesties in the 17th century. Those imprisoned in 1798 were released in 1802, and those who took part in the 1848 rising were pardoned a decade later. An amnesty for political prisoners took place fairly quickly in the 1916 and 1924 period.

Many people were involved in securing the Good Friday deal, but Mansergh played a pivotal role within the Irish Gov-ernment delegation. Indeed, his involvement was central to the success of the negotiations. "Centrally located among the Irish officials was Martin Mansergh," Mitchel McLaughlin of Sinn Féin observed, "People came with different expectations. Mar-tin was an important part of keeping the big picture in view."[52]

There was praise from many quarters. In a hand written note, President Mary McAleese said: "With greatest respect and admiration for the work of your patient, scholarly genius. Well done."[53]

A letter of thanks was received from his employer. Bertie Ahern observed: "Since independence, few public servants have played a role in the advancement of the welfare of our country and nation that can compare with your extraordinary contribution." The letter went on: " … you deserve, I believe, to be seen as one of the principal architects of the Agreement now reached … the process bears your finger-prints at every stage."[54]

The Taoiseach also acknowledged the importance of Mansergh's contacts with the Republican Movement: "Your credibility among those in that group who were seeking to embrace the path of democratic politics was a very valuable asset in this whole process."[55]

On 22 May 1998 the Good Friday Agreement received popular endorsement in separate referendums in Northern Ireland and the Irish Republic. The turnout south of the border was 56%, with the agreement and the changes to Articles Two and Three receiving the support of just over 94% of voters. The turnout in the North at 81% was the highest in any poll there since 1921. Some 71% of voters backed the Good Friday Agreement. However, a Coopers and Lybrand exit poll indicated that while 96% of Catholics favoured the agreement it had the support of only 55% of Protestants. There were deep divisions within the Protestant/unionist community over the Good Friday Agreement. These divisions would surface again and again over the following months and years.

But any euphoria over what had been achieved on Good Friday was short-lived. There were ugly scenes in the lead-in to the annual Orange Order march at Drumcree in Co Down. In the early hours of 12 July, three young boys lost their lives in a firebomb attack on their home at Ballymoney in Co Antrim. The Quinn brothers – Richard (11), Mark (10) and Jason (9) – were Catholic and lived in a predominantly Protestant housing estate. Worse – if that was at all possible – was actually to follow.

On 15 August 1998 a car bomb ripped through the centre of Omagh on a busy Saturday afternoon. The attack on the Co Tyrone town left 29 people dead. Hundreds more were injured. The so-called Real IRA, a republican dissident group opposed to the Good Friday Agreement, was behind what was the single biggest loss of life in the North since 1969. There was widespread condemnation of the attack.

Mansergh had long been a vocal critic of the dissident republican groups. "Ideological rigidity is nearly always associated with the politics of failure, as the real and the ideal move further and further apart. The unwitting repetition of history decades later is often frustrating."[56]

He battled republicans on their own territory, dissecting republican ideology and history to illustrate the weakness in their claims of legitimacy:

This leaves by default, through *reductio ad adsurdum*, a tiny breakaway and unaccountable secret army, the legal and lawful government and law-givers (no separation of powers there) of not the real but a metaphysical 32-county Irish Republic by mandate of the people – back in 1918, when women under 30 did not have the suffrage! The voice of the living men and women of Ireland, voting democratically today, in this preposterous scheme of things counts for nothing."[57]

Yet despite these criticisms Mansergh was prepared to meet and deal with republican hard-liners. The initial contacts with the leadership of the Provisional IRA – albeit via Sinn Féin – were undertaken in the aftermath of the 1987 Enniskillen bombing. Those meetings took place without any tangible evidence that they might spawn a peace process.

There was also contact with representatives of the Irish Republican Socialist Party (IRSP), the political wing of the Irish National Liberation Army (INLA) in 1996, once more facilitated by Fr Alex Reid at Clonard. Gerry Ruddy of the IRSP recalled the emphasis on "nationalist Ireland coming together as a strong force to democratically push forward an agenda for a united Ireland."[58] Progress, stalled while the IRA was off-ceasefire, but resumed following the summer of 1997 with Fianna Fáil back in government and the IRA ceasefire restored.

At a meeting in Portlaoise on 8 August 1998 – a week prior to the Omagh bombing – the INLA informed the Irish Government advisor of their plans to call a ceasefire. The so-called Real IRA bombed Omagh the following week, prompting the INLA to bring forward the announcement ending their military campaign. Contact was subsequently made with representatives of the 32-County Sovereignty Committee, the group commonly accepted as representing the Real IRA. However, the organisation continued with its campaign of violence.

All these contacts were undertaken with the objective of ending the conflict in Northern Ireland. The work was painstakingly slow but progress was made. On 10 September 1998 the first official meeting between the leaders of unionism and northern republicanism in 75 years took place when David Trimble and Gerry Adams met for direct discussions. Four days later at Stormont the Northern Ireland Assembly convened for the first time.

The new government in Northern Ireland consisted of ten departments, with six North-South implementation bodies and six North-South areas of co-operation. The six agreed implementation bodies include inland waterways, food safety, trade and business development, special EU programmes, the Irish and Ulster Scots languages and aquaculture/marine matters.

Mansergh had been prepared to be hard-line about cross-border contacts in the Good Friday talks. He believed that the North-South bodies were one of the most positive aspects of the peace process. The rationale was clear: cross-border interaction would help to underpin peace and stability in Northern Ireland and would contribute to employment and prosperity in the future.

During the negotiations leading to the Good Friday Agreement there was a view that these bodies had been 'too much too soon' for unionists. However, Mansergh believed the importance of the bodies should neither be exaggerated nor played down:

> Democratic decisions by the people, and nothing else, will determine the constitutional status of Northern Ireland, which will not be changed over the heads of the people of Northern Ireland without their agreement and participation.[59]

David Trimble was in agreement, offering this view a few days later:

> Only a fool would pretend the cross-border bodies represent a tool for levering Northern Ireland out of the United Kingdom. Unionists needn't take my word for it. Ask Martin Mansergh, the Taoiseach's special advisor and well-known anti-unionist.[60]

Despite the Good Friday Agreement and the formation of an executive, political life in the North was a stop-start affair. "Political progress is slow and difficult. One cannot expect peace to solve in one year what violence has failed to solve in 25 years. The long peace follows the long war," Mansergh had said in 1995. Three years later the arms issue continued to slow progress. The true intentions of the IRA remained unclear. The Ulster Unionists were unwilling to allow the arms issue drift indefinitely. Decommissioning became, in Mansergh's words, "a wearisome and repetitive business for all concerned."[61] However, there were some moments of humour:

> Flicking through the pages of *Frankfurter Allgemeine Zeitung*, I came across this remarkable photograph of guerrilla soldiers belonging to an Islamic Front organisation in Algeria depositing their weapons, in what looked like a wood, as part of an agreement with the Government. I copied it to some of my colleagues with the caption, 'Decommissioning at last!'[62]

On 1 December 1999 leading figures from the worlds of politics, business, academia and the media gathered at the British Ambassador's residence in South County Dublin. The guest of honour at the dinner engagement was Peter Mandelson, the Northern Ireland Secretary. That night power was transferred from London to the new institutions in Northern Ireland. Mandelson had travelled to Dublin to sign, along with his Irish counterpart, the documents that would transform legal and constitutional relations between Ireland and Britain.

Mandelson paid tribute to many of those involved in the process including Garret FitzGerald who was a guest that evening. He also thanked Mansergh for his work in steering republicans towards the Good Friday settlement. In reply, Mansergh said: "We couldn't have done it without you."[63]

The belief within Fianna Fáil was that an irresistible dynamic now existed to create a united Ireland within a matter of decades. This was the language that unsettled unionists. In

any event their constitutional and political future was uncertain, according to Mansergh who remarked that

> ... Unionists may, like white South Africans, or some
> of the Eastern European elites prior to 1990, find
> themselves considering the unthinkable, and ask
> themselves what actually at the beginning of the 21st
> century is so unacceptable about forming a new Irish
> State, incorporating, as desired, devolution in the
> North.[64]

The Fianna Fáil advisor was sceptical about the argument
that the changing demographic profile in favour of nationalists
in the North would produce a majority for unity within a
generation. In 1998 he expressed the hope that there would be
"healthy democratic competition" with unionists persuading
enough Catholics that they were best served by a continuation
of the Union, and with nationalists trying to persuade enough
Protestants that their best interests were best served by a united
Ireland.[65]

Ten

The Political Survivor

Niccolò Machiavelli was born in Italy in 1469 at the height of the Renaissance. His upbringing on a small farm outside Florence was frugal – his father, an insolvent debtor, was barred from public office. The young Machiavelli "learnt to do without before he learnt to enjoy".[1] But driven by ambition he climbed the career ladder in the Florentine administration. As a diplomat and a civil servant, he saw at close quarters political power being used and abused. In the classic text *The Prince*, Machiavelli set down the principles for achieving power and success.

Martin Mansergh was familiar with the work of the archetypal backroom advisor. The Fianna Fáil employee was invited to the Listowel Writers' Week in 1996. His address drew heavily on the Italian master. He cited the qualities of a good advisor by reference to Machiavelli: "A man entrusted with the task of government must never think of himself but of the prince, and must never concern himself with anything except the prince's affairs."

This was undoubtedly a characteristic of Mansergh's tenure as advisor to Fianna Fáil. Haughey followed by Reynolds and latterly Ahern were his princes. But the Mansergh/Machiavelli roles were not totally paralleled as, interestingly, Mansergh noted that although Machiavelli served as a political advisor, that did not imply that all political advisors were Machiavellis. Nor did the Fianna Fáil advisor ever have to suffer the fate of Machiavelli who endured 'four twists on the rack' when his political mentor was forced from office.

When he went to work for Charles Haughey in 1981 one of the tasks allocated to Mansergh was speech-writing. He went on to become the principal wordsmith for Fianna Fáil during the Haughey years. This role continued under Reynolds and Ahern although increased responsibilities related to the North lessened his input into general day-to-day speeches.

The profession of political speech-writer can be under-estimated but Mansergh was not shy in poking fun at its status which, he said

> ... hovers somewhere below that of the advertising copywriter and shares a nickname with horses that also ran ... Human vanity being what it is, those so engaged, and there are many of us, are naturally inclined to regard their better handiwork when finally moulded and well delivered by the speaker as works of art.[2]

The speeches written by Mansergh were peppered with quotations from political figures and poets. There was a particular fondness for the works of William Shakespeare. In the final month of Haughey's tenure as Taoiseach and Fianna Fáil leader there were many references in Dáil debates to Shakespeare. In his final Dáil contribution Haughey quoted from *Othello*: "I have done the State some service, and they know't, No more of that." To Mansergh's delight, Mary Holland, a columnist in the *Irish Times*, wrote the following day: "It is difficult to imagine when we will have another Taoiseach (or a speech-writer) who looks to one of Shakespeare's most sublime tragedies to sum up more than three decades in public life."[3]

The arrival of Reynolds in Government Buildings signalled a new stage in Mansergh's career as a political advisor. The gambles for peace sanctioned by the new Taoiseach necessitated an even greater focus on Northern Ireland policy. There was increased public profile for the Fianna Fáil advisor. The back-room figure moved into the spotlight. Alongside the media attention prompted by the IRA ceasefire in August 1994, there was some months later, a high-profile appearance at an

Oireachtas Committee investigating the collapse of the 1992-94 Fianna Fáil/Labour coalition. In more recent times, under Ahern, the advisor gave more media interviews and in May 2002 moved directly into the political domain by contesting the South Tipperary constituency in the general election.

But at the start of 1992 the emerging peace process was the only priority. Nonetheless there were other issues distracting Mansergh and Fianna Fáil from that agenda. Indeed, the new Reynolds-led coalition immediately became embroiled in controversy when Harry Whelehan, the Attorney General, judged that he had a constitutional obligation to prevent a pregnant teenage rape victim from leaving the jurisdiction to have an abortion. Despite the legal arguments in what became known as the X-case, Mansergh was not wholly convinced of the necessity for the action taken by Whelehan. There was turmoil in Government and, not for the last time, it was associated with the Attorney General.

Relations within the Fianna Fáil/PD coalition were strained throughout 1992. The PDs recalled remarks made by Reynolds in 1990 when he told a Fianna Fáil gathering that the coalition pact was a "temporary little arrangement" which he hoped would not "be there all that long". That wish came through in the aftermath of evidence given by Reynolds to the Beef Tribunal on 28 October 1992.

The tribunal was investigating irregularities in the Irish beef industry. The PD leader Des O'Malley had given highly critical evidence about Reynolds's actions on the beef sector when he was a minister. The Taoiseach responded to his Tánaiste: "He puffed up Goodman's claim for what I regard as cheap political gain. He was reckless, irresponsible and dishonest to do that here in the Tribunal."[4]

Mansergh was not involved in advising Reynolds on his appearance at Dublin Castle and was unimpressed by his performance there: "He did not seem to appreciate, by whoever had cynically advised such a macho response, that this was bound to bring down the Government ... "[5] Not surprisingly the evidence from Reynolds precipitated the collapse of the Fianna Fáil/PD coalition.

The ensuing general election delivered an enormous electoral blow to Fianna Fáil with the party losing nine seats. The Fianna Fáil first preference vote at 39.1% was the lowest since 1927. Mansergh described the general election as "a nightmare."[6] But if Fianna Fáil were the election losers then the real winners were Labour which won 33 seats – a gain of 18 seats.

A possible heave against Reynolds was delayed as the opposition parties bickered about forming a coalition administration. The Fine Gael leader John Bruton had a difficulty with a multi-party government that included Democratic Left (DL), a left-wing party with a chequered past. His preference was to agree a deal between Fine Gael, Labour and the Progressive Democrats. But the Labour leadership was not impressed with the idea. They had agreed a policy agenda with DL which was the basis for their negotiations with Fine Gael.

Progress was slow. Another flank was opened up with a decision to contact Fianna Fáil, although initially this was designed to pressure Bruton into agreeing a deal. However, when the overtures came from Labour, Fianna Fáil was ready. Bertie Ahern had signalled that contact could come and had sought approval from Reynolds to prepare the ground for potential discussions with Labour. Mansergh was asked to examine the policy positions favoured by Spring and his colleagues.

When Fianna Fáil received the position paper agreed between Labour and DL, Reynolds handed it to his senior advisor. Mansergh immediately set to work on drafting a response aimed at breathing life into a possible deal. Within a matter of hours, Labour received a position paper for the formation of a partnership government with Fianna Fáil. The document was perfectly pitched to Labour's policy constituency. According to one of Spring's team, "Mansergh prepared a draft that in a way trapped us. It was very finely calibrated that we had to talk to them, we were sucked in."

Fergus Finlay, one of Labour's key advisors, later wrote:

> Martin Mansergh had read the arithmetic too. In the immediate aftermath of the election, he had approached Albert Reynolds, and pointed out that at

least the mathematical possibility existed that a Fianna Fáil and Labour Government could be put together. Albert had given him *carte blanche* to prepare something, in case of an approach, and Martin had spent the preceding two weeks – when otherwise he would only have been clearing his desk anyway – researching all of our positions and writing the kind of response that we were sure to find attractive.[7]

There were many considerations at work. Mansergh was aware that the peace process would most likely fail without Fianna Fáil's involvement in government. Moreover, his own political leanings were orientated in the social democratic and liberal direction of the Labour Party. "Being somewhat left-of-centre ideologically it suited me very well," Mansergh observed.[8]

Ruairi Quinn, the Labour Party deputy leader, was impressed with the document: "They virtually said 'Yes, anything you want and anything else besides'."[9] Quinn was intrigued when told that Mansergh had written the response. The two met had had their first real conversation at a meeting of the British-Irish Association in Cambridge some years earlier. The Labour politician recalled: "I found him intellectual, erudite and knowledgeable; not a green republican at all."[10]

Senior politicians from Fianna Fáil and Labour led the negotiations on a policy platform. Mansergh was co-ordinating the Fianna Fáil response. As the talks continued Labour's Fergus Finlay noted that Mansergh was "extremely important" within the Fianna Fáil delegation. When policies were agreed, Mansergh and his Labour counterparts would finalise the text.

The Programme for the Fianna Fáil/Labour coalition was written in Mansergh's office in Government Buildings. He had a pivotal role in drafting the historic document which cemented the first coalition Government between the two parties. Those writing the text were frequently able to influence the thrust of the document, in particular through nuances in language. Quinn remarked: "Lessons were learnt when we were negotiating with Fine Gael some years later. Whoever writes the text and controls the PC [Personal Computer] has an extra control over the final shape of the document."[11]

From his observation of Mansergh during the negotiations in late 1992, Quinn noted how the Fianna Fáil advisor stood out:

> His was the only political contribution that was coming from Fianna Fáil, the rest was all depart-mental. They were putting stuff out to the civil ser-vants who would come back with 'that would or could not be done'. I had never met a Fianna Fáil ideologue before. He was the first. He was much more rigorous and much more substantial than I was given to understand. Most of the Fianna Fáilers I had met, the likes of Bertie Ahern, struck me as pragmatic politicians who did basically what the civil servants said they could do. Here was someone who was trying to think through a political position from a republican point of view, republican in a mainstream European liberal sense, as I understood it.[12]

The formation of the Fianna Fáil/Labour Government in late 1992 radically changed the advisory system. Part of deal that cemented the Programme for Government was Fianna Fáil acceptance of Labour's demand for a well-oiled mechanism to ensure the programme platform was being implemented. Eunan O'Halpin of Trinity College, Dublin argued that Labour invented "a new kind of official, operating within the civil service but with a political brief."[13] These were the programme managers, who worked alongside a series of special and political advisors. Although central to the Fianna Fáil side of the Government – and pivotal to the party's advisory structure – Mansergh in fact retained the Special Advisor title.

The programme managers met weekly – the day after the cabinet meeting – with the objective of reviewing progress under the Programme for Government on a department-by-department basis. They also sought to identify blockages in the system, to facilitate interdepartmental exchanges on matters of common interest and shared responsibility, and also to provide a forum where difficulties could be speedily resolved.

There was much criticism of the arrangement – some saw the combination of special advisors and programme managers as the precursors of a full blown ministerial cabinet system along European lines. However, proponents of the new system argued that it was an *ad hoc* arrangement to deal with the different party objectives in a coalition government.

The Fianna Fáil advisor spoke about the benefit of having individuals like himself as part of the governmental system; individuals who were free to operate across the civil service and political boundaries. In such instances, politicians were not constrained in the material they discussed and did not have to differentiate between political and non-political subjects. Mansergh observed that it was desirable to have people who were tuned in to the politician's philosophy and political aims in a way that a neutral civil service could not replicate.

There is no rulebook to determine the nature of the relationship that should exist between advisor and political master. Each individual advisor is probably best placed to make the required judgement. In the case of Martin Mansergh, the political advisor very much shared the political outlook of the party he served. Indeed a lack of sufficient distance from his political masters was a problem, according to Garret FitzGerald, the former Fine Gael leader:

> He can be political but you don't have to go over-
> board. There should be some element of detachment.
> The ability to do a useful job requires an advisor to
> retain some objectivity in what they do. Obviously
> they need to do propaganda but they don't need to
> fool themselves.[14]

Fergus Finlay, the long-time Labour Party official, identified two characteristics of a good advisor – emotional detachment from issues and also an ability to ignore personal interests when providing advice. During the two years they worked together, Mansergh never once talked about the impact of governmental decisions on his personal situation, Finlay observed. There was, however, more difficulty in creating distance from policy issues. Finlay noted:

> The thing Martin cares most passionately about – Northern Ireland – he is in fact most detached from. But in relation to other areas, the party political stuff – which shouldn't matter – he is not dispassionate enough.[15]

Political and policy advisors were only emerging as a feature of the Irish governmental system when Mansergh went to work for Haughey in 1981. In those first years of government involvement, advisors did not have any clearly defined role within departments. Individuals like Mansergh tended to operate primarily as the confidants of individual politicians: they did not work across departments in pursuit of a party's or a government's agenda.

Indeed, successive governments had relied heavily on the civil service for policy advice since the foundation of the State. The first systematic appointment of advisors from outside the civil service only occurred with the formation of a Fine Gael/Labour coalition in 1973 when several Labour party ministers appointed non-civil servants as their advisors. The system was built upon when subsequent governments employed greater numbers of advisors although the development was not without problems.

There was deep resentment in 1981 when Mansergh arrived to work for Haughey. As noted previously, many in the civil service would have been antagonistic to the idea of one of their own opting to work for the controversial Fianna Fáil leader. But a less hostile attitude existed when Mansergh returned to the Department of the Taoiseach in early 1982 – during his second term working for Haughey in government his status had changed from civil servant to political advisor.

Moreover, as Mansergh gained experience, his years of service to Fianna Fáil meant there was no advisor more rooted in the nuances of his party. This fact most likely strengthened his standing within the governmental system. His previous existence at the Department of Foreign Affairs also provided him with an advantage – he knew how the system worked and he knew most of the main players.

The ability of a non-civil-servant advisor to operate seamlessly as a cog in the official system remained important to Fianna Fáil. Indeed, the party placed greater trust in the civil service to defend its own particular interests than other political parties. In government Fianna Fáil tended to blur the distinction between the political and the civil service. O'Halpin observed that perhaps that was because the party was so accustomed to government that its leaders were less worried about the problems of policy co-ordination in a coalition arrangement. Bertie Ahern remarked:

> The thing about Martin Mansergh is that he always works very, very well with civil servants. There is never any friction. And I think they probably feel as comfortable as I would that he'd be around there with his sources of knowledge.[16]

In many ways Mansergh, despite his political advisor position, adhered to the employment rules laid down for civil servants. He was drawn to a characteristic of the advisor as determined by Machiavelli in *The Prince*:

> It is an austere ideal, but can be lived, at any rate for a time. This is why we have a largely anonymous civil service, and why the most effective advisor or intermediary is often the obscure one who excites little or no public interest.

He saw his function as a political advisor as implementing the wishes of the party leader, fleshing out ideas and lines of argument to assist in achieving political goals and fight political battles, and also to act as a confidant and a sounding board. Advice was offered within his general remit and outside it only when invited or encouraged to do so. "As an advisor, I am always conscious of the democratic mandate earned by elected politicians, which gives them the right to make the ultimate political judgements and decisions which I have a duty to respect," Mansergh observed. [17]

During his 11 years working for Haughey, Mansergh had had a relatively low public profile. There were occasional letters to the papers, a handful of conference speeches and the *Spirit of the Nation* book. But in general, he had successfully maintained a backroom role, a fact illustrated by Seán Duignan, who had been Political Editor for RTÉ for much of the 1980s.

Duignan accepted the position of Government Press Secretary when Reynolds became Taoiseach in 1992. In his memoir of that period, he wrote: "Of all the luminaries surrounding Reynolds, the one I most wanted to meet was the notoriously reclusive Martin Mansergh who had always seemed to me as a most unlikely Solider of Destiny."[18] The lack of contact was all the more remarkable given that throughout the 1980s, both Duignan and Mansergh would have fulfilled their respective roles within the near-claustrophobic environs of Leinster House.

Duignan recalled the early days of the new Reynolds-led Government when:

> Initially, Mansergh kept his distance but I continued working on him and he eventually came around. As with so many savants, he was almost painfully shy at one level and brutally candid at another, but, once he trusted you, he could be extraordinarily forth-coming.[19]

This was a character trait identified by many people who worked with Mansergh including junior officials who served under him in the Department of Foreign Affairs. All recounted the initial wariness, which disappeared when Mansergh believed sufficient trust had been established.

Over the following two-and-a-half years, Duignan came to associate two things with Mansergh:

Although cast primarily as a theorist, he was also one of the most practical persons I ever met. Whatever the problem or calamity, he never wasted time bemoaning fate or seeking to apportion blame. Instead, he would immediately set about identifying counter-measures to try to nullify the setback or, if possible, actually turn it to advantage.[20]

The area of responsibility most associated with Mansergh was naturally Northern Ireland. However, he took a strong interest in economic policy. The Fianna Fáil advisor admitted that if he were starting his career over he would give greater consideration to joining the Department of Finance. There were occasions when the two areas overlapped. In April 1982 he led a delegation of executives from leading semi-state companies in the Republic to Belfast. The objective was to establish and promote contacts between businesses on both sides of the border. The delegation visited the Harland and Wolff shipyard, and the *Belfast Telegraph* the following day noted that "loyalist workers were riveted by his religion and slightly Anglo-Irish accent."[21]

Mansergh was also involved with the influential Tax Strategy Group (TSG) that examined and developed taxation and social welfare proposals ahead of the annual budget. The importance attached to the TSG was reflected in its membership which included some of the most senior civil servants from the Department of Finance, the Revenue Commissioners and the Department of the Taoiseach.

The working papers of the TSG have been released since 1999 under the Freedom of Information Act. Tax and financial experts keenly study these documents to gleam insights into the dynamics of policy formation. One article on the TSG written by a tax manager at the accounting firm KPMG noted: "The most interesting feature, and potentially the most significant, is the presence of Dr Martin Mansergh ... "[22]

Outsiders were intrigued by the Fianna Fáil employee especially after he survived the departure of his mentor Charles Haughey. Albert Reynolds would also described Mansergh as his top advisor although their time working together was relatively short The Fianna Fáil/Labour coalition which came into office at the end of 1992 had 101 of the 166 seats in the Dáil. But not even this commanding parliamentary position could save the Government when its two leading figures clashed and fell out.

Tensions within the coalition were raised following revelations about the policy of issuing Irish passports to non-nationals who invested in Irish businesses. Officials opened the files to convince the Labour Party that there was no impropriety in the operation of the scheme. Mansergh, along with his Labour counterpart Fergus Finlay, drafted proposals to reform the scheme. However, the affair damaged Dick Spring as he took much of the opposition and media criticism.

Outwardly, however, the Government appeared solid. There was the commanding Dáil majority and in August 1994 there was the historic achievement in getting the IRA to end its military campaign. But just at the time when republicans called their ceasefire the political relationship between Reynolds and Spring was at breaking point over the publication of the report of the Beef Tribunal.

The report was published on 29 July 1994 following a bizarre episode in which Labour officials were temporarily denied access to Government Buildings to examine the contents of the lengthy document delivered by Judge Liam Hamilton. Reynolds argued that he was exonerated by the report and proceeded to selectively issue those portions of the report which appeared to support this contention. Spring was on the verge of resignation and would have done so but for the delicate state of the peace process.

Further strains in the Reynolds-Spring relationship developed from early September over the appointment of a President of the High Court. Convention decreed that the Attorney General be given first choice on any judicial appointment that arose during his tenure in office. Harry Whelehan had indicated his interest in the position but there was resistance from within the Labour Party. Whelehan had been responsible for instigating the X-case and also for advice offered about the confidentiality of discussions at cabinet meetings.

The controversy simmered over subsequent weeks with both Reynolds and Spring abroad at different intervals on official business. Their lack of direct communication about the matter later emerged as one of the reasons why the apparently straightforward matter of a judicial appointment could split what had been until that point a genuinely successful administration. Matters eventually came to a head with revelations concerning a delay by the Attorney General's office in processing the extradition papers of paedophile priest Brendan Smyth. A complex and byzantine series of events followed but Labour withdrew from the Government after Reynolds was accused in the Dáil of failing to reveal to the house all relevant information in his possession.[23]

An Oireachtas Committee later investigated the circumstances surrounding the collapse of the Reynolds-led Government. The hearings were televised and attracted much attention. For many media and political figures, as well as the general public, this was the first time they got to see and hear Mansergh. He was the star witness providing a *tour de force* with his evidence which sought to rehabilitate Reynolds and place some coherence on the events in Government Buildings in early November 1994. In the *Sunday Independent*, journalist Gene Kerrigan wrote: "He was superb. The tone and substance of his evidence was both refreshing and impressive."[24]

Mansergh described the confused atmosphere in Government Buildings as Fianna Fáil ministers and officials sought to save their coalition with the Labour Party. He relayed the view that relations within the Government soured after newspaper reports, citing Labour sources, described Reynolds as "punch-drunk following the IRA ceasefire" and acting like "the High King of Ireland on a roll". Whatever hope there was of a compromise over the High Court vacancy appeared to have disappeared as the Taoiseach's resolve to appoint Whelehan hardened.

Mansergh was appalled at the Labour briefing and offered the view that he would not have permitted himself, nor would he have been permitted, to brief the media in a manner so derogatory to the Tánaiste: "It is totally destructive of trust to attack a partner in Government, and especially its head, in that fashion. It is nevertheless indicative of the subterranean tensions created by the breakthrough on the North ... The Taoiseach was politically soaring and had to be pulled down to earth."[25] This interpretation was, however, rejected by Labour Party officials who also gave evidence to the committee.

As the Whelehan controversy worsened in September and October 1994 Mansergh supported the Taoiseach's position. However, he was concerned that the High Court appointment should not be allowed to cause the breakup of the Government. On more than one occasion he expressed the view that Whelehan was pitching his claim rather high. The Fianna Fáil advisor later said he regretted not urging more forcibly greater caution, as the claims to the High Court Presidency were not "worth the risk of political martyrdom and the loss of a good Government."[26]

Mansergh recalled the scenario created by Seán Duignan, who in the presence of Reynolds "often whimsically painted the picture of Mr Justice Harry Whelehan safely ensconced as President of the High Court, metaphorically waving goodbye and saying 'Nice to have known you' to Fianna Fáil retreating towards the Opposition Benches."[27]

The row soon turned to crisis. There was renewed Labour resistance to the appointment of the Attorney General when it emerged that there had been a seven-month delay in processing extradition papers in the case of Brendan Smyth, a Roman Catholic priest wanted in Northern Ireland on sex abuse charges. The delay was sourced to the office of the Attorney General. Explanations for the delay failed to satisfy Spring and his colleagues. Yet still Reynolds pursued the appointment.

Mansergh spent Thursday 10 November at a meeting on Northern Ireland involving British Government officials. During a break he was informed that the cabinet had approved Whelehan's appointment at a meeting earlier the day. It was with "some surprise and some foreboding" that he learnt that the Labour ministers had withdrawn from the cabinet meeting before the decision was made.

The situation rapidly deteriorated. The following days were about trying to save the Fianna Fáil/Labour Government. Mansergh was assigned responsibility for drafting the speech which Reynolds would deliver in the Dáil setting out the context and background to the Smyth case and the handling of the extradition request. There were attempts to get Whelehan to delay his swearing in and also to stand aside from the position. The atmosphere was confused. There was, according to Mansergh, passing reference to another abuse case – the Duggan case – involving an ex-monk and similar delays in processing warrants.

Fianna Fáil ministers and officials later insisted that it was only on the following Tuesday evening that the potentially serious implications of the Duggan case dawned. By that time Reynolds had delivered his speech in the Dáil – without any reference to Duggan. Claims that the Dáil had been misled due to the withholding of information about the Duggan case were "specious" according to Mansergh. Fianna Fáil argued that the Duggan case was irrelevant and the Taoiseach had not misled the Dáil when he failed to mention the case.

But Eoghan Fitzsimons, the new Attorney General, claimed Reynolds had been told about the Duggan case on Monday, advice that ended any hope of Spring and his colleagues re-entering government. Only weeks after securing a historic IRA ceasefire the coalition collapsed over a crisis that was difficult to comprehend, let alone explain. Reynolds was left to wonder what might have been had his senior advisor been on hand, rather than at a meeting on the peace process, on the day he decided to forge ahead with the Whelehan appointment.

In his contribution to the Oireachtas Committee, Mansergh cast doubt on the judgement of Fitzsimons, downplayed the importance of the Duggan case and portrayed Labour as a party run by unelected advisors. There were barbed references to Fergus Finlay who in turn took the opportunity when giving evidence to counter Mansergh's interpretation of the Government's collapse. Finlay later wrote: "When I discussed the fall of that Government with Martin Mansergh, a few days after it happened, he told me that "the Taoiseach was engaged in a power play that went hideously wrong – what he wanted, he had to have, and that was the end of the matter."[28] This was a recollection rejected by the Fianna Fáil advisor.

One of the more surprising aspects of the final months of the Fianna Fáil/Labour administration was there was such little communication between Mansergh and Finlay on matters of political controversy. The two advisors were engaged in post-IRA ceasefire negotiations but appear to have avoided talking about the cracks emerging in the Government they both served.

The Government with the largest ever Dáil majority lasted little over two years. The suddenness of the collapse – and the confusion about the causes of the collapse – left most senior Fianna Fáil figures bewildered as the party settled into the opposition benches for the first time since 1987. Bertie Ahern took over the helm from Albert Reynolds. The new Fianna Fáil leader faced a difficult task in rejuvenating and reuniting his party. Mansergh would later observe that Ahern "conducted the retreat from office in good order".[29]

There were many changes but Mansergh's own personal stock was high. The decision not to accept John Bruton's job offer met with widespread admiration within Fianna Fáil. The Fianna Fáil advisor now had someone from his own generation as his political boss. Mansergh was four years older than the new Fianna Fáil leader. Moreover, they were contemporaries in terms of high-level involvement in Fianna Fáil. Mansergh started working for Haughey in January 1981, becoming Head of Research for Fianna Fáil six months later. Ahern was first elected to the Dáil in the 1977 Fianna Fáil landslide election and, in early 1982, Haughey appointed the Dublin deputy as Government Chief Whip.

The two men came from vastly different backgrounds which provided fodder for the *Phoenix*, a satirical magazine that published a spoof diary chronicling Ahern's inner-most thoughts while sending-up his Dublin accent: "I have me new doctorate up on de wall already and it's a beauty. Dat's tree now which is even more dan Mansergh has and him with de huge brain."[30]

Ahern quickly got used to receiving weekend phone calls

from his advisor in Co Tipperary. The Dubliner, who led Fianna Fáil, was amused at the thought of his Oxford-educated official in wellingtons tending to cattle on the family farm. When he became Taoiseach in the summer of 1997, Ahern enjoyed several foreign trips in the company of his Special Advisor. Mansergh would often arrive on the government jet with five or six books as reading material for the journey. He would sometimes bring some obscure reference to the attention to the Taoiseach or get animated after discovering an incorrect fact. The error would rarely be forgotten as sometimes weeks later Mansergh would arrive in the office saying, "Look, I told you it was wrong," – he would have located the original reference in the National Archives or the National Library.

Despite the differences in background Ahern and Mansergh had soldiered in a common cause for many years. They were both loyal supporters of Charles Haughey. Moreover, Ahern took advice from Mansergh when delivering his first public speech on Northern Ireland. They also worked closely on the implementation of the social partnership model of govern-mental decision-making when Fianna Fáil was returned to office after the 1987 general election. Mansergh had also liased with Ahern in preparing the ground for the formation of the Fianna Fáil/Labour Government in late 1992. He spoke of Ahern's "decency and shrewdness and simplicity of life-style".[31]

The salient characteristic displayed by Ahern when he was elected party leader was a conciliatory approach. He set about healing the internal divisions that were the legacy of the Haughey and Reynolds leaderships. His frontbench was drawn from the different factions within Fianna Fáil. There were changes in the advisory team. Mansergh was retained as Head of Research but new faces arrived. He was no longer the sole party advisor as Ahern moved to strengthen the media and research personnel employed by Fianna Fáil. However, when it came to policy on Northern Ireland, Mansergh remained the most influential player, especially as Ahern maintained and developed lines of contact with all political sides in the peace process. The Fianna Fáil leader observed:

He is a good guy to say 'what way do you think we should play this or play that? I don't think I ever asked Martin for a view on something where I didn't get one. Martin wouldn't be the kind of guy who'd say, 'Well, I don't know anything about that, you need to check somewhere else.' If Martin hadn't got it – he'd go research it for you.[32]

Their relationship was defined by Northern Ireland. In opposition up to the summer of 1997, Ahern and Mansergh sought to bolster the peace process especially after the first IRA ceasefire ended. Fianna Fáil started negotiations with the Progressive Democrats to form a minority coalition Government in June 1997. Mansergh was assigned the task of getting a renewal of the IRA ceasefire so as to allow serious multi-party talks to commence.

Over the following twelve months Ahern placed the peace process at the top of his policy agenda, culminating in the Good Friday Agreement. Mansergh was central to the Easter 1998 deal although unlike when Reynolds was Taoiseach he was no longer pivotal to all aspects of the process. This was not unexpected, as the atmosphere and mechanics had changed since 1994. No longer were senior republicans unknown quantities while the range of issues had substantially expanded. Mansergh had responsibility for the key constitutional aspects of the deal and also for liasing with the republican leadership.

In recent times, his principal areas of involvement remained the North and general policy formation. However, the presidential election in 1997 provided evidence of Mansergh's interest in the internal world of Fianna Fáil politics. In April 1997 Fr Alex Reid met Mansergh to discuss prospects for restoring the IRA ceasefire. During their discussions, Reid asked about the presidential elections and the possibility of Mary McAleese getting the Fianna Fáil nomination. McAleese was an academic at Queens University in Belfast, where she had retreated after failing in the late 1980s to start a political career in the Republic. After an unsuccessful attempt at winning a Dáil seat for Fianna Fáil in the 1987 general election,

McAleese was on a list of potential Seanad nominees with Mansergh, although neither was eventually appointed.

"He was … sounding me out about it," Mansergh recalled of Reid's intervention. "My reply would have been that we were concentrating on the general election. I tried neither to be too encouraging or discouraging. At that distance it looked like somewhat of an outside prospect."[33] The Fianna Fáil advisor then met the Queens academic at the National Concert Hall in Dublin in late June. They chatted at the interval. Mansergh mentioned names worth contacting to build support for a potential bid for the party's nomination.

The opportunity to convince Bertie Ahern of the case for her nomination came on 9 September. Mansergh greeted McAleese in the front hall in Government Buildings and escorted her to the Taoiseach's office. The Belfast-born lawyer spoke for fifteen minutes and was questioned about her presidential ambitions. "Her quarter-of-an-hour monologue on her vision of the presidency was a *tour de force*. Very persuasive, flowing and articulate," Mansergh recalled.[34] McAleese went on to beat Albert Reynolds for the Fianna Fáil nomination and in October 1997 was successfully elected as the Republic's eighth Head of State.

The following years revealed another facet of the Mansergh ideological outlook. Several members of Bertie Ahern's 1997-2002 coalition Government sparred with the European Union on a diverse range of issues. The atmosphere fed into an emerging public questioning of Ireland's role in the EU and the value of membership in the absence of significant inflows of resources from Brussels. The relationship between the Republic and the EU moved into unpredictable territory in June 2001 when voters in Ireland opted to reject the latest treaty on European integration.

Mansergh was appalled. He had a deep attachment to the European ideal, was fluent in French and German and each day read a selection of continental newspapers. His language reacting to the Nice Treaty defeat was far more strident than any member of the Government. "How can anyone calling themselves republican turn their back on the historic links

284

between Ireland and Continental Europe … or still think of sovereignty in terms that are 505 years out of date?" he asked at a seminar to mark the anniversary of the Battle of Kinsale.[35]

In clear and concise terms the Fianna Fáil advisor repudiated the arguments of those opposed to the Nice Treaty – the financial benefits for agriculture and the wider economy; the justifications for a EU Rapid Reaction Force and the folly of a European Super-State with no tax-raising powers. "If we do not spend more time thinking seriously about Europe soon, I suspect we will have plenty of time to think about it in cool and sober detachment at our leisure," Mansergh warned.[36]

In a sense there was a divergence of view between Mansergh and the political thrust of the first Ahern-led Fianna Fáil/PD Government. The coalition tilted to the right favouring reductions in taxation, adopting a neutral attitude to the EU and a less-than-benign line on the value of continuing with the social partnership model. Much of this thinking emanated from Charlie McCreevy, the Fianna Fáil finance minister and the PD leader Mary Harney. Mansergh was on the opposite side of the ideological spectrum to the two leading ministers in the coalition Government. Not alone did he push more enthusiastically for the Nice Treaty, but he also defended social partnership against business sector and internal governmental attack. Critics were warned to "think many times over before throwing it over, and also about the effects on business confidence of a breakdown or abandonment of the process".[37]

The influence of any one advisor is difficult to determine. Mansergh was obviously critically important to Haughey during the 1980s as Fianna Fáil clawed its way out of opposition. In all likelihood, Albert Reynolds would not have cemented a programme for government with the Labour Party in 1992 without Mansergh's involvement. He was vital to all three party leaders in developing the peace process. The extent of his influence on Ahern in other policy areas was probably less than under the two previous incumbents of the senior political position in Fianna Fáil. Mansergh was orientated to the left-of-centre. Ahern and his Government with the PDs moved to the right-of-centre. The enthusiasm for the Nice Treaty and protection of social partnership were two areas of divergence. Nevertheless, Mansergh remained a key member of the Ahern advisory team, and he was not unprepared to bat for his political boss.

In an uncharacteristic intervention, the Fianna Fáil employee entered the public debate over Ahern's relationship with Celia Larkin in May 2001. The marriage of Bertie and Miriam Ahern ended during the 1980s. The couple, who had two daughters, had legally separated although divorce was not an option considered by either. Nevertheless, Ahern was involved in a subsequent relationship with Larkin, a member of the Fianna Fáil organisation in his constituency. She also joined his staff when he was appointed a Government minister in 1987.

Ahern made no secret of his personal situation, revealing details of his failed marriage in a television interview in the early 1990s. When Ahern was elected leader of Fianna Fáil at the end of 1994, he told his first news conference that Larkin was his partner. She accompanied him to official engagements and when he became Taoiseach in July 1997 assumed the role previously filled by the spouse of the head of government. In this regard, Larkin accompanied Ahern on official visits abroad and their names appeared together as co-host of State functions.

The arrangement caused some unease among Catholic Church and Church of Ireland leaders but they generally remained silent on the issue. Public criticism was left to lay-conservatives who at regular intervals took their displeasure to the RTÉ airwaves and the letters page of the *Irish Times*.

The relationship became a source of great comment and controversy when in February 2001 the Catholic Archbishop of Dublin, Desmond Connell was appointed to the rank of cardinal by the Vatican. The honour was widely welcomed. The Fianna Fáil/Progressive Democrat Government decided to host a State reception for Connell. It was scheduled for May 2001 at Dublin Castle. However, controversy arose when the invitation to the reception was issued in the name of Ahern and Larkin. Some believed the inclusion of Larkin's name on the invitation placed the new cardinal in an awkward position. The Catholic hierarchy remained silent on the issue although members of the Church of Ireland decided to air their annoyance in public.

The Church of Ireland Archbishop of Dublin, Dr Walton Empey said the wording of the invitation was "insensitive", but that the Church of Ireland had always been "pastorally sensitive" where marriage breakdown was concerned. Then one prominent member of the Church of Ireland decided to decline the invitation. Dean Robert McCarthy objected, saying the invitation from Ahern and his partner put "lesser relationships" on a par with marriage.

Mansergh was aware of McCarthy's views on the matter. An interview request to the Fianna Fáil advisor came from RTÉ's *Morning Ireland* radio programme. He had only previously given a limited number of media interviews, almost all were related to Northern Ireland and the peace process. But the comments from a senior member of his own church raised his annoyance.

The normal practice when asked to write for a newspaper or to do a broadcast interview was to inform the Government Press Secretary Joe Lennon, who would then check with Ahern. However, on this occasion Mansergh agreed to the interview prior to checking. He was motivated by a sense of indignation and the view that if he did not speak out nobody else would do so. "It was somewhat of a risky thing to do. It certainly was not within the terms and conditions of employment of a Special Advisor," he laughed.[38]

On *Morning Ireland*, he did not hold back in his criticism of Dean McCarthy, who he regarded as a friend:

> But I'm afraid I regarded his remarks as gratuitously discourteous to the elected head of government, and indeed discourteous to his loyal and devoted companion, Celia Larkin, and I didn't like to see that coming from within my own church.[39]

The comments were being made in a personal capacity but it was an unusual speaking engagement for the Special Advisor to the Taoiseach. "The basic point I wanted to make is I don't think people have the right to judge the integrity of other people's relationships," he said. Mansergh said Larkin played "a distinguished role" in assisting Ahern in representing the country "and I would personally be proud of both her and him."

He accepted that Church leaders had every right to stress the value and importance of marriage in society but asked what happened in situations of marriage breakdown:

> Clearly the Catholic Church doesn't approve of divorce. So is the formal position for someone caught in a position of marital breakdown that they should be without loyal, faithful and devoted companionship from the other sex for the rest of their lives? I personally would find that very harsh.

The President could be seen as a role model but not the holders of the office of Taoiseach. When asked if Ahern should have considered whether the invitation would cause offence, Mansergh replied: "In the case of the Dean, since he wasn't going to go to the reception anyway because he was hosting one himself, it seems to be that he was going out of his way to seek offence." He said McCarthy tended to be "forward with his comments" and had adopted a "holier than thou" attitude. McCarthy later said the comments were "value judgements" and that criticism of his stance was akin to "shooting the messenger."

There was amazement – and admiration – within Government and Fianna Fáil circles as the comments were broadcast at breakfast time on national radio. It was the most high profile intervention by Mansergh in his 20 years as a political advisor. It was an indication of the transition from backroom advisor to front row political activist, a move that was confirmed over a year later when he was selected as a Fianna Fáil general election candidate. But the motivation in May 2001 was as much about church politics as about defending his political boss.

The Manserghs had long been active Church of Ireland members. The Southcotes created and first occupied the family vault in St Mary's churchyard in Co Tipperary over which

Richard Martin Southcote built a large obelisk. Relations of Martin Mansergh were members of the Select Vestry which in 1795 decided to build an elaborate steeple for the church. However, the steeple caused numerous problems and the church was condemned in 1818. A new church was built in 1832. Anyone sitting in the pews in St Mary's today would find themselves surrounded by references to the Mansergh family; plaques on the church walls remembering relations and the pulpit donated in the memory of another family member. The Manserghs paid £300 for the family pew box.

Moreover, three members of the family served in the Church of Ireland, including Brian Mansergh who was curate in Tipperary from 1789 to 1805. There have been other church links in more recent times. Martin Mansergh's brother-in-law was an Anglican priest in England but departed for the Catholic Church over the ordination of women priests.

Mansergh took a strong line on the history and position of the Church of Ireland in contemporary Ireland. Attempts to portray Protestants as the discriminated minority in the post-1921 Free State were forcefully challenged. He argued that labelling Ireland in the initial decades after independence as a 'Catholic country' should not be seen as a negative but rather as a statement of reality – 95 per cent of the population were members of that faith. The fact that Ireland was a Catholic country did not prevent there being a Protestant Ireland was Mansergh's observation.

This exercise tended to downplay the discrimination meted out to Protestants in the early years of the State's existence, even if it was low-level and carried no official sanction:

> That Irish people should initially have wanted to demonstrate pride and attachment to a faith, which had suffered persecution, and which, after that had ceased, was scarcely accorded the full recognition and official favour to which it was entitled, is only natural, and they would hardly expect to be always inhibited by the consideration that people of other

faiths who had, where they could, opted out of the State …

Protestants had, Mansergh argued, significance out of all proportion to the numerical weight of the small minority they were associated with. He remarked that Protestant institutions, including Trinity College, Dublin, the Royal Dublin Society and the Rotunda Hospital, continued to play an important role in Irish life. There was fault on both sides:

> If Catholicism was oppressive during these years, it was primarily so to its own members. The Trinity ban is a case in point. The prejudices and disadvantages that subsisted were on both sides.[40]

An interpretation of the ethos underpinning the 1937 Constitution also placed him at odds with many commentators who criticised the influence of Roman Catholic values in the text. There was, Mansergh argued, very little in the Constitution that other denominations could find objectionable. The exception, he admitted, was the ban on divorce although even it left a loophole, allowing tacit recognition of foreign divorces, that the minority were most likely to avail of at that time.

Mansergh sought to examine the Church-State and intra-church relationship from a broad perspective. It was correct in that much of the wrong – for example, the *Ne Temere* decree on inter-church marriages – was church- rather than State-sponsored. However, he was on weaker ground in attempting to associate members of his own flock with the staunch Catholicism evident in the early decades after independence. "Many Protestants in fact shared vicariously in the sense of national pride felt by Catholics of the time of the Eucharistic Congress in 1931, as more recently during the Pope's visit."

The accuracy of these observations is difficult to discern, but they would raise the ire of many within the Church of Ireland. However, Mansergh was also vocal in arguing against a simplistic labelling of members of his church. No more than there was one paradigm of Irishness was there one paradigm of

Protestantism. "Collectively, we are neither relics of the old Ascendancy, honorary Catholics, craven Uncle Toms, or the unionist or any other party at prayer."[41] But there was little sympathy for those from his tradition who had not come to terms with the political and constitutional changes heralded by the Anglo-Irish Treaty – if some Protestants felt less Irish, they often had only themselves to blame.

The contrast was always with Northern Ireland and the treatment given to the Catholic minority by their Protestant neighbours for the first half century after partition. This argument was augmented by reference to his personal situation. When he joined the civil service in the mid-1970s the English-born Protestant observed a prevailing spirit that was "one of scrupulous fairness to minorities". Over the subsequent 30 years, Mansergh prospered. Indeed, no other Fianna Fáil official survived as long, over the course of three different leaderships while also managing to make the level of contribution to party and national life as made by Mansergh.

He once quoted one of Parnell's lieutenants who described his political leader as 'someone who knows what to do in a crisis'. The definition met with approval from the Fianna Fáil advisor, and it could equally apply to himself. Mansergh observed closely many leading political figures. The lessons learnt were useful tools to have in 2002 when he decided upon a new career path.

Eleven

Electoral Ambitions

Bertie Ahern passed the traditional bowl of shamrock to George W Bush. There were smiles for the cameras from the Taoiseach and the President of the United States. "A hundred thousand welcomes to you all," Bush said as he greeted his Irish visitors at the White House. "I probably am not going to try to say that in Gaelic. But I have learnt to pronounce Taoiseach," the US President quipped.

Saint Patrick's Day arrived early in the White House in March 2002. It was Wednesday morning, four days before the Irish national holiday. But the Bush schedule was already packed. Talk of war with Iraq was high on the news agenda as the fallout from the attacks on 11 September continued to preoccupy the US administration in Washington. When the photographers were finished, and the small talk for the media was completed, the Taoiseach and the US President moved into the Oval Office. "Today, Ireland's supporting the coalition against terrorism, and we're proud of your support," Bush observed. Sporting a green tie, the American President listened as Ahern briefed him on developments in the Northern Ireland peace process.

When the meeting concluded and Bush made to bid farewell the Irish delegation, Ambassador Egan gestured to the Irish Special Advisor. "That man," Egan said to Bush as he pointed at Martin Mansergh, "that man is contesting the forthcoming elections in Ireland." The American President moved closer to the Fianna Fáil candidate for South Tipperary. "Are you suffering from some form of mental incompetence?" Bush asked, smiling broadly. There was laughter all round as the US

President wished Mansergh well.

There was some puzzlement about his appearance in the American capital only weeks ahead of the general election. The academic Paul Arthur approached him, enquiring of how many votes there were in Washington. But Mansergh was learning fast. "I may be in Washington, but tonight I'll be going into every home in South Tipperary," he replied. And indeed, on the main evening news on RTÉ television, as Bertie Ahern was interviewed about his meeting with the US President, there on the Taoiseach's shoulder was the Fianna Fáil candidate for South Tipperary.

The decision to redirect his career brought many changes. There was bemusement from long-time colleagues when they first caught sight of Mansergh with a newly acquired mobile phone. But emerging from the background was not without the occasional hiccup. In March 2002, as Ahern was about to be interviewed outside the White House, Joe Lennon, Ahern's Press Secretary, moved to tidy up the Special Advisor. An unseemly scarf dangling from Mansergh's overcoat pocket was removed. But to Lennon's horror just as the cameras started recording, Mansergh opted to give the scarf greater prominence. As so on the RTÉ news there was Mansergh nodding behind the Taoiseach with the scarf wound around his neck. "He looked like something out of the Taliban," one onlooker remarked.

As Mansergh's public profile developed after the 1994 IRA ceasefire, two interesting proposals regarding the advisor were made to Bertie Ahern. In the summer of 1997, with Fianna Fáil about to return to government with the Progressive Democrats, Ahern received a hand-written letter from County Galway. The correspondent proposed the appointment of Mansergh as Minister for Foreign Affairs because he was the "best candidate around for the job and to negotiate and sell the republican ideal".

Another letter was received in the Department of the Taoiseach in early September 1997, again suggesting a promotion for Mansergh. Mary Robinson had announced her intention not to seek a second term as Irish President. Albert

Reynolds looked as if he would be the Fianna Fáil candidate. The name of Mary McAleese had not yet emerged. However, one supporter from Co Kilkenny lobbied the Taoiseach not to look beyond his own office. Nine reasons were put forward in favour of Mansergh as the Fianna Fáil candidate for the presidential election. If anything they offered a sense of the image of Mansergh held by the wider public. He was a nationalist; a Protestant; a pacifist; educated; not a politician; a linguist; not a woman so comparisons with Robinson would be avoided; unknown to the public and not a member of the Dáil so there would be no threat to the parliamentary position of Ahern's minority coalition.

Ahern obviously did not pursue either proposition, but Mansergh had himself considered the possibility of leaving his advisory role to enter the cut-and-thrust of parliamentary politics. Others had successfully made such a move, including Séamus Brennan, who served as Fianna Fáil general secretary before entering the Dáil and later became a cabinet minister. And Ted Nealon of Fine Gael had been a government press officer before winning a Dáil seat in Sligo-Leitrim.

In the immediate aftermath of the 1987 general election, with Fianna Fáil set to form a minority government, speculation mounted as to who would be rewarded with ministerial positions in a new Haughey administration. Several newspapers carried stories that Mansergh would be appointed to the Seanad and given a ministerial role with responsibility for Northern Ireland. Garret FitzGerald had used this unorthodox, but constitutionally permissible, route in 1981 when James Dooge, who was not a member of the Dáil, was appointed as Minister for Foreign Affairs. The procedure was facilitated by the fact that the Taoiseach had the right to nominate 11 of the 60 members of Seanad Éireann.

The possibility of a Seanad nomination was discussed in Co Tipperary. Correspondence from his Uncle Gregor to his father in February 1987 observed: "Yes, I think the election was pretty satisfactory," while adding later in the letter, "Martin was here yesterday and I'm hoping he might get a senatorship, certainly he deserves it." Among the other names mentioned for inclusion in Haughey's list of Seanad nominees was academic Mary McAleese. However, neither Mansergh nor the future Irish President were among the names eventually appointed by the new Taoiseach.

The possibility of membership of the Upper House arose again two years later in the aftermath of the 1989 general election. Fianna Fáil entered the contest leading a minority single-party government, but when the results were known, the party had to forge its first ever coalition arrangement so as to remain in power. A number of those appointed to the Seanad in 1987 by Haughey had been successfully elected to the Dáil in 1989. In the period before the new Seanad was elected the Taoiseach had the ability to fill those vacancies.

Haughey wanted to nominate Mansergh. He had rewarded other associates like PJ Mara in similar circumstances during previous interludes. However, the official advice given to Haughey was that if Mansergh was nominated he could not remain in his position as Special Advisor; the two roles were legally incompatible. Faced with the prospect of losing his trusted advisor, Haughey decided not to proceed with the nomination.

Some years later, the Labour Party advisor Fergus Finlay again raised the idea of Mansergh's appointment to the Upper House. A Seanad vacancy arose in early 1998 after Seán Ryan, a Labour Party politician, was elected to the Dáil in a by-election in Dublin North. Ryan had been a member of the Seanad since 1997. Given that the Government had a majority in the Seanad, the task of filling the vacancy essentially fell to Bertie Ahern. Finlay argued for the nomination of Mansergh to the Upper House as "some small recognition for a historic contribution to peace".[1]

The gesture would undoubtedly have been well-received by the Fianna Fáil advisor, but were a choice available Mansergh's preference was membership of Dáil Éireann. He had long been attracted to the idea of representing the South Tipperary constituency that took in his family home outside Tipperary Town. Indeed, for many years he had been a member of the local Dan Breen Cumann.

On several occasions, Mansergh sought to stand as a Dáil candidate for Fianna Fáil. This motivation was driven by a historical appreciation of the position of parliamentary life in the affairs of state. In addition, there was also the type of desire to serve which had originally prompted him to join the civil service.

It is open to question whether or not the advisor would actually have made a successful party politician. One senior Fianna Fáil figure – who was familiar with Mansergh – was emphatic with asked about the entry of Mansergh into national politics:

> I don't think he was cut out for the hurly-burly of politics. He would be unable to look you in the eye and tell a lie, and in politics you have to be able to lie and cheat. I don't think he would have made the contribution he made, if he was elected to the Dáil.

Over the last 25 years Mansergh paid considerable attention to the local media in Co Tipperary. One of the first articles he published after joining Fianna Fáil from the civil service in July 1981 appeared in the *Clonmel Nationalist* newspaper. That somewhat turgid article sought to explain the Irish experience within the European Monetary System.

When the Fianna Fáil Government collapsed at the end of 1982, Mansergh made his first move towards direct political involvement. He was one of five candidates who sought the party nomination for what was then the South Tipperary and West Waterford constituency. Fianna Fáil won two of the seats in the four-seat constituency at the general election earlier in 1982. The party decided to run three candidates at the second general election in that year. These candidates were selected by local constituency delegates at a convention chaired by Gerry Collins, the Limerick West TD and cabinet minister. The two outgoing Fianna Fáil TDs – Seán Byrne and Seán McCarthy – were nominated without a vote.

The 256 delegates were then asked to fill the one remaining vacancy on the party ticket in South Tipperary from the other three candidates. When the votes were cast Tom Ambrose received 114 votes and Denis McInerney received 112 with Mansergh coming in a poor third with 30 votes. He was duly eliminated and his transfers helped Ambrose, a secondary school teacher from Clonmel, to secure the nomination. In a speech to the convention after the results were announced, Mansergh pledged his loyalty to the party and predicted that Fianna Fáil would be returned to power.

In fact, the result of the subsequent general election put Fianna Fáil out of government. Mansergh returned to his role as Head of Research. Speculation about his political ambitions continued. In early 1984, the *Tipperary Post* newspaper reported that he was about to be selected as a candidate for the Dun Laoghaire constituency, and if elected to the Dáil it seemed certain he would at least be appointed a Minister of State. Mansergh reacted swiftly to the report. In a letter to the *Tipperary Post*, he said the article was "based on pure speculation and is indeed inaccurate in certain particulars".[2]

He failed, however, to expand on the errors in the report, which was prompted by news that he had joined the Fianna Fáil cumann that covered his Dublin home in Killiney. It was possible that he would have had a better chance of election as a candidate for the more liberal Dun Laoghaire constituency. But the matter was never actively pursued, although the possibility of standing in the constituency was raised on several occasions in subsequent years.

Mansergh had decided that should he enter national politics, it would be in South Tipperary. In the aftermath of his unsuccessful selection convention in late 1982, he toyed with the idea of building a stronger base in the constituency. He was travelling at weekends to Friarsfield, but the possibility of contesting the local elections in 1985 offered the prospect of establishing an electoral base from which to seek a Dáil nomination at the subsequent general election. The option was discussed and opinion canvassed. However, he was reluctant to leave his role as party advisor in Leinster House and Haughey was not prepared to lose a key aide as Fianna Fáil prepared the ground for its return to government. At the 1985 local elections, the husband of Philippa Mansergh Wallace, his first cousin and owner of Grenane, was an unsuccessful Fianna Fáil local election candidate.

The possibility of embarking upon a political career re-emerged in 2000 with the death of Michael Ferris of the Labour Party. South Tipperary was now a three-seat constituency. At the 1997 general election Noel Davern of Fianna Fáil, Theresa Ahern of Fine Gael and Ferris had won the seats.

In April 2000 the *Irish Examiner* newspaper carried a story with the headline: "Ahern Advisor Mansergh To Stand For Fianna Fáil In By-election." The story quoted "informed sources" as saying Mansergh had been approached by the party hierarchy and that he had expressed an interest in contesting an internal party selection convention. Unsure of Mansergh's ability to overcome a convention comprising local party members in South Tipperary, Fianna Fáil officials were testing the waters.

He would have been a loss to the advisory team surrounding Bertie Ahern and, in particular, his key role in the peace process may ultimately have undermined any attempt at a Dáil election bid. It was made clear in briefings that Mansergh would only be a candidate if he secured the nomination without local opposition. The selection had to be guaranteed. He was not going to suffer the embarrassment of returning to Government Buildings after losing a selection convention in South Tipperary. Senior party sources confirmed that Mansergh was extremely interested in the vacancy.

On the day the story broke Mansergh was attending a meeting of the General Council of County Councils in Monaghan. A statement was issued on a plain white sheet of paper with no letterhead or contact details for further elaboration. But the content was confirmation. It was a clear expression of interest:

> Fianna Fáil is a very democratic party, and a Convention will decide whom it wishes to put forward as a candidate for the Dáil to join Minister Noel Davern. It would be a great honour to have the opportunity to

represent and serve the people of Tipperary. No decision has been taken yet about whether I should put my name forward. I am keen to continue in public service in whatever capacity I can contribute best.

While there was some support from senior party officials, local rivals were quick to scotch the possibility, saying they were better placed in the constituency than the Dublin-based political advisor. Without local backing his candidacy was not going to progress. There was a further difficulty. Fianna Fáil headquarters commissioned a private opinion poll of the constituency. The results indicated that Mansergh's "name recognition" was poor. On the evidence of the poll the party would not stand a chance of winning the by-election. However, members of the party hierarchy argued for taking a chance.

Several met in Fianna Fáil headquarters on Upper Mount Street in Dublin. They poured over the opinion poll data and assessed the advantages and disadvantages of Mansergh vis-à-vis one of the local party members in South Tipperary who were manoeuvring for the nomination. "Let him have a crack at it. Take a risk and have a flyer," one senior Fianna Fáil advisor said. Another to argue in favour of Mansergh as the by-election candidate was John O'Donoghue, the cabinet minister and Kerry South TD.

In the end, the opinion poll data killed off the nascent Mansergh candidacy, and – according to one Fianna Fáil official – "he withdrew gracefully". Barry O'Brien, one of the local representatives to question the wisdom of Mansergh's candidacy, contested the by-election for Fianna Fáil. O'Brien was drubbed at the polls, beaten into third place on a dismal first preference vote. It was Fianna Fáil's worse ever by-election performance. A second by-election in Tipperary South was held in 2001 following the death of Theresa Ahern of Fine Gael. Michael Maguire was selected as the Fianna Fáil candidate, but once more the party vote in the constituency failed to impress.

Fianna Fáil had only a handful of selection conventions to hold towards the end of 2001, before the full list of the party's general election candidates would be chosen. Bertie Ahern had repeatedly said his preference was to hold the general election in the summer of 2002. Few had initially believed the Fianna Fáil Taoiseach, but as the months passed it was clear the party's coalition government with the Progressive Democrats was likely to be one of the most durable administrations in the history of the State.

Officials at Fianna Fáil headquarters in Dublin were unsure what to do about Tipperary South. The three-seat constituency was unlikely to deliver more than one seat for the party. The results of the by-elections in 2000 and 2001 had been disastrous for Fianna Fáil. The possibility of selecting a single candidate – outgoing TD Noel Davern – was discussed. But the long-term implications of a single-candidate strategy included the concession that a second seat was being discounted and the danger that even minimal representation would be threatened at a future contest when Davern stood down.

A view was growing among Fianna Fáil members in South Tipperary that it was time to be bolder in their choice of running mate for Davern. One of those who reintroduced the idea of Mansergh contesting the general election was Michael Maguire, the unsuccessful candidate at the 1997 general election and the by-election in 2001.

Mansergh was approached. His brother Nicholas, while encouraging, laughed and made a reference to soldiers marching towards the Somme. The potential candidate was receptive to the idea but had one demand; he would only go forward if he came through a selection convention. Any proposal to simply have him added as the second candidate by Fianna Fáil headquarters was being vetoed.

News of his interest reached the media in January 2002, by which time the aspiring candidate was working the phones and sending out letters to the delegates, who would select the two general election hopefuls. There was a brief interlude for the Fianna Fáil advisor when he departed for a few days to Sri Lanka, to advise on that country's developing peace process. The ability to translate this national – and international standing – into a credible vote-getting position in Tipperary South was one of the unknown aspects about the Mansergh candidature.

There was a huge crowd at the convention, which was held in the Cahir House Hotel in the middle of February. There were three names seeking the nominations – Mansergh, Davern and Barry O'Brien, who had failed in the 2000 by-election. The Minister for Defence, Michael Smith, chaired the meeting telling delegates that Fianna Fáil was "ready for the fray". The three candidates were invited to sign the party pledge, which committed them to not contesting the election as an independent should they fail to secure the Fianna Fáil nomination.

The voting process took less than an hour. There were 185 delegates. The quota was 63 votes. When Smith announced the first round result, Davern secured the backing of 97 delegates; Mansergh had 52 votes while O'Brien trailed into third place with 36 votes. As Davern was 34 votes in excess of the quota, the outgoing TD took the first place on the Fianna Fáil ticket. As had been expected, the second slot was a contest between Mansergh and O'Brien. The second count involved the distribution of Davern's surplus 34 votes. Mansergh took 24 of these votes while O'Brien secured 10 additional votes. Smith announced the second round result: Mansergh was on 76 votes with O'Brien taking 46 votes. Twenty years after he was defeated at a Fianna Fáil selection convention, the party's long-time advisor was a general election candidate in Tipperary South.

The Defence Minister then asked the three candidates to address the meeting. Mansergh's was not the typical acceptance speech delivered at Fianna Fáil selection conventions. He had no difficulty following the traditional route in applauding the outgoing Government for its economic and other policy successes. But there was an additional quality which char-acterised the personal satisfaction the Fianna Fáil advisor felt at being given the opportunity to contest the general election in Tipperary South.

Mansergh said he was more honoured than he could say by his success, while the support received from a great-niece of Dan Breen was a source of some pride. "My ambition has always been to serve Ireland and Tipperary in which lives, since early childhood, my deepest attachments. A good philosophy would be – contribute nationally, benefit locally. As Charles Kickham once wrote, 'there's a deal to be done', meaning a great deal to be done," the newly selected candidate told the party convention.

There was also an acknowledgement of the formidable challenges ahead: "to shake the certainties and foregone conclusions beloved by those who like to discount long in advance of any election the people's choice." Neither opinion polls nor the views of political pundits would put him off this task. He recalled that when he joined Haughey's advisory team in early 1981, a civil servant colleague had predicted that he would not last six weeks. The incumbent Fianna Fáil TD Noel Davern followed his new running mate in addressing the delegates. "You're not as innocent as you look," Davern remarked to Mansergh before adding with a wry smile, "and I'm not as stupid as I look."

Tipperary South had all the appearances of a constituency that the political commentators would talk about as 'no change'. Davern had first won his seat in 1968, having succeeded his brother, who in turn succeeded their father, a TD since 1948. The two by-elections – in 2000 and 2001 – had seen the independent Seamus Healy and Tom Hayes of Fine Gael installed in Leinster House. Conventional wisdom had it that the voters of Tipperary South, casting their ballots for the third time in three years, were unlikely to remove their relatively new political representatives. But that sedate scenario was upset when Mansergh came through the Fianna Fáil selection convention.

There was considerable attention from the national media. The morning after the Tipperary South selection convention, a smiling Mansergh was the main photograph on the front page of the *Irish Times*. Some days later the same newspaper asked him to write an article for its main opinion page, explaining why he wanted to be a member of Dáil Éireann. There was positive coverage in the other national newspapers, all of which were bemused by the election decision.

His appearance was humorously described as "middle-aged Harry Potter" in a *Sunday Business Post* profile.[3] But there were some subtle changes including new glasses which replaced the large black-rimmed models he had worn in previous years. In addition, the candidate – who was commuting between his day job in Government Buildings and evening meetings in Tipperary – had to be contactable, and so he acquired his first mobile phone. However, if anything, the media coverage confirmed just how little was known about one of the most influential individuals in Fianna Fáil and Irish political life.

There was an opportunity to make firmer introductions over the following weeks as the candidate sought to turn his increased profile into votes in South Tipperary. The annual Fianna Fáil Árd Fheis in March 2002 became in effect a pre-election rally. In previous years, Mansergh was the principal drafter of the keynote speech delivered by the party leader. While maintaining this role, he also had in 2002 the status of candidate, and in a general election year, new and promising party candidates were openly promoted.

Mansergh was one of those who addressed the Árd Fheis during live coverage on RTÉ television. With the exception of the selection convention speeches, it was his first public party political address. The candidate for Tipperary South spoke about the peace process but added a local flavour. He offered "warm congratulations" to the craftsmen and management at Tipperary Crystal, who were responsible for the specially commissioned bowl used by the Taoiseach to present shamrock to President Bush in Washington.

During Bertie Ahern's leader's address, time was set aside for several video inserts. These pre-recorded videos were in effect a means to promote general election candidates. Mansergh briefly spoke about republicanism and the Good Friday Agreement against the backdrop of Tipperary Town. The backroom advisor was working hard to promote his local links and to show that he was indeed a credible candidate.

The Fianna Fáil campaign strategy in Tipperary South was agreed between the two candidates. There would be a joint poster carrying photographs of Mansergh and Davern. Similarly in their respective election literature there would be generous references to each other. However, if Mansergh was to make the transition from political advisor to political representative, then Davern's seat had to be the target. This was a reality he downplayed throughout the campaign: "The objective of my participation is to increase the representation of the party. As far as I am concerned I want to come in behind Noel Davern," Mansergh declared.[4]

The phrase 'Contribute Nationally, Benefit Locally' was adopted as his election slogan, placing emphasis on his access at national political level. The prospect of Tipperary South gaining a cabinet minister if he was successfully elected was commented upon by the media and also by his own supporters. The candidate was understandably reluctant to directly mentioned future elevation but he did leave the idea open:

> It has been put forward by various candidates in Tipperary South that they would just concentrate on local politics. The point I would make is if you want to be in a position to make the strongest possible case for things in the local area, it is desirable that you are contributing nationally."[5]

Bertie Ahern was also reluctant to speculate when he was asked whether or not Mansergh would be left on the back-benches, should he win a Dáil seat. "Eh, I don't know (laughs). I've plenty of talent. If they're all elected I'll have plenty of talent. He's a hugely useful person in whatever role he'll play and if he is elected he'll be a very good representative of the people of South Tipp," the Fianna Fáil leader remarked.[6] Privately, Ahern was pleased that his advisor had taken on the challenge, but while admiring the interest and enthusiasm, he considered it a near-impossible task to win a second Fianna Fáil seat in Tipperary South.

From the time he was first mooted as a candidate, representations from the public in South Tipperary started to arrive with the Fianna Fáil advisor. The numbers increased significantly once he came through the party convention. An office was opened on the main street in Tipperary Town. Potential voters came with their problems and requests.

Firsthand experience of the 'parish-pump' element of Irish political life was quickly gained.

The level of representations increased further once Bertie Ahern called the general election at the end of April 2002. However, it was a feature of Irish political life that Mansergh had seen at close and senior quarters:

> Politicians carry, in most cases voluntarily, the huge burden of expectations of society, in relation to the solution of both large problems and local or individual ones. When I worked for Charles Haughey, who had an unusual ability to get things done, every morning I opened a newspaper, I could read urgent pleas from half a dozen places calling on him to intervene personally, often over the heads of Ministers or other agencies, and sort out some impasses that had arisen.[7]

Every morning during the campaign Mansergh would meet with his long-time secretary Evelyn Egar. She ran the election office and collated the representations that the candidate received on the hustings and also which came into the office by phone, in the post and in person. All of these queries were followed up with local and central government.

Mansergh had an advantage over most candidates in that he knew the corridors of powers and had direct access to the personnel who wielded that power. During a visit to Garryshane National School there was a query about the capacity of the school to physically match the expansion in student numbers. Mansergh was learning fast. He responded: "I'll get in touch with the Department of Education straightaway and send it personally to the Minister, in a way in which he will actually receive it, and not be spirited away by some civil servant."[8]

There were many successful outcomes as recorded in the local newspapers. For example, the *Clonmel Nationalist* reported that Mansergh announced Brian Cowen's decision to approve a grant for the Tipperary Song of Peace Festival. Another article reported news of a grant for a local sports centre that had been "communicated personally by Dr Martin Mansergh".

It was a far cry from Government Buildings although the aspiring TD did not seem to mind the clientalist aspect of his new role. "There is undoubtedly great satisfaction to be had in helping a neighbour or local community, in an area where your family had lived for generations, and seeing projects in which you have played some role coming to fruition," Mansergh remarked.[9]

During the general election campaign the national media came to observe the Tipperary South candidate on the canvass. There was repeated questioning as to why he would swop his high-level advisory role for the job of Fianna Fáil TD. Journalist Kevin Myers was one of those bemused by the choice:

> The inverse career of Martin Mansergh, Special Advisor to the Taoiseach on Everything, moves another cog in reverse today when Mr Ahern visits him at his election headquarters in Thurles. Most politicians start off at the bottom and gradually work their way through cumann, town council, county council, the Dáil, a minister's office or two and finally, Roinn an Taoisigh. Martin Mansergh, like Merlin is doing it backwards. He began his career in the Taoiseach's office and now, after two decades of eminence, he has his eyes and his heart set on a seat in Tipperary South. A place on Thurles Town Council is probably the next appetising prospect shimmering on his horizon.[10]

But standing for election had been a long-time objective. Indeed, after 20 years Mansergh was approaching the end of his tenure as a political advisor. There had been many achievements but, in reality, there was unlikely to be anything in the years ahead remotely equivalent to the peace process or the Good Friday Agreement.

The role as advisor had limitations; power and influence was delegated by elected authority. The primacy of the elected representative was something Mansergh recognised and accepted:

> Is there a difference between public service and politics? I speak as one who has moved between one and the other. In many respects, they are similar and complementary activities. Politics is or ought to be a form of public service. Being a member of a democratic political party is a vehicle for public service, and should not be an end in itself.[11]

The highest form of democratic participation was being chosen to serve by the people in parliament. As an advisor Mansergh believed it was important to limit his own participation so as not to cut across the primary role of elected decision-makers. However, the long experience as a Fianna Fáil advisor positioned him to take on a more public role for the party when the opportunity arose.

Mansergh resigned as Special Advisor to Bertie Ahern when the general election was called. From his Tipperary home at Friarsfield House he started on a three-week campaign to win a Dáil seat. The two Fianna Fáil candidates agreed on joint canvass literature – a four-page leaflet introduced by Bertie Ahern with a page each for Davern and Mansergh outlining their respective careers.

Mansergh set out his experience as a public servant and policy advisor to three Taoisigh. The content emphasised his peace process involvement, membership of the Tax Strategy Group and assistance provided to local projects such as the Excel Heritage Centre in Tipperary and restoration of the Warehouse near Ballingarry. Among his priorities were to be an active voice for the constituency in the legislative and committee work of the Dáil on national issues; to promote investment in sub-standard school accommodation and public health facilities and to support employment and living standards in Tipperary.

From morning to night he criss-crossed South Tipperary in search of votes. He participated in debates with rival candidates on local radio, spoke at public meetings organised by communities lobbying on local issues, and knocked on doors in towns like Cashel, Cahir and Clonmel. The representations continued to arrive on everything from difficulties with planning permissions to overcrowded classrooms.

There was general recognition for the Fianna Fáil advisor who, while stressing his Tipperary connections, was a Dublin-based candidate. 'You're Bertie's man' was a comment from some voters, who were handed the joint canvass leaflet as well as his personal card.

Those settling in for a drink in the pubs were informed of his role on the Tax Strategy Group and how he had objected – unsuccessfully – to a recent tax increase on cider, an important piece of information as the drink was produced by Bulmers in Clonmel. One woman asked about his doctorate as she told her boyfriend to order a pint of Guinness and a glass of Cidona. When told about the research area, she jokingly replied: 'So tell us about the French Revolution.' The drinks waited on the bar counter as the straight-faced candidate began an explanation about the rights and wrongs of the events several hundred years ago, so dear to his heart.

The exchange captured the part-naive, part-awkward canvass style that Mansergh brought to the election campaign in Tipperary South. Reporters following the candidate on the canvass witnessed similar experiences. Kathy Sheridan in the *Irish Times* observed: "He pauses beside a couple of uniformed schoolgirls in Donohill. 'Did the bus drop you here?' he enquires politely. They nod. Silence. 'Well, lovely uniform you have anyway.' The girls look wary. Silence. 'Oh dear, you are looking at me very suspiciously,' he murmurs ruefully, as his team collapses into hilarity."[12]

And yet alongside such naivety, Mansergh displayed a steely determination to prove he was worthy of being a candidate and that he had the ability to win a Dáil seat. Although his home was in Dublin, he was no blow-in to Tipperary. The farming background helped in the predominantly rural constituency. The local Fianna Fáil organisation was impressed with the work their new candidate put into the contest.

Privately they conceded the task was near impossible in a three-seat constituency with a well-established party TD. Nevertheless, there was open recognition of the possibilities for Tipperary South if Mansergh was a Dáil deputy.

The voters had their say on 17 May 2002. When the ballots were counted Mansergh was placed fourth of the eight candidates chasing the three seats. The three outgoing TDs were well-positioned to be re-elected. When the candidates with the lower preferences were eliminated Hayes, Davern and Healy secured the seats. Mansergh, who polled 5,233 first preference votes, was off-the-pace but avoided elimination. The Fianna Fáil vote in the constituency increased by 1.25% on the 1997 performance, but more significantly there was no re-run of the disastrous outcomes in the two by-elections held in the intervening period. The result was "very satisfactory and a step in the right direction," according to one senior Fianna Fáil official.

The general election signalled a new chapter in the career of the long-time Fianna Fáil advisor. The intellectual attachment to the party had long been evident from the research work and also the peace process involvement. The 2002 election campaign allowed Mansergh to publicly display his emotional attachment to Fianna Fáil. His background and upbringing told him that it was a duty to serve the people. The highest form of political representation was securing sufficient votes to enter Leinster House as a Dáil deputy. The fulfilment of that goal did not come in 2002, and may wait for another day.

A further signal of future intentions was made with the decision to contest the Seanad Éireann elections in the summer months of 2002. The possibility of receiving one of the Taoiseach's nominations was once again mooted, but Mansergh was determined to stake out his own ground. In any event there was no phone call from Bertie Ahern guaranteeing a place among the 11 nominees that he would select.

The fortnight that followed the general election was spent preparing for the Seanad contest and also clearing out his office in Government Buildings. Two decades of material had to be shifted through: some was disposed but much documentation that may have some historical import when it is made accessible went to the National Archives. Throughout June and into July, Mansergh travelled the country in search of votes.[13] The electorate in Seanad elections is limited to national politicians and local councillors. Success is determined by an ability to make personal contact which as many voters as possible. Mansergh travelled over 5,000 miles hoping his strong name recognition and solid general election performance would convince a sufficient numbers of voters to support him.

His message was unambiguous – membership of the Seanad would allow him to remain politically active in South Tipperary, to contribute publicly to the nation's affairs and to further the peace process. Outside the Fianna Fáil constituency Mansergh hoped to attract support from Sinn Féin which due to its small number of elected representatives had no candidates seeking election. Crucial support also came from the Progressive Democrats. As part of the Government deal with Bertie Ahern, the PDs had promised to support Fianna Fáil candidates in the Seanad elections. Mansergh benefited from this support which saw him comfortably elected to Seanad Éireann.

It was an long-time ambition realised and in doing so he had overcome those in Fianna Fáil who doubted his ability to operate beyond the role of backroom advisor.

But with his Seanad success Mansergh had moved from political advisor to elected representative. The new role held few of the constraints associated with his previous position, particularly when speaking on topical and contentious subjects. The term as a member of the Seanad would allow many views and opinions previously uttered only in private to be aired publicly. Some idea of the political position he may adopt can be drawn from a confidential paper prepared for the Fianna Fáil parliamentary party mid-way through the life of the first Bertie Ahern Government.[14]

Entitled *The Positioning of Fianna Fáil*, the six-page document was also a synopsis of Martin Mansergh's outlook on contemporary Irish politics. He was politically left-of-centre but also a pragmatist. The area of core political belief was on Northern Ireland and his deeply held belief in constitutional republicanism. He wrote:

In many respects, Fianna Fáil is positioned extremely well, as it continues to hold the central position in Irish politics. Maintenance and consolidation of that depends on continued agility and adaptability, and the ability to fight off constant challenges.

The party had "huge strengths and some dangerous weaknesses," according to Mansergh. The strengths included: representing mainstream opinion; having a unique record of achievement and delivery in government; and being the party of economic development coupled with close working relations with the trade union movement – "while regularly accused of conservatism, Fianna Fáil has in many ways managed to be the real Labour party," Mansergh claimed.

However, when identifying the six "weaknesses or vulnerabilities" that faced his party, Mansergh indicated a great deal about his own personal political leanings.

The first trouble spot was the controversy associated with the Haughey era. "An open and forward approach is essential. Great prudence is required so as not to create new material for controversy," was the Mansergh advice. He also warned about opposition tactics in painting Fianna Fáil as a conservative party – "It is important to maintain a young and modern image and to be seen to be abreast of the changing needs of society." There was also mention of the need to increase the position of women within the party.

Mansergh also dealt with the lessening political and policy differences between Fianna Fáil and Fine Gael. He wrote: "There is a lot to be said for a political system built around two parties that are not hugely dissimilar (viz. the US system) with Fianna Fáil the main player and Fine Gael very much the alternate … "

The growth of Sinn Féin and the possible threat it posed to Fianna Fáil was also discussed:

> Fianna Fáil has to be at the forefront of developing a new constitutional republican philosophy suited to the [Good Friday] Agreement and to the reconciliation of the main traditions on the island. In this

311

task, Fianna Fáil does not carry the recent baggage of Sinn Féin, has a far broader and more credible agenda, and has succeeded more than any other Southern party in establishing a working relationship with mainstream Unionism and Loyalism ...

In one final area – identified by Mansergh in the confidential internal party paper – there was evidence of some personal unease with the policies of the first Ahern-led Fianna Fáil/PD coalition:

> One of the biggest risks when settled into government is over-confidence. This includes using power in ways that are both unnecessary and unpopular. There are, for example, various suggestions floating around for new taxes (tourism) or new charges (water supply, tolling ring-roads). In the current financial climate, such decisions would be an absolute gift to the Opposition, and would not be understood by the public.

A further divergence in political stance between Mansergh and the government he served was also evident from the list of main challenges identified. The prioritisation of issues tended to confirm Mansergh's position on the left within Fianna Fáil which at that time was involved in a coalition government with the Progressive Democrats and positioned to the right economically. The main challenges were set down as:

> effective measures to reduce and overcome social exclusion (which gives a continued opening to the Left) and regional disparities, including raising of incomes in the poorer areas of both rural and urban Ireland. Determined tackling of bottlenecks, and waiting lists etc, in transport, housing and health.

Mansergh also mentioned the case "in a measured way" for some constitutional reform including removing any sexist bias in the text of the Constitution. This rather limited reference also provided evidence of another facet of the Mansergh political composition. Colleagues who worked with him admitted that he was not the man for fundamental policy reform or radical constitutional crusades.

It was a line of thinking to which his father also subscribed. In an interview with the *Irish Times* in 1982, Nicholas Mansergh offered the insight that:

> Great men are apt to think when they hold powerful office that there are all sorts of options before them, but when you look at it very closely, there are very few and maybe just one. A skilful political leader will always disguise this and pretend it is his decision. The constraints upon a political leader are so considerable that he is in a very strong position if ten per cent of the decision making process is in his own hands. After all ten per cent can be an awful lot.[15]

Martin Mansergh himself quoted the high priest of political advisors, Machiavelli: "The innovator makes enemies of all those who prospered under the old order, and only lukewarm support is forthcoming from those who would prosper under the new."[16]

But if Mansergh did not favour the big political or policy gesture, there were genuine political achievements for his 21 years as a Fianna Fáil advisor. Included in their number were sustaining Fianna Fáil in opposition in the 1980s; advancing the social partnership process and facilitating the formation of the first Fianna Fáil/Labour coalition.

The assessment was not, however, without the views of his critics. They listed the unswerving loyalty to Haughey; sacrificing his liberal credentials as the party he served pursued a conservative policy course and a lack of understanding of the unionist tradition. But the scale was tipped in his favour because of the Mansergh-Adams dialogue and all that it spawned. Whatever about the future, already Martin Mansergh had made an indelible contribution.

Notes

One

1 The Mansergh surname is believed to originate from an Irish-Scandinavian background. About 1,000 years ago Scandinavian settlements were established along the east coast of Ireland. It would seem that a unified force of Irish and either Danish or Norwegian soldiers invaded the north-western part of England. Some stayed and put down roots including the forefathers of Martin Mansergh. It was several centuries later before the family name was re-introduced to Ireland.

2 George Mansergh died in 1636 leaving an estate valued at £74-14s-7d.

3 Mansergh Clann Rally Address, 1996.

4 National Library of Ireland, D.22676.

5 Smyth, p.132.

6 A son of Robert Mansergh, the youngest of the three brothers who came to Ireland, was an Alderman of Cashel from 1686 until his retirement in 1710. On two occasions he stood unsuccessfully for Mayor of the Corporation of Cashel. Over 200 years later Martin Mansergh would canvass this area for votes in the 2002 general election in the Irish Republic.

7 Richard Martin Mansergh built Friarsfield in the 1850-1860s for his second and favourite son.

8 Mansergh Clann Rally Address, 1996.

9 Bowen, p.9.

10 McGrath, p.273.

11 There was little unrest in Co Tipperary or from the Grenane tenants during the 1798 Rebellion although a relation was killed by the rebels. Richard St George Mansergh arrived at Araglin in Co Cork to quell local action but was killed with a rusty scythe. Three locals were later hanged for the murder. 200 years later Martin Mansergh was a member of the Irish government's 1798 Commemoration Committee. At a ceremony in Araglin he expressed his "deepest regret and sorrow" for the tragedy brought upon his relation and the local community at the time.

12 National Archives of Ireland, PPC 3321.

13 Report of the Assistant Commissioners, Ireland, Sixth Report, Appendix B. no 22, pp. 247-51.

14 Mansergh Clann Rally Address, 1996. John Mansergh – eldest son of RMS Mansergh – was chairman of the Tipperary Town Relief Committee.

During the 1840s the committee raised money, supervised public works and ordered food including ten tonnes of Indian meal. In a letter written to the Relief Board in July 1846, John Mansergh noted "the urgent necessity of a further supply of money to employ the great number of labourers who have not yet got work. By complying with our request we trust to be enabled to avert the threatened famine, want of employment and its frightful consequences."

[15] Mansergh, 30 October 2001.
[16] Mansergh, N, 1997, p. 234.
[17] Mansergh, N, 1997, p. 124.
[18] Griffith Valuation, Ord.S.59.
[19] Mansergh Clann Rally Address, 1996.
[20] Massy-Dawson, p. 107.
[21] Massy-Dawson, p. 107.
[22] The Ogilvy family from whom Ethel Mansergh's mother was drawn included a relation who was physician to one of the Russian Czars although it has been speculated that he may even have been a son of the ruler of Russia. Ethel Mansergh's brother was one of those who died in the 'A1' submarine disaster in 1904.
[23] Bowen, p.17.
[24] Interestingly, with this marriage the surname 'St George' entered the Mansergh family. Martin Mansergh's grandfather was baptised Philip St George Mansergh. Several surnames by marriage such as St George, Southcote, Otway and Stepney have been maintained between generations of the Mansergh family through their use as second or third Christian names. For example, Martin Mansergh's second and third Christian names are George and Southcote.
[25] Gashell, 1914.
[26] Gashell, 1914.
[27] Bowen, p.22.
[28] Hart, p.81.
[29] Dooley, p.188. A relation who owned Templemore Abbey was less lucky. The property was destroyed by fire in 1922.
[30] Spectator, 26 November 1994.

Two
[1] Dooley, p.259.
[2] Kennedy, p.30.
[3] Dooley, p.219.
[4] Bowen, p.196.
[5] Mansergh, M, in Walshe, pp.45-46.
[6] Mansergh, M, 2000, p.149.
[7] *Irish Times*, 11 June 1983.

[8] Interestingly, the young Nicholas Mansergh had not been dissimilar in appearance to Eamon de Valera. There is a family story that, on one occasion when returning from a tennis competition in Limerick he was arrested along with his older brother Gregor. The local officers believing they had made a fine capture placed the two Mansergh siblings into a cell for the night, until to their later embarrassment they accepted they had not arrested the leader of the Anti-Treaty faction and his colleague.

[9] Lee, p.xiv.

[10] Mansergh, N, 1997, p.123.

[11] Lee, p.xiii.

[12] Lee, p.xiii.

[13] *Irish Times*, 1 July 2000.

[14] Mansergh, 11 April 1997.

[15] Mansergh, N, 1997, p.125.

[16] Diary entry, 6 August 1934.

[17] Diary entry, 19 January 1935.

[18] Mansergh, N, 1997, p.121.

[19] Diary entry, 3 February 1934.

[20] Letter from RTE to N. Mansergh, 31 August 1939. The nature of the proposed radio programme is not obvious from the content of the letter.

[21] Report October 1944, from private papers of N. Mansergh.

[22] Lysaght, p.28.

[23] *Irish Times*, 6 August 1982.

[24] *Irish Times*, 6 August 1982.

[25] Private Correspondence, February 1945.

[26] Private papers of N. Mansergh

[27] *Irish Times*, 11 June 1983.

[28] *Irish Times*, 30 April 2001.

[29] *Irish Times*, 30 April 2001.

[30] Interview with author, 4 April 2002.

[31] *Irish Times*, 30 April 2001.

[32] Mansergh, N, 1997, p.127.

[33] Mansergh, N, 1997, p.128 Indeed, Cosgrave gave Mansergh some assistance with his first book; Mansergh recorded the politician's "quiet sub-acid humour" in a diary entry from 22 October 1934.

[34] Mansergh, N, 1997, p.144.

[35] Mansergh, N, 1997, p.222.

[36] Mansergh, N, 1997, p.222.

[37] Mansergh, N, 1997, p.222.

[38] Mansergh, N, 1997, p.130.

Three

[1] Quoted in Power, 1995, p.120.
[2] Quoted in Power, 1995, p.123.
[3] Quoted in Power, 1995, p.123.
[4] Quoted in Power, 1995, p.123.
[5] Quoted in Power, 1995, p.121.
[6] Quoted in Power, 1995, p.120.
[7] Hobson, p.249.
[8] Paxman, p.157.
[9] Interview with author, 5 December 2001.
[10] Canterbury School, 1965.
[11] Dooley, p.57.
[12] Quoted in Power, 1995, p.124.
[13] Interview with author, 5 December 2001.
[14] Interview with author, 5 December 2001.
[15] Mansergh, M, in Walshe, 1998, p.43.
[16] Mansergh, M, in Walshe, 1998, p.47.
[17] Interview with author, 5 December 2001.
[18] Mansergh, 1981.
[19] Interview with author, 5 December 2001.
[20] Quoted in Power, 1995, p.121.
[21] Many years later, Mansergh said he was "very disappointed" to hear a former teacher from Canterbury, "from whom I would have expected better", express the view that there was too much history in Ireland.
[22] Interview with author, 5 December 2001.
[23] Interview with author, 5 December 2001.
[24] Quoted in Pearce, p.80.
[25] Quoted in Power, 1996, p.118.
[26] Hobson, p.192.
[27] www.oxford.ac.uk.
[28] *Oxford Times*, November 1970.
[29] Quoted in Power, 1996, 120.
[30] Quoted in Logue, p.127.
[31] Interview with author, 5 December 2001.
[32] Quoted in Power, 1996, p.119.
[33] Mansergh, M, in Walshe, 1998, p.47.
[34] Mansergh, 3 February 2000.
[35] Interview with author, 5 December 2001.
[36] Quoted in Power, 1996, p.117-8.
[37] Quoted in Power, 1996, p.118.
[38] Quoted in Power, 1996, p.118.
[39] Interview with author, 5 December 2001.

[40] *Irish Times*, March 1971.
[41] *Irish Times*, November 1973.
[42] Interview with author, 4 April 2002.
[43] London *Times*, June 1972.
[44] Quoted in Power, 1995, p.124.
[45] Dooley, p.73.
[46] Quoted in Power, 1995, p.124.
[47] *Irish Times*, March 1974.
[48] Interview with author, 5 December 2001.
[49] Quoted in Power, 1995, p.124.
[50] Interview with author, 5 December 2001.
[51] Interview with author, 5 December 2001.
[52] Interview with author, 5 December 2001.
[53] Quoted in Power, 1996, p.120.
[54] Quoted in Power, 1996, p.121.
[55] Quoted in Power, 1996, p.121.
[56] Quoted in Power, 1996, p.121.
[57] Interview with author, 5 December 2001.
[58] Quoted in Power, 1996, p.122.
[59] Interview with author, 4 March 2002.
[60] Interview with author, 5 December 2001.
[61] The "events" in question being the Arms Trial.
[62] Interview with author, 14 November 2001.
[63] Martin Mansergh and his brother Nicholas jointly own the family
    property at Friarsfield in Co Tipperary.
[64] Interview with author, 14 November 2001.
[65] Interview with author, 28 November 2001.
[66] *Nationalist*, 9 January 1988.
[67] *Irish Examiner*, 24 November 2000.

Four

[1] Interview with author, 8 January 2002.
[2] *Irish Press*, 27 December 1981.
[3] Ross, p.17.
[4] Gallagher, 1981, pp.279-82.
[5] Sinnott, p.67.
[6] Mansergh, 16 May 2001.
[7] Mansergh, 16 May 2001.
[8] *Études Irlandaises*, 2000, p.151.
[9] Mansergh, November 2000.
[10] Finlay, p.136.
[11] Interview with author, 4 April 2002.
[12] Mansergh, 6 May 1997.

[13] Interview with author, 15 January 2002.
[14] *Irish Times*, 6 September 1994.
[15] Duignan, p.15.
[16] Interview with author, 28 November 2001.
[17] Interview with author, 14 November 2001.
[18] Interview with author, 15 January 2002.
[19] Interview with author, 28 November 2001.
[20] Interview with author, 27 November 2001.
[21] Mansergh's papers are now held by the National Archives.
[22] Interview with author, 14 November 2001.
[23] Interview with author, 8 January 2002.
[24] *Irish Times*, 24 April 2001.
[25] Interview with author, 5 December 2001.
[26] Interview with author, 5 December 2001.
[27] Interview with author, 8 January 2002.
[28] Interview with author, 8 January 2002.
[29] Interview with author, 28 November 2001.
[30] Mansergh, 25 February 1998.
[31] Interview with author, 5 December 2001.
[32] Interview with author, 8 January 2002.
[33] Interview with author, 5 December 2001.
[34] Interview with author, 5 December 2001.
[35] Interview with author, 4 March 2002.
[36] Interview with author, 27 November 2001.
[37] Interview with author, 14 January 2001.
[38] Mansergh, 20 September 1986.
[39] Mansergh, 6 May 1997.
[40] Mansergh, 20 September 1986.
[41] Mansergh, 16 May 2001.
[42] Mansergh, 20 September 1986.
[43] Mansergh, 20 September 1986.
[44] *Business and Finance*, May 1984.
[45] Mansergh, 16 May 2001.
[46] Mansergh, 20 September 1986.
[47] Interview with author, 5 March 2002.
[48] Mansergh, 16 May 2001.
[49] Mansergh, 16 May 2001.
[50] Mansergh, 16 May 2001.
[51] Mansergh, 16 May 2001.
[52] Mansergh, 16 May 2001.
[53] Mansergh, 16 May 2001.
[54] Mansergh, 1 March 1997.

[55] Mansergh, 1 March 1997.
[56] Mansergh, 6 May 1997.
[57] Mansergh, 6 May 1997.
[58] *Sunday Press*, May 1984.
[59] *Sunday Press*, May 1984.
[60] *Études Irlandaises*, 2000, p.143.
[61] *Études Irlandaises*, 2000, p.145.
[62] *Études Irlandaises*, 2000, p.143.
[63] *Études Irlandaises*, 2000, p.163.
[64] Mansergh, 16 May 2001.
[65] Mansergh, 6 May 1997.
[66] Arnold, 2001, p.228.
[67] *Irish Independent*, 2 November 1999.
[68] *Irish Independent*, 2 November 1999.
[69] *Études Irlandaises*, 2000, p.155.
[70] Hannon and Gallagher, p.126.
[71] Mansergh, 16 May 2001.

Five

[1] Private Correspondence, 16 July 1987.
[2] Department of Taoiseach Memorandum, January 1981.
[3] Joyce and Murtagh, p.155.
[4] Interview with author, 4 April 2002.
[5] Interview with author, 4 April 2002.
[6] *Irish Times*, 28 August 2001.
[7] Interview with author, 28 November 2001.
[8] Interview with author, 8 January 2002.
[9] Interview with author, 14 January 2002.
[10] Mansergh, 5 April 1986.
[11] *Sunday Times*, 23 August 1981.
[12] *Belfast Telegraph*, April 1982.
[13] *Sunday Press*, 27 December 1981.
[14] *Sunday Press*, 27 December 1981.
[15] *Sunday Press*, 27 December 1981.
[16] Hesketh, p.160.
[17] Hesketh, p.155-58.
[18] *Nationalist*, 23 April 1983.
[19] Some years later, commenting on the 1992 X-case, Mansergh revised his own opinion: "I at least was not surprised by the eventual Supreme Court judgement … "
[20] *Irish Times*, 9 February 1983.
[21] *Nationalist*, 9 January 1988.
[22] Private Correspondence, 22 May 1983.

[23] Mansergh, 20 September 1986.

[24] Whyte, p.415.

[25] Interview with author, 28 January 2002.

[26] *Sunday Press*, 27 December 1981.

[27] *Sunday Press*, 27 December 1981.

[28] Mansergh, p.335.

[29] Bew and Gillespie, p.141.

[30] Interview with author, 4 April 2002.

[31] Interview with author, 8 January 2002.

[32] Mansergh, 20 September 1986.

[33] Mansergh, 6 January 2002.

[34] Mansergh, 13 October 1999. He also mentioned that one of his godfathers, John Collins, was a founder of the Campaign for Nuclear Disarmament, CND.

[35] *Irish Times*, 28 August 2001.

[36] *Irish Times*, 28 August 2001.

[37] Interview with author, 4 April 2002.

[38] Interview with author, 15 January 2002.

[39] Private Correspondence, 5 June 1982.

[40] Private Correspondence, 22 June 1982.

[41] Private Correspondence, 11 October 1982.

[42] *Nationalist*, 23 April 1983.

[43] *Irish Times*, 28 August 2001.

[44] *Irish Times*, 28 August 2001.

[45] Interview with author, 4 April 2002.

[46] Interview with author, 4 April 2002.

[47] Interview with author, 4 April 2002.

[48] *Irish Times*, 28 August 2001.

[49] Interview with author, 4 March 2002.

[50] Interview with author, 8 January 2002.

[51] Interview with author, 8 January 2002.

[52] Ryan, p.79.

[53] Ryan, p.79.

[54] Mansergh, 17 May 1996.

[55] Mansergh, 17 May 1996.

[56] Mansergh, 17 May 1996.

[57] *In Dublin*, 5 March 1987.

[58] Quoted in Power, 1996, p.123.

[59] *Sunday Independent*, 11 June 1989.

[60] Interview with author, 27 November 2001.

[61] Mansergh, 1986, p.xxviii.

[62] Interview with author, 15 January 2002.

[63] Interview with author, 4 March 2002.
[64] Mansergh, November 2000.
[65] Mansergh, 17 May 1996.
[66] Interview with author, 14 January 2002.
[67] *Irish Times*, 28 August 2001.
[68] *Irish Times*, 29 August 1997.
[69] Mansergh, 17 May 1996.
[70] Michael Smurfit was an investor in UPH, which sold a site to Chestvale Property which in turn sold it to Telecom Éireann, of which Michael Smurift was chairman.
[71] Collins and O'Shea, p.35.
[72] Mansergh, 17 May 1996.
[73] Mansergh, 25 February 1998.
[74] Mansergh, 25 February 1998.
[75] Interview with author, 4 April 2002.
[76] *Irish Independent*, 24 January 1992.
[77] *Irish Independent*, 24 January 1992.
[78] *Irish Independent*, 24 January 1992.
[79] Interview with author, 4 April 2002.
[80] Mansergh, 17 May 1996.
[81] Mansergh, 17 May 1996.
[82] Mansergh, 17 May 1996.
[83] Tribunal of Inquiry, p.107.
[84] Interview with author, 4 April 2002.
[85] Interview with author, 14 January 2002.
[86] Mansergh, 6 May 1997.
[87] Mansergh, 6 May 1997.
[88] Mansergh, 6 May 1997.
[89] Mansergh, 6 May 1997.
[90] Tribunal of Inquiry, pp.72-73.
[91] *Irish Times*, 28 August 2001.
[92] Mansergh, 5 February 1998.
[93] Mansergh, undated review.

Six

[1] Breen, p.34.
[2] Breen, p.40.
[3] Mansergh, Nicholas, 1991, p.3.
[4] Mansergh, 25 January 1998.
[5] *Études Irlandaises*, p.201.
[6] Mansergh, Nicholas, 1991, p.3.
[7] Mansergh, 5 June 1982.
[8] Duignan, p.15.

[9] Quoted in Cox et al, p.14.
[10] Quoted in Cox et al, p.14.
[11] *Études Irlandaises*, p.196.
[12] Mansergh, 1 August 1998.
[13] *Études Irlandaises*, p.195.
[14] Interview with author, 17 April 2002.
[15] *Études Irlandaises*, p.208.
[16] Mansergh, 21 October 1995.
[17] *Études Irlandaises*, p.195.
[18] Mansergh, 30 October 2001.
[19] Mansergh, 30 October 2001.
[20] *Études Irlandaises*, p.199.
[21] Mansergh, 30 October 2001.
[22] Mansergh, 30 October 2001.
[23] Mansergh, 30 October 2001.
[24] Mansergh, 30 October 2001.
[25] Mansergh, 30 October 2001.
[26] Mansergh, 5 June 1982.
[27] Mansergh, 30 October 2001.
[28] *Sunday Business Post*, 11 September 1992.
[29] *Belfast Telegraph*, 4 November 1997.
[30] *Irish Times*, 6 October 2000.
[31] Interview with author, 12 March 2002.
[32] Mansergh, 16 May 2000.
[33] Interview with author, 30 January 2002.
[34] Nic Craith, p.6.
[35] Letter from MM to Lord Laird, undated but from February 2001.
[36] Letter from MM to Lord Laird, undated but from February 2001.
[37] Letter from Lord Laird to MM, 19 February 2001.
[38] Interview with author, 30 January 2002.
[39] Interview with author, 30 January 2002.
[40] Interview with author, 12 March 2002.
[41] Letter from MM to Reform Movement, 25 January 2001.
[42] Letter from MM to Reform Movement, 25 January 2001.
[43] Mansergh, 30 October 2001.
[44] Quoted in Cox et al, p.9.
[45] Quoted in Cox et al, p.10.
[46] Mansergh, 24 January 2001.
[47] *Études Irlandaises*, p.203.
[48] Mansergh, 3 February 2000.
[49] Mansergh, 3 February 2000.
[50] Quoted in Cox et al, p.11.

[51] Quoted in Cox et al, p.11.
[52] Mansergh, May 2000.
[53] Interview with author, 21 March 2002.
[54] In fact, the Irish Free State became a recognised entity in international law on 6 December 1922.
[55] *Irish Times*, 19 August 2000.
[56] Mansergh, May 2000.
[57] *An Phoblacht/Republican News*, 5 March 1998.
[58] *Irish Echo*, April 1998.
[59] Mansergh, May 2000.
[60] Mansergh, Frank Cahill Lecture, 1995.

Seven

[1] Mansergh, 23 June 2001.
[2] Mansergh, 23 June 2001.
[3] Mansergh, 23 June 2001.
[4] Arthur, p.212.
[5] Quoted in Cox et al, p.16.
[6] Quoted in Cox et al, p.16.
[7] Bew and Gillespie, p.166.
[8] Quoted in Cox et al, p.15
[9] Arthur, p.192.
[10] Arthur, p.196.
[11] Quoted in Cox et al, p.16.
[12] Quoted in Cox et al, p.16.
[13] Interview with author, 29 January 2002.
[14] Bow and Gillespie, p.191.
[15] Quoted in Cox et al, p.16.
[16] Quoted in Cox et al, p.14.
[17] Quoted in Cox ct al, p.13.
[18] Quoted in Cox et al, p.12.
[19] Mansergh, 16 October 1994.
[20] It later emerged that Martin McGuinness held secret meetings with an emissary of the British Government and that communications between London and Sinn Féin had been established since 1990.
[21] Quoted in Cox et al, p.12.
[22] Finlay, p.15.
[23] Quoted in Cox et al, p.12.
[24] Interview with author, 17 April 2002.
[25] Interview with author, 17 April 2002.
[26] Interview with author, 17 April 2002.
[27] Interview with author, 17 April 2002.
[28] Interview with author, 17 April 2002.

[29] Interview with author, 8 January 2002.
[30] Interview with author, 17 April 2002.
[31] Interview with author, 17 April 2002.
[32] Interview with author, 17 April 2002.
[33] Duignan p.104.
[34] Mansergh, 16 September 1995.
[35] Mallie and McKittrick, 1996, p.87.
[36] Quoted in Cox et al, p.17.
[37] Mansergh, 16 September 1995.
[38] Interview with author, 4 April 2002.
[39] Mallie and McKittrick, 1996, p.88.
[40] Interview with author, 4 April 2002.
[41] Interview with author, 21 March 2002.
[42] Interview with author, 6 August 2002.
[43] Mansergh, University of Reinnes, September 1995.
[44] Interview with author, 16 April 2002.
[45] Interview with author, 21 March 2002.
[46] *Irish Times* 21 October 2000.
[47] Interview with author, 16 April 2002.
[48] *Études Irlandaises*, p.197.
[49] Interview with author, 16 April 2002.
[50] Interview with author, 21 March 2002.

Eight
[1] Gallagher and Hannon, p.118.
[2] Gallagher and Hannon, p.118.
[3] Gallagher and Hannon, p. 118.
[4] *Irish Times*, 6 September 1994.
[5] Duignan, p.15.
[6] Gallagher and Hannon, p.116.
[7] Gallagher and Hannon, p.117.
[8] Delaney, p.341.
[9] Quoted in Cox et al, p.21.
[10] *Sunday Times*, 2 January 2000.
[11] Delaney, p.319.
[12] Quoted in Cox et al, p.21.
[13] Interview with author, 29 January 2002.
[14] Interview with author, 14 January 2002.
[15] Interview with author, 14 January 2002.
[16] Mansergh, 6 May 1997.
[17] Interview with author, 29 January 2002.
[18] Duignan, p.101.
[19] Interview with author, 29 April 2002.

[20] Interview with author, 16 April 2002.
[21] Quoted in Cox et al, p.16.
[22] Interview with author, 16 April 2002.
[23] Interview with author, 16 April 2002.
[24] Interview with author, 16 April 2002.
[25] Interview with author, 16 April 2002.
[26] Interview with author, 16 April 2002.
[27] Finlay, p.188.
[28] Mallie and McKettrick, 2001, p.116.
[29] Quoted in Cox et al, p.18.
[30] Major, p.449.
[31] Duignan, p. 104.
[32] Dáil Debates, 31 November 1993.
[33] Interview with author, 30 April 2002.
[34] Quoted in Cox et al, p.12.
[35] McKittrick et al, p.1328.
[36] Duignan, p.102.
[37] Finlay, p.245.
[38] Duignan, p.121.
[39] Duignan, p.122-23.
[40] Quoted in Mallie and McKittrick, 2001, p.134.
[41] Quoted in Cox et al, p.19.
[42] Duignan, p.126.
[43] Finlay, p.204.
[44] Bew and Gillespie, p.285.
[45] Finlay, p.151.
[46] Quoted in Mallie and McKittrick, 2001, p.147.
[47] Quoted in Bew and Gillespie, p.288.
[48] The description was rejected by leading Irish and US political figures. Jean Kennedy-Smith described the comments Seitz made about her in his memoirs as "unfortunate".
[49] *Études Irlandaises*, p.198.
[50] *Études Irlandaises*, p.198.
[51] Interview with author, 17 April 2002.
[52] Mallie and McKittrick, 2001, p.165.
[53] Finlay, p.236
[54] Quoted in Mallie and McKittrick, 20.01, p.169.
[55] Interview with author, 29 January 2002.
[56] *Études Irlandaises*, p.205

Nine

[1] Mansergh, 16 September 1995.
[2] Mansergh, 16 September 1995.

[3] Mansergh, 19 April 1998.

[4] *Études Irlandaises*, p.196.

[5] Mansergh, 29 February 2000

[6] Interview with author, 29 January 2002.

[7] Interview with author, 4 March 2002. FitzGerald also said of Mansergh's rejection of the job offer: "There was a lack of cohesion between the Department of the Taoiseach and the Department of Foreign Affairs at that time, and having Martin Mansergh in the mix – God knows what would have been the consequences. In fact it would have complicated things, I suspect."

[8] Interview with author, 9 January 2002.

[9] Information supplied by John Bruton, 9 January 2002.

[10] Interview with author, 9 January 2002.

[11] Mansergh, 14 October 1995.

[12] Mansergh, 16 September 1995.

[13] Mansergh, 3 October 1996.

[14] Interview with author, 9 January 2002.

[15] Interview with author, 9 January 2002.

[16] Interview with author, 9 January 2002.

[17] Interview with author, 9 January 2002.

[18] Interview with author, 12 March 2002.

[19] Letter from British Prime Minister to MM, 20 December 1994.

[20] *Irish Times*, 24 April 1995.

[21] *Études Irlandaises*, p.210.

[22] *Études Irlandaises*, p.210.

[23] Interview with author, 4 April 2002.

[24] Interview with author, 29 January 2002.

[25] Interview with author, 12 March 2002.

[26] Major, p.482.

[27] Major, p.482.

[28] Interview with author, 29 January 2002.

[29] Defence & Foreign Affairs' Strategic Policy.

[30] Mansergh, London paper 1998.

[31] Mansergh, London paper 1998.

[32] Interview with author, 17 April 2002.

[33] Interview with author, 12 March 2002

[34] Quoted in Cox et al, p.12.

[35] Quoted in Cox et al, p.12.

[36] *Irish Times*, 14 February 2000.

[37] Interview with author, 4 April 2002.

[38] *Belfast Telegraph*, 4 November 1997.

[39] *News Letter*, 5 November 1997.

[40] *News Letter*, 24 December 1997.

[41] Mansergh, 19 May 1998.

[42] Letter from Taoiseach to MM, 11 May 1998.

[43] De Breadun, p.100.

[44] Quoted in Mallie and McKittrick, 2001, p.231.

[45] *Magill*, May 1999, p.55.

[46] Interview with author, 12 March 2002.

[47] Interview with author, 14 January 2002.

[48] Interview with author, 12 March 2002.

[49] Interview with author, 14 January 2002

[50] Mallie and McKittrick, 2001, p.249.

[51] Hennessey, p.49.

[52] Interview with author, 21 March 2002.

[53] Note from President to MM, undated.

[54] Letter from Taoiseach to MM, 11 May 1998.

[55] Letter from Taoiseach to MM, 11 May 1998.

[56] Mansergh, 10 July 1998.

[57] Mansergh, 10 July 1998.

[58] Interview with author, 12 March 2002.

[59] *Irish Times*, 2 October 2000.

[60] *Irish Times*, 6 October 2000.

[61] Mansergh, 29 February 2000.

[62] Mansergh, 29 February 2000. The IRA eventually started to decommission in 2001.

[63] McIntyre, p.5

[64] Mansergh, 30 October 2001.

[65] Mansergh, June 1999.

Ten

[1] Machiavelli, p. 8.

[2] Mansergh, 17 May 1996.

[3] *Irish Times*, February 1992.

[4] The charges that Reynolds made in the Tribunal against O'Malley were rejected by the PD leader and ultimately precipitated the collapse of the coalition between Fianna Fáil and the PDs.

[5] Hannon and Gallagher, p.126.

[6] Hannon and Gallagher, p.126.

[7] Finlay, p.136.

[8] *Irish Examiner*, 18 February 2002.

[9] Interview with author, 15 January 2002.

[10] Interview with author, 15 January 2002.

[11] Interview with author, 15 January 2002.

[12] Interview with author, 15 January 2002.

[13] O'Halpin Research Paper, DCU 1996.

[14] Interview with author, 4 March 2002.

[15] Interview with author, 15 May 2002.

[16] Interview with author, 14 January 2002.

[17] Report of Sub-committee, p. 318.

[18] Duignan, p.14.

[19] Duignan, p.15.

[20] Duignan, p.15.

[21] *Belfast Telegraph*, May 1982.

[22] Kelly, KPMG.

[23] In the Dáil and in media interviews Reynolds rejected claims that the house had been misled or that there was an intention to mislead.

[24] *Sunday Independent*, 15 January 1995.

[25] Report of the Sub-committee, p.319.

[26] Report of the Sub-committee, p.325.

[27] Report of the Sub-committee, p.319.

[28] Finlay, p.264.

[29] Mansergh, 6 May 1997.

[30] *Phoenix*, 23 April 1999.

[31] Mansergh, 6 May 1997.

[32] Interview with author, 14 January 2002.

[33] McCarthy, p.155.

[34] McCarthy, p.170.

[35] Mansergh, 6 January 2002.

[36] Mansergh, 6 January 2002.

[37] *Irish Times*, 7 May 2002.

[38] Interview with author, 4 April 2002.

[39] RTÉ *Morning Ireland*, February 2000.

[40] Mansergh, 1981.

[41] Mansergh, 3 October 1996.

Eleven

[1] *Sunday Times*, 12 April 1998.

[2] *Tipperary Post*, January 1984.

[3] *Sunday Business Post*, 17 February 2002.

[4] *Irish Examiner*, 18 February 2002.

[5] *Irish Examiner*, 18 February 2002.

[6] *Irish Times*, 26 March 2002.

[7] Mansergh, 3 October 1996.

[8] *Irish Times*, 14 May 2002.

[9] *Irish Times*, 14 February 2002.

[10] *Irish Times*, 1 May 2002. The reference to Thurles was obviously in error as the town is in Tipperary North and not Tipperary South where Mansergh was a candidate.

[11] Mansergh, 3 October 1996.

[12] *Irish Times*, 14 May 2002.

[13] His nomination papers for the Agricultural Panel had been signed by the Irish Thoroughbred Breeders' Association reflecting his family's involvement in the horse sector.

[14] 'The Positioning of Fianna Fail', private paper prepared by Martin Mansergh, circa 1998/99.

[15] Taken from unedited version of 1982 *Irish Times* interview in Nicholas Mansergh private papers

[16] Mansergh, 17 May 1996.

Bibliography

Martin Mansergh has written and spoken widely on a variety of subjects. These contributions are listed by date-order starting with material from 1981. The footnote referencing system employed in the book lists Mansergh's material by the date of delivery or publication. Other research material was sourced in publications including the *Irish Times*, the *Irish Independent*, the *Irish Examiner, Aimsir Óg* and *Times Change: Quarterly Political and Cultural Review.*

The Impact of Cultural Revival, Commentary on Culture and Anarchy by FSL Lyons, 1981.

In Memory of the 'Patriot' Ireland of 1782: Historical Role-Reversals and the Potential for Cultural Convergence, SDLP Conference Belfast, June 1982.

Parnell and the Leadership of Nationalist Ireland, Parnell Society Co Wicklow, April 1986.

The Driving Force of Irish Democracy, Fianna Fáil Conference, September 1986.

Revisionism, UCD, September 1987.

The Irish Constitution – 50 Years On, Trinity College, Dublin, October 1987.

The Significance of Wolfe Tone and His Legacy, Trinity College, Dublin, November 1990.

Parnell and The Leadership of Nationalist Ireland in McCarthy, Donal (ed.), *Parnell. The Politics of Power,* 1991.

The Background to the Peace Process in *Irish Studies in International Affairs,* Vol.6 (1995)

The Rights of Man in Ireland and the Role of Lawyers in 1798, Kings' Inns, February 1991.

Freedom and a New Dawn of Peace, Sean Treacy Commemoration, October 1994.

Towards An Agreed Ireland, Fianna Fáil meeting UCD, February 1995.

The Orange Order – A Part of Our Two Traditions?, Drogheda,
June 1995.
The Framework Document, Fianna Fáil Conference, March 1995.
Elizabeth Bowen and the Anglo-Irish Tradition, Farahy Church,
August 1995.
*Building the Bridge to Peace: The Questions of Principle and
Ideology*, University of Rennes, September 1995.
*From the Treaty of Limerick to the Framework Document – The
Political Economy of a Peace Settlement*, Wexford Historical
Society, October 1995.
'A Nation at Peace Once Again'? The Legacy of Thomas Davis,
Mallow, Co Cork, October 1995.
Untitled Briefing Notes, Basque Region, October 1995.
The Peace Process in Historical Perspective, in *Études Irlandaises*, No
25-1 1996, pp. 195-211.
Gloomy Scenarios, Sunday Tribune review of *On the Eve of the
Millennium* by Conor Cruise O'Brien, February 1996.
Machiavelli, Shakespeare and Irish Politics, Listowel Writers'
Week, May 1996.
A Brief History of the Mansergh Family and Grenane, Grenane
House, September 1996.
What Became of Tim Healy?, Review of Frank Callanan biography
of Healy, 1996.
*Creating a New Era of Understanding and Trust, Church of Ireland
Gazette*, January 1997.
*'The Freedom to Achieve Freedom'. The Political Ideas of Collins and
De Valera*, UCC, March 1997.
A Tribute to an Historian Father, Hodges Figgis Dublin, April
1997.
A Great Tradition – The Spirit and Identity of Fianna Fáil, Fianna
Fáil Conference, May 1997.
In Memoriam Gordon Wilson, Gorey Co Wexford, June 1997.
'A Deal to be Done'. Charles Kickham, The Tipperary Patriot,
Tipperary, August 1997.
The Republican Ideal Regained in Porter, Norman, (ed.), *The
Republican Ideal: Current Perspectives*, 1998.
Elizabeth Bowen and the Anglo-Irish tradition, in Walshe, Eibhear
(ed.), *Elizabeth Bowen Remembered* The Farahy Address, 1998.

The Ambush at Soloheadbeg, Annual Commemoration Lecture, January 1998.

The Remains of Medieval Tipperary, Fethard, Co Tipperary, January 1998.

The Value of Historical Commemoration and its role in peace and reconciliation, with special reference to 1798 and 1848, Butler House Kilkenny, February 1998.

The Assassination of St George and Uniacke, Araglin Co Cork, February 1998.

A Passionate Attachment to the Ideal – Erskine Childers, Childers Memorial Lecture, February 1998.

A Fallen Republican Leader – General Liam Lynch, Annual Lynch Commemoration, April 1998.

The Belfast/Good Friday Agreement, Dublin West Fianna Fáil meeting, May 1998.

The 1798 Rebellion and Its Meaning for Today, Wexford, June 1998.

The Agreement Viewed from Dublin, Agreed Ireland Forum London, June 1998.

Thomas Maguire and the Stretching of Republican Legitimacy review of *Dileacht* by Ruairi O Bradaigh, July 1998.

Dr William Drennan, Son of the Manse, and Father of Irish Constitutional Republicanism, John Hewitt Summer School, August 1998.

The Challenges of the Good Friday Agreement and the Consolidation of Peace, Irish Association, November 1998.

Padraic Pearse and the Creation of an Irish National Democracy, Dublin Civic Museum, November 1998.

The Famine, Solomon Gallery Dublin, December 1998.

Twentieth Century Irish Leaders: Reassessment Eamon de Valera – The Reputation of a Statesman, Douglas Hyde Summer School, July 1999.

Untitled Address, PDFORRA Conference, October 1999.

Memory and Mission – Christianity in Wexford 600 to 2000AD, Ferrcarrig Hotel, November 1999.

The Early Stages of the Irish Peace Process in McCarthy, Clem, Accord. An international review of peace initiatives, December 1999.

The Political Legacy of Sean Lemass in *Études Irlandaises*, No 25-1 2000, pp.141-72.

Background to the Peace Process, in Cox et al, 2000, pp.8-23.

The Uses of History. Government Policy and the onset of the recent Northern Ireland Troubles as seen through the State Papers in the late 1960s, UCC, February 2000.

Lessons from the Northern Ireland Peace Process, Jerusalem, February 2000.

Republicanism in a Christian Country – Past, Present and Future, All Hallows' College, March 2000.

Roger Casement and the idea of a broader nationalist tradition: His impact on Anglo-Irish relations, Royal Irish Academy, May 2000.

Unititled Script, US Congressional Staff Briefing, Washington, May 2000.

The Arms Crisis, 30 Years On, Review of *The Arms Trial* by Justin O'Brien, October 2000.

The Future of the Irish Economy and Social Partnership, Fianna Fáil Forum, November 2000.

Liam Mellows and the Struggle Against Imperialism, Liam Mellows Commemoration Co Wexford, December 2000.

The Government of Ireland Act, 1920 on the 80th anniversary of its introduction: The political significance of an historical legacy, UCD, January 2001.

The Significance of St. Patrick's Day, Ulster Society, 2001.

The Legacy of Kinsale – A 400 Year Perspective, Kinsale Local History Society, March 2001.

Cross Border Bodies – Laying the Groundwork, IBIS, May 2001.

Reflections on the History of Fianna Fáil, Fianna Fáil Forum, May 2001.

A Pioneer in State-Building, National Library, May 2001.

The Legacy of the Hunger Strikes 20 Years On, Parnell Square Dublin, June 2001.

Fianna Fáil – The Achievements of 75 Years, Fianna Fáil meeting, September 2001.

Irish Unionism and its legacy, Collins Barracks Dublin, October 2001.

The *Legacy of Kinsale – A 400 Year Perspective*, Battle of Kinsale Winter School, January 2002.

Secondary Reading

Arnold, Bruce, *Charles Haughey: His Life and Unlucky Deeds*, 1993

Arnold, Bruce, *Jack Lynch: Hero in Crisis*, 2001.

Arthur, Paul, *Special Relationships: Britain, Ireland and the Northern Ireland Problem*, 2000.

Bew, Paul and Gillespie, Gordon, *Northern Ireland A Chronology of the Troubles 1968-1999*, 1999.

Bowen, Kurt, *Protestants in a Catholic State: Ireland's Privileged Minority*, 1983.

Collins, Neil and O'Shea, Mary, *Understanding Corruption in Irish Politics*, 2000.

Cox, Michael, Guelke, Adrian and Stephen, Fiona (eds.), *A Farewell to Arms? From 'longwar' to long peace in Northern Ireland*, 2000.

Curwen, John F., *Records relating to the Barony of Kendale*, 1924.

De Breadun, Deaglan, *The Far Side of Revenge*, 2001.

Delaney, Eamon, *An Accidental Diplomat*, 2001.

Dunphy, Richard, *The Making of Fianna Fáil power in Ireland, 1932-48*, 1995.

Dooley, Terence, *The Decline of the Big House in Ireland*, 2001

Duignan, Seán, *One Spin on the Merry-go-round*, 1995.

Finlay, Fergus, *Snakes and Ladders*, 1998.

FitzGerald, Garret, *All in a Life: An Autobiography*, 1991.

Gashell, *Ulster Leaders: Social and Political*, 1914.

Hannon, Philip, and Gallagher, Jackie (eds.), *Taking the long view: 70 years of Fianna Fáil*, 1996.

Hart, Peter, "The Protestant Experience of Revolution in Southern Ireland" in English, Richard and Walker, Graham (eds.), *Unionism in Modern Ireland*, 1996.

Hennessey, Thomas, *The Northern Ireland Peace Process: Ending the Troubles*, 2000.

Hesketh, Tom, *The Second Partitioning of Ireland?: The Abortion Referendum of 1983*, 1990.

Howard J. and Crisp, Frederick, (eds.), *Visitation of Ireland*, 1899.

Kelly, Jed, *Taxation Policy and the Tax Strategy Group*, KPMG 1999.

Kennedy, Liam, *Colonialism, Religion and Nationalism in Ireland*, 1996.

Lee, Joseph, in Mansergh N, *Nationalism and Independence: Selected Irish papers*, 1997

Logue, Paddy, (ed.), *Being Irish: Personal Reflections on Irish Identity Today*, 2001.

Logue, Paddy, (ed.), *The Border: Personal Reflections from Ireland, North and South*, 2000.

Lysaght, Charles, *Brendan Backen Memorial Lecture 2001*, in Churchill Review, Volume 38, 2001.

Major, John, *John Major: The Autobiography*, 2000.

Mallie, Eamon, and McKittrick, David, The *Fight for Peace: The Secret Story Behind the Irish Peace Process*, 1986.

Mallie, Eamon, and McKittrick, David, *Endgame in Ireland*, 2001.

Mansergh, Nicholas, *The Unresolved Question: The Anglo-Irish Settlement and Its Undoing, 1912-72*, 1991.

Mansergh, Nicholas, *Nationalism and Independence: Selected Irish papers*, 1997

Marnane, Denis G., *Land and Violence: a History of West Tipperary from 1660*, 1985.

Massy-Dawon & Poore Pedigrees, 1937

Mitchell, George, *Making Peace*, 1999.

McCarthy, Justine, *Mary McAleese, The Outsider*, 1999.

McGrath, Thomas, *Interdenominational relations in pre-Famine Tipperary* in Nolan, W, (ed.), *Tipperary: History and Society*, 1985.

McIntyre, Donald

McKittrick, David, Kelters, Seamus, Feeney, Brian and Thornton, Chris, *Lost Lives – The stories of the men, women and children who died as a result of the Northern Ireland troubles*, 1999.

Nic Craith, Mairead, *Cultural Diversity in Northern Ireland and the Good Friday Agreement*, 2001.

Nolan, W, (ed.), *Tipperary: History and Society*, Geography Publications, 1985.

O'Brien, Brendan, *The Long War: The IRA and Sinn Féin to Today*, O'Brien Press, 1993.

O'Halpin, Eunan, *Partnership programme managers in the Reynolds/Spring coalition, 1993-94*, 1996.

O'Malley, Padraig, *The Uncivil Wars in Ireland Today*,

Paxman, Jermey, *The English*, 2000.

Power, Sean, (ed.), *Those Were the Days*, 1995.

Power, Sean, (ed.), *Egg on My Face*, 1996.

Report of the sub-Committee of the Select Committee on Legislation and Security, 1995.

Rowan, Brian, *Behind the Lines: The Story of the IRA and Loyalist Ceasefires*, 1995

Ryan, Tim, *PJ Mara*, 1992.

Sinnott, Richard, *Irish Voters Decide*, 1995.

Smyth, William, *Property, patronage and population – reconstructing the human geography of mid-seventeenth century County Tipperary*, in Nolan, W, (ed.), *Tipperary: History and Society*, 1985.

Walsh, Dick, *The Party: Inside Fianna Fáil*, 1986.

Whyte, John, *Interpreting Northern Ireland*, Oxford 1990.

Whyte, John, *Church & State in Modern Ireland 1923-1979*, 1980.

Index

British Commonwealth *see*
  Commonwealth
British Government 76, 163,
  168-9, 204, 207-8, 213, 230, 236,
  240-1
  secret contacts with IRA 214-15
British Intelligence 202
British Northern Ireland
  Constitution Act 251
Brooke, Charlotte 191
Brooke, Peter 191
Bruton, John 77-8, 83, 205, 231-3,
  235-6, 240, 281
Burke, Dick 122-3
Bury, Robin 160
Bush, George W. 292
Butler, Sir Robin 201, 208, 214-15
Byrne, Seán 296

C

Cahill, Bernie 137
Cahill, Joe 224
Canary Wharf bomb 239
Carroll, Lewis 54
Cassidy, Donnie 126
Catholic Church 37, 288-91
Catholic Emancipation 16
Cayman Islands 144
Chilcott, John 201, 230
Childers, Erskine 29
Childers, President Erskine 36, 79
Church of Ireland 16, 53, 112,
  113-14, 286-91
see also Protestants
Churchill, Winston 35
City of London bomb 213
civil rights campaign 162-3
Civil War 24, 28, 29, 42, 73, 92,
  96-7, 226, 228
Clinton, Bill 101, 220-1, 224, 240,
  243, 256
Clonmel Nationalist 113, 296, 305
Colley, George 120-1, 123
Collins, Gerry 296

Collins, Michael 73, 95-6
Commemoration Committee 163
Commonwealth 30-1, 38-9, 156
Commonwealth Experience, The 39
Conference on Security and
  Co-operation in Europe 65
Connell, Archbishop Desmond
  286
Conservative Government in UK
  76, 163, 168-9, 204, 236, 241
Constitution 109-10, 290
  abortion referendum 111-14
  Articles Two and Three 110,
    176-7, 197-8, 214, 233, 248,
    250-3, 258-9
  sexist bias in 312-13
contraception 58-9, 95, 111, 113,
  114-16, 126
Coogan, Tim Pat 182
Cosgrave, W.T. 42, 91, 228-9
Costello, John A. 38
Council of Ireland 162
Cowen, Brian 305
Cromwell, Oliver 13-14, 52
Cromwellian settlement 13-14, 30,
  191
Cruise O'Brien, Conor 123
Cumann na nGaedheal 73, 91-2

D

Daily Telegraph 203
Dalton, Tim 244, 247
Davern, Noel 298, 300-1, 304, 307
Davis, Thomas 91
de Brun, Bairbre 250
de Chastelain, John 243
de Gaulle, Charles 95
de Valera, Eamon 31, 36-7, 41-2,
  72-4, 92, 95-8, 100, 105, 170, 226
  and Irish neutrality 119
*De Valera and the Ulster Question
  1917-173* 97-8
Deasy, Austin 68, 186
Declaration of Independence 156

M

Macaulay, Thomas Babington 142
Machiavelli, Niccolò 266, 274, 313
MacLíammóir, Micheál 48, 50
MacSharry, Ray 103
Magee, Roy 211
Maginnis, Ken 158, 258
Maguire, Frank 168-9
Maguire, Michael 299, 300
Mair, Peter 75
Major, John 101, 194, 199, 201,
    203-4, 208-9, 211-12, 215-16, 221,
    232, 234, 236, 239-41
Mandela, Nelson 95
Mandelson, Peter 264
Mansergh, Arthur Henry
    Wendworth 23
Mansergh, Brian 14-15, 289
Mansergh, Diane (mother) 40-1,
    44
Mansergh, Ethel (grandmother)
    21, 22-3, 27-9, 45
Mansergh family
    Church of Ireland members
        288-9
    and Cromwellian settlement
        13-14
    home in Co Tipperary 12, 149
    unionists 16, 22
Mansergh, General Sir Robert
    (godfather) 22
Mansergh, George 12
Mansergh, Gregor (uncle) 21, 25,
    30, 34, 72, 104, 114, 125, 294
Mansergh, Liz (wife) 56-7, 62-4,
    66, 131, 186
Mansergh, Major Charles
    Stephney 22-3
Mansergh, Martin
    ancestors 8, 11-25
    birth 8, 44
    brothers and sisters 44, 53-4
    candidate for Seanad Éireann
        309-10

candidate for South Tipperary
    292-313
and ceasefire 196-226
children 58, 63-4
comments on Fianna Fáil 75-6,
    311
in Department of Foreign
    Affairs 62-3, 66-7
and Haughey 7, 10, 40-1, 51, 63,
    67, 70-101, 144-8, 168, 274,
    276, 281, 285, 305, 313
Head of Research 71, 76, 81, 83,
    106-7, 109, 232, 281-2, 297
Irish embassy, Bonn 63-6
joins Fianna Fáil 7, 9, 67-8, 70-
    102
letters to *Irish Times* 58-9, 61,
    114
marriage 57-8
move to Co Tipperary 58, 60
and Northern Ireland 9, 105,
    116, 122, 151, 154, 168-265,
    273, 276, 283, 310, 313
republican beliefs 149-67
Special Advisor to Taoiseach
    7-8, 84-5, 197, 237, 240, 271,
    282, 295, 307, 313
speech-writing 85, 105, 267
threatened by loyalist
    paramilitaries 244-5
upbringing and education 8, 44-
    69
Mansergh, Nicholas (brother) 15,
    50, 300
Mansergh, Nicholas (father) 19,
    21, 25-46, 61, 72, 96, 114, 125,
    149-50, 162, 313
Mansergh, PSG (grandfather)
    20-2, 24-6, 27-30
Mansergh, Richard Southcote 46,
    289
Mansergh, RMS 17-19
Mansergh Wallace, Philippa 298
Mara, PJ 105, 129-30, 131-2, 142,
    198, 295